LIFE IN DIXIE

DURING THE WAR

1861-1862-1863-1864-1865

MARY A. H. GAY

J. H. Segars, Editor

Mercer
University
Press
2000

© 2001 Mercer University Press
6316 Peake Road
Macon, Georgia 31210-3960
All rights reserved

Originally published in 1892.

Foreword © by J. H. Segars, 2000.

0-86554-723-8 (cloth bound)
0-86554-749-1 (paperback)

The essay "A Brief Sketch of the Life and Literary Career of Mary Gay" (© 1979) and the index (© 1979)are used courtesy of the DeKalb Historical Society.

∞The paper used in this publication meets the minimum requirements of American National Standard for Information Sciences—Permanence of Paper for Printed Library Materials, ANSI Z39.48-1984.

CIP data are available from the Library of Congress

FOREWORD

The Civil War continues to be the most scrutinized period of American history, yet, readers still search for notable sources that will lead them to a deeper understanding of this—our greatest national—conflict. To meet this demand for information, historians are hard at work writing "definitive" studies that will explain the causes and effects of the war and provide insight into the mindsets of the participants. This undertaking, of course, is not always easy to accomplish.

Unfortunately, there are a number of authors who report the Civil War with a "new millennium" perspective and demonstrate a lack of understanding about life in the 1860s. "If we view history only through the lens of contemporary political considerations, we risk misunderstanding the motivations and beliefs of people at the time and losing the diversity of historical experience" says Elizabeth Fox-Genovese, professor of history at Emory University. Some researchers do not spend enough time sifting through the extant accounts of the very people who survived the period and, as a result, contemporary analyses may contain errors, omissions, and questionable statements that seem to based on regional mythology rather than historical fact. Consequently, knowledgeable readers remain confused about this period of history and, in particular, about the roles and mindsets of those who participated in the Civil War.

Ironically, many people study this conflict by only reading books that are narrowly focused on the military operations of Union and Confederate generals. Others are interested in the biographies of political leaders or prominent civilians who were most often from privileged societies. Some of the best sources of information, however, are found in the original letters, diaries, and first person accounts penned by enlisted soldiers, women, and minorities—ordinary people who constituted the largest segment of the American population involved in the Civil War.

Bell Irvin Wiley was among the first in a line of eminent historians to conduct serious studies into the lives of common soldiers, women on the home front, and African Americans. The writings of these "plain folk " provide a true rendering of American history and include historical events that many not be so well known today. Moreover, with the inclusion of eye-witnessed descriptions and the candid observations of *all* of the participants, readers can gain a better understanding of the war while uncovering some of the mysteries of one of the greatest epochs of human experience.

Some of the most compelling accounts of the Civil War were written by Confederate women. Many of the feminine memoirs are continuing to receive literary acclaim and a number of volumes sell well in reprint editions. Examples of the most popular titles include the following: Mary Boykin Chesnut's *A Diary From Dixie*, first published in 1905 and later made famous in C. Vann Woodward's Pulitzer Prize winning edition of 1981; Phoebe Yates Pember's *A Southern Woman's Story* (1879); Varina Howell Davis' *Jefferson Davis: Ex-President of the Confederate States* (2 volumes, 1890); Sarah Morgan Dawson's *A Confederate Girl's Diary* (1913); Belle Boyd's *Belle Boyd: In Camp and Prison* (1865); Mary Anna

Jackson's *Memoirs of Stonewall Jackson, by His Widow...*" (1895); Mary Ann Loughborough's *My Cave Life in Vicksburg, with Letters of Trial and Travel* (1864); Kate Cumming's *A Journal of Hospital Life in the Confederate Army of Tennessee from the Battle of Shiloh to the End of the War...*" (1866); and Eliza Frances Andrews' *The War-Time Journal of a Georgia Girl, 1864-1865* (1908).

There are other narratives, however, that are not as well known but are of equal importance. One of these, entitled *Life in Dixie During the War, 1861-1865*, was written by Mary Ann Harris Gay (1829-1918) of Decatur, Georgia. Mary Gay was not only an eloquent chronicler of the war but an active participant as well; and her first hand reporting brings to life harrowing true life adventures that occurred against a backdrop of human defiance, suffering, and bitter defeat.

Throughout the war Mary Gay provided assistance to her beloved Confederate solders but to others who were in poverty, discomfort, and distress. The turmoil and devastation brought on by the battle of Atlanta, however, brought the greatest disruption to thousands of Georgians. Miss Gay encountered innumerable dangers and privations and on several occasions risked her life to hide military contraband and to transport information (and Confederate citizens) between battle lines. She was described by veterans, both North and South, as "unusually brave and fearless."

Although from a wealthy family, Mary Gay identified with the common folk that lived in her beloved DeKalb County, Georgia. This strong woman gave most of her financial resources to the Southern war effort and provided material assistance to the poor, homeless refugees of Atlanta. Unfortunately, the Gay family never recovered from the financial losses; but, the poverty and starvation that they endured proved to be small sacrifice compared to the many wartime deaths of friends, neighbors, and family members. The hardest blow came when Mary Gay's brother, a Confederate officer, was killed at the Battle of Franklin (Tennessee).

Mary Gay received encouragement to write *Life in Dixie During the War* from Captain William L. Ritter, a Confederate soldier who was encamped with Hood's army in Decatur, Georgia. This book first appeared in 1892 and praise came quickly from the old veterans and their descendents, and from prominent personalities of the South to include Confederate generals, southern governors, and renown journalists. By 1898, *Life in Dixie During the War* was being published in a third printing and Sam Cunningham, the founding editor and publisher of the *Confederate Veteran,* reported that "many books have been written on the subject, but we doubt if any of them are of deeper interest than 'Life in Dixie During the War.'" *Confederate Veteran* (1898, Vol. VI) also featured the following review:

> While possessing all the charms of romance, it is a recital of facts concerning the war, which occurred in the hear of the Confederacy. Written in the first person, it has an unusual vividness of style. The author's descriptions are truly remarkable. The reader seems to be living in those days and a witness to the scenes described. Historic facts are brought out regarding the siege of Atlanta which are perhaps found nowhere else. The author spared no pains in preparation of the book. Not the least of its merit is its pure English diction,

with unsurpassed pathos in many of its pages. The heroism of men, the daring of boys, and the endurance of women are alike skillfully painted.

Throughout the war, Mary Gay considered herself to be a Confederate soldier; and, afterwards, she remained steadfast in her devotion to the principles of the "Lost Cause." This unsung Georgia heroine remained active in the Agnes Lee Chapter of United Daughters of the Confederacy and lived a quiet, simple life until her death at the age of eighty-nine in 1918.

Civil War historians have long recognized the importance of Mary Gay's life and literary work. James I. Robertson, Jr. of Virginia Tech writes: "Mary Gay's *Life in Dixie during the War* is one of the few authentic personal narratives we have of life in Atlanta during the Civil War. Miss Gay was in her late thirties when Sherman's army came to the city. Thus, she possessed a maturity that enabled her to pass adult judgment on what transpired." Richard M. McMurry, Civil War author and doctoral student of Bell I. Wiley, states: "I grew up in Decatur (Georgia) and heard about Mary Gay for years. Later, when I began my own graduate work at Emory and since then as a Civil War historian, I have had occasion to use her reminiscences many times. I know that many other historians have also found the book to be valuable for their own projects."

For contemporary readers, Mary Gay's remarkable book reads like a historical novel and is considered to be one of the best first person accounts of the American Civil War. *Life in Dixie During the War* served as a primary source for Margaret Mitchell's *Gone With the Wind* and Miss Gay's true life experiences can easily be seen in the depictions of the characters Scarlett O'Hara and Melanie Wilkes.

Harrowing ordeals and heart wrenching experiences are felt by readers who are now far removed from Mary Gay's time and place. Cyndy Coan, an educator in Rabun County, Georgia, says, "In reading Miss Gay's work one does not see words on a page; rather, the words leap forth to transcend time, and they play out as scenes before the reader's eyes. This woman's bravery, perseverance, tenacity and devotion to duty prove her to be as much of a solder as any man who wore the butternut or gray." While a southern partisan, Mary Gay was not a meek and defenseless woman; instead, she lived a thrilling, dangerous life and served as a bold witness to "the suffering and struggle, defeat and despair, triumph and hope that is human history. " This inspiring story, *Life in Dixie During the War,* is a southern classic and we are most fortunate to have Mary Gay's rare book back in print.

J. H. Segars (2000)

Sources:

Confederate Veteran Magazine: "A Noble Georgia Woman" (Vol. XXVII, March, 1919); "Unique and Thrilling War Stores" (Vol. VI, August, 1898); Captain James Dinkins column (Vol. III, July, 1895). *Life in Dixie During the War, 1861-1862-1863-1864-1865* by Mary A. H. Gay. Introduction by Jim Cherry and Dorothy Nix; DeKalb Historical Society reprint, 1979.

Personal correspondence from James I. Robertson, Jr., Richard M. McMurry, and Cynthia A. Coan (June, 2000).

LIFE IN DIXIE

DURING THE WAR.

1861 - 1862 - 1863 - 1864 - 1865.

MARY A. H. GAY.

THE THIRD EDITION. (*ENLARGED.*)

ATLANTA, GA:
CHARLES P. BYRD,
1897.

CONTENTS.

INTRODUCTION.

I am asked to write a few words of introduction to these reminiscences of a lady who, in the pleasant afternoon of a life devoted to deeds of mercy and charity, turns fondly and sympathetically to the past. But there is nothing to be said. What word of mine could add to the interest that inheres in this unpretentious record of a troubled and bloody period? The chronicle speaks for itself, especially to those who remember something of those wonderful days of war. It has the charm and the distinction of absolute verity, a quality for which we may look in vain in more elaborate and ambitious publications. Here indeed, is one of the sources from which history must get its supplies, and it is informed with a simplicity which history can never hope to attain.

We have here reproduced in these records, with a faithfulness that is amazing, the spirit of those dark days that are no more. Tragedy shakes hands with what seems to be trivial, and the commonplaces of every-day life seem to move forward with the gray battalions that went forth to war.

It is a gentle, a faithful and a tender hand that guides the pen—a soul nerved to sacrifice that tells the tale. For the rest, let the records speak for themselves.

JOEL CHANDLER HARRIS.

PREFACE.

By way of preface to "Life in Dixie During the War," I scarcely know what to say. I have long felt that it was the duty of the South to bequeath to posterity the traditions of that period; for if we do it not ourselves they will be swallowed up in oblivion. Entertaining this opinion, I have essayed the task of an individual effort, and hope that others may follow my example.

No woman who has seen what I have seen, and felt what I have felt, would be apt to write with less asperity; and yet, now that we have come back to the United States, and mean to stay in it, let the provocation to depart be what it may, I would not put into practice an iota of the war-time feeling. In thus expressing myself, I am sure I represent every Christian in my own beautiful Southland.

There was one for whom these sketches would have had a special interest. An inspiring motive for writing them was that they would be read by my nephew, Thomas H. Stokes, of Atlanta, the only child of the brother so often mentioned. But, ere he had had more than a glimpse of them, he was called away by an Inscrutable Providence, in his pure and beautiful young manhood, as we trust to a Land of Peace more in keeping with his noble, true, and tender heart, than earth with its sin and strife. "Blessed are the pure in heart; for they shall see God."

MARY A. H. GAY.

Decatur, Georgia.

INTRODUCTORY REMARKS.

The tocsin of war has resounded from Mason and Dixon's line to the Gulf of Mexico, from the snow-crested billows of the Atlantic to the tranquil waves of the Pacific.

War! War! War! is the battle cry of a people, who, long suffering and patient, but now, goaded to desperation and thoroughly exasperated, are determined, at all hazards, to protect the rights for which their forefathers fought, bled and died ; and which their own Thomas Jefferson embodied in an instrument of writing which, for beauty of diction and wisdom of thought, will go sounding down the corridors of time, so long as time itself shall last—unequaled, unparalleled ; and which was adopted without a dissenting voice by the ablest convocation of men ever assembled in national councils as their declaration of human rights and liberties.

Thus, under auspices favorable to the happy and speedy development of a new and glorious country, commenced the government of the freest and happiest people on earth, under the administration of George Washington—an administration which caught the eye of the world and called forth its admiration ; and which the most censorious never had the temerity to attack ; an administration which secured for the country the alluring title, " The land of the free and

the home of the brave." And its fame went abroad
in story and in song, and every nation on earth sought
its blessings and advantages, and it grew to be a
mighty country.

Coeval with the settlement of this beautiful continent by the white man, there came, or rather, there
was brought, a race of people which needed the fostering care as well as the strong arm of slavery to
kindle the latent spark of intellectual fire which had
smoldered for centuries, in, as President Cleveland
would say, "innocuous desuetude."

This race of people came not as pioneers in the
building up of this great nation, but as a menial race,
sold into bondage by their own kith and kin, and not
to be endowed with elective franchise nor representation in its councils. It was held in bondage alike in
Massachusetts and in South Carolina. Under the
auspices of slavery, it became a powerful factor in the
building up of the staple industries of the country—
the Southern portion of it directly, the Northern portion indirectly, and it received in return more than any
other people in bondage has ever received—as a usual
thing, good wholesome food, comfortable homes and
raiment, and tender treatment in sickness. When
they failed to receive these benefits, their masters
were improvident and careless alike of the comfort of
their own wives and children, and they, too, showed
hard usage and neglect. This is not said by way of
apology for any treatment received at the hands of
Southern slaveholders by this vassal race. I repeat
that no people held in bondage ever received so many
benefits.

Slavery, as all other institutions, had its evils, and those evils were far greater to the slaveholder than to the slaves. Climatic and other considerations rendered the system of slavery unprofitable in the Northern States of this great and growing republic, and the men at the helm of their respective governments agitated the subject of emancipation.

Having given themselves time to bring the greater number of their slaves South and sell them, they nominally freed the others by legislative enactment ; and by this great and magnanimous action, there were so few left that to this day, as attested by Northern tourists, a "darkey," or a "colored person," is an object of curiosity and great interest.

The country, North and South, was too prosperous. The agitators could stand it no longer. Discord and strife took the place of harmony and peace in the halls of congress, and in the senate chamber of the United States. Men who could in no other way acquire prominence, became conspicuous as champions of an "oppressed and down-trodden race," and were swift to slander the white people of the South. Our slaves were taught that murder, rapine, arson, and every species of wickedness known in the catalogue of crime which, in any way, could weaken, yea, destroy the South, was service most acceptable.

The country was in the clutches of an organized mob, determined to precipitate it into the jaws of dissolution. By way of confirming this statement the following resolutions are reproduced.

These resolutions were adopted by a large and representative body of men at Worcester, Massachusetts,

soon after Fremont's defeat in 1856, and long before
Governor Gist of South Carolina, and other Southern
leaders, began to take measures for a peaceable separation, rather than to be forcibly expelled :

"*Resolved*, That the meeting of a state disunion
convention, attended by men of various parties and
affinities, gives occasion for a new statement of principles and a new platform of action.

"*Resolved*, That the conflict between this principle
of liberty and this fact of slavery has been the whole
history of the nation for fifty years, while the only result of this conflict has thus far been to strengthen
both parties, and prepare the way of a yet more desperate struggle.

"*Resolved*, That in this emergency we can expect
little or nothing from the South itself, because it, too,
is sinking deeper into barbarism every year. Nor
from a supreme court which is always ready to invent
new securities for slaveholders. Nor from a president
elected almost solely by Southern votes. Nor from a
senate which is permanently controlled by the slave
power. Nor from a house of representatives which,
in spite of our agitation, will be more proslavery than
the present one, though the present one has at length
granted all which slavery asked. Nor from political
action as now conducted. For the Republican leaders
and press freely admitted, in public and private, that
the election of Fremont was, politically speaking, the
last hope of freedom, and even could the North cast a
united vote in 1860, the South has before it four years
of annexation previous to that time.

"*Resolved*, That the fundamental difference between mere political agitation and the action we propose is this, it requires the acquiescence of the slave power, and the other only its opposite.

"*Resolved,* That the necessity for disunion is written in the whole existing character and condition of the two sections of the country—in social organizations, education, habits and laws—in the dangers of our white citizens of Kansas and of our colored ones in Boston, in the wounds of Charles Sumner and the laurels of his assailant—and no government on earth was ever strong enough to hold together such opposing forces.

"*Resolved,* That this movement does not seek merely disunion, but the more perfect union of the free States by the expulsion of the slave States from the confederation in which they have ever been an element of discord, danger and disgrace.

"*Resolved,* That it is not probable that the ultimate severance of the union will be an action of deliberation or discussion, but that a long period of deliberation and discussion must precede it, and this we meet to begin.

"*Resolved,* That henceforward, instead of regarding it as an objection to any system of policy that will lead to the separation of the States, we will proclaim that to be the highest of all recommendations and the grateful proof of statesmanship ; and we will support politically and otherwise, such men and measures as appear to tend most to this result.

"*Resolved,* That by the repeated confession of Northern and Southern statesmen, the existence of the union is the chief guarantee of slavery, and that

the despots of the whole world and the slaves of the
whole world have everything to hope from its destruction and the rise of a free Northern republic.

"*Resolved*, That the sooner the separation takes
place the more peaceable it will be; but that peace or
war is a mere secondary consideration in view of our
present perils. Slavery must be conquered ; peaceably
if we can, forcibly if we must."

To keep before the people of the United States,
North and South, the hostility of the then controling
spirit of the North towards the South, the above
resolutions cannot be repeated too often. Nor were
they an isolated example of party fanaticism. The
stock and staple of the entire republican press was
slander of the Southern people; and like noxious
weeds it well nigh rooted out all that was elevating to
man, and ennobling to woman. The pulpit became a
rostrum from which bitter invective of the South
flowed in Niagaran torrents ; and the beautiful fields
of Poesy were made to yield an abundant crop of
briar and bramble and deadly Upas.

The burden of every song, of every prayer, of
every sermon, was the " poor down-trodden slave" of
the South. What wonder that seed thus constantly
and malignantly sown sprang up and bore a crop of
discontent which nothing short of "separation" from
the enemy could appease. We, too, felt that under the
existing circumstances peace or war was a mere
secondary consideration in view of our perils in the
union, and took measures to withdraw from a sectional
union of States that had ceased to respect State
sovereignty outside of its own borders.

The insults and taunts and the encroachments of fifty years had welded the people of the South into a compact party organization, animated for all substantial purposes by one sentiment and one glorious principle of patriotism, and never was there a movement in the annals of nations that had a more unanimous support. And when the tocsin of war resounded from one end of the country to the other, and reverberated over hills and through valleys, the sons and sires in the beatiful Sunny South, from the high born and cultured gentleman in whose veins flowed the blue blood of the cavalier, to the humblest tiller of the soil and the shepherd on the mountain sides, buckled on the paraphernalia of warfare and reported for duty. To arms! To arms! was the patriotic appeal of a people who had no other redress; and I repeat with emphasis that never a people responded with more chivalrous alacrity or more earnestness of purpose.

I was too well versed in the politics of the country, too familiar with the underground workings of the enemy, to hesitate. I, too, enlisted in the struggle, and in the glorious efforts to establish "home rule and domestic felicity," not literally in the ranks of the soldier, but in the great army of women who were willing to toil and to suffer, and to die, if need be, for the cause of the South.

I had but one brother, a darling young half brother, Thomas J. Stokes, who had gone to Texas to practice his chosen profession. With all the intensity of my ardent nature I loved this brother, and would have died that he might live ; and yet with all the perils involved, it was with a thrill of pride that I read his long letter breathing, pulsing, with the patriotism illsutrated by our ancestry in the revolutionary struggle for American Independence. And now this noble brother and myself, though widely separated, enlisted in aid of the same great cause ; the perpetuity of constitutional rights. He to serve on the battle-field, and I to care for the sick and wounded soldiers, or to labor in any capacity that would give greatest encouragement to our cause.

Life in Dixie During the War.

Notwithstanding the restful signification of "Alabama," the State bearing that name had passed the ordinance of secession, and mingled her voice with those of other States which had previously taken steps in that direction.

Then followed a call for a convention, having in view the election of a President of a new Republic to take its place among the nations of the earth, and to be known throughout the world as the Southern Confederacy. As an intensely interested spectator I was at that convention; and will remember, to my dying day, that grand spectacle. Yea, that was a grand and solemn occasion—that of issuing a mandate "Let there be another nation, and to all intents and purposes there was another nation." In the course of human events it requires centuries to evolve such moral courage and sublimity of thought and action; and the proceedings of that day will stand out in bold relief as the acme of patriotic greatness.

Ah ! that scene at the capitol of the State of Alabama, when Jefferson Davis, the chosen leader of the

Southern people, took the oath of office and pledged undying fidelity to the best interests of his own sunny land.

On that momentous occasion not a word was uttered denunciatory of the States we were seeking to leave in their fancied superiority, and the great concourse of people there assembled was too familiar with the history of the times to require recapitulation of the causes of the alienation which led by rapid ascent to the summit of discontent, and determination to no longer submit to the domination of an enemy.

That scene being enacted as a preliminary, a call was made for Alabama's quota of volunteers to defend the principles enunciated and the interests involved.

The Magnolia Cadets, under the leadership of Captain N. H. R. Dawson, of Selma, were among the first to respond. I accompanied my cousins of Alabama to see this company of noble, handsome young men mustered into the military service of their country. It was a beautiful sight! Wealthy, cultured young gentlemen voluntarily turning their backs upon the luxuries and endearments of affluent homes, and accepting in lieu the privations and hardships of warfare ; thereby illustrating to the world that the conflict of arms consequent upon the secession was not to be " a rich man's war and a poor man's fight."

I saw them as they stood in line to receive the elegant silken banner, bearing the stars and bars of a new nation, made and presented to them by Miss Ella Todd and her sister, Mrs. Dr. White,. of Lexington, Kentucky, who were introduced to the audience by Captain Dawson as the sisters of Mrs. Abraham

Lincoln, the wife of the president of the United States. I was thus made aware that Mrs. Lincoln and hei illustrious husband were Southerners. I have since been in the small, mud-chinked log cabin in Elizabethtown, Kentucky, in which he was born, and in which his infancy and little boyhood were domiciled. Mrs. White had married an Alabamian, and as his wife became a citizen of his State. Her sister, Miss Todd, was visiting her at the enactment of the scene described, and under like circumstances, also became a citizen of Alabama. She married the valiant gentleman who introduced her to the public on that memorable occasion.

I have sought and obtained from Mrs. Mary Dawson Jordan, of Chattanooga, Tennessee, a daughter of Captain Jordan, a complete record of the names of the officers and members of this patriotic company of Alabama's noble sons—native and adopted—which I subjoin as˙ an item of history that will be read with interest by all who revere the memory of the Lost Cause and its noble defenders.

Muster Roll of the "Magnolia Cadets."

N. H. R. DAWSON, Captain.

(Enrolled for active service at Selma, Ala., on the 26th day of April, 1861. Mustered into service on the 7th day of May, 1861, at Lynchburg, Va.)

Commanded by Col. Ben Alston of the Fourth Alabama Regiment of Volunteers.

1. N. H. R. Dawson, Captain.
1. Shortbridge, Jr., Geo. D., 1st Lieutenant.
2. McCraw, S. Newton, 2nd Lieutenant.

3. Wilson, John R. 3rd Lieutenant.
1. Waddell, Ed. R., 1st Sergeant.
2. Price, Alfred C., 2nd Sergeant.
3. Daniel, Lucian A., 3rd Sergeant.
4. Goldsby, Boykin, 4th Sergeant.
1. Bell, Bush W., 1st Corporal.
2. Garrett, Robert E., 2nd Corporal.
3. Brown, James G., 3rd Corporal.
4. Cohen, Lewis, 4th Corporal.
1. Melton, George F., Musician.
2. Marshall, Jacob, Musician.

PRIVATES.

1. Adkins, Agrippa
2. Adams, William S.
3. Avery, William C.
4. Byrd, William G.
5. Beattie, Thomas K.
6. Briggs, Charles H.
7. Bohannon, Robert B.
8. Baker, Eli W.
9. Bradley, Hugh C.
10. Cook, Thomas M.
11. Cook, James W.
12. Cook, Benson.
13. Caughtry, Joseph R.
14. Cole, George W.
15. Cleveland, George W.
16. Clevaland, Pulaski.
17. Cunningham, Frank M.
18. Coursey, William W.
19. Daniel, John R.
20. Densler, John E.
21. Donegay, James G.
22. Friday, Hilliard J.
23. Friday, James L.
24. Friday, John C.
25. Ford, Joseph H.
26. Grice, Henry F.
27. Haden, James G.
28. Harrill, Thornton R.
29. Hannon, Wm. H., Sr.
30. Hannon, Wm. H., Jr.
31. Hooks, William A.
32. Hodge, William L.
33. Jones, William.
34. Jordan, James M.
35. Jackson, Felix W
36. King, William R.
37. Kennedy, Arch.
38. Kennedy, George D.

39. Lamson, Frank R.
40. Lane, William B.
41. Lowry, Uriah.
42. Lowry, William A.
43. Littleton, Thomas B.
44. Luske, John M.
45. Lamar, John H.
46. Mather, Thomas S.
47. Martin, James B.
48. May, Syd M.
49. May, William V.
50. Melton, Thomas J.
51. Miller, Stephen J.
52. Mimms, George A.
53. Moody, William R.
54. Mosely, Andrew B.
55. McNeal, George S.
56. McKerning, John W.
57. Overton, John B.
58. Overton, Thomas W.
59. O'Neal, William.
60. Paisley, Hugh S.
61. Pryor, John W.

62. Pryor, Robert O.
63. Peeples, Frank W.
64. Raiford, William C.
65. Reinhardt, George L.
66. Robbins, John L.
67. Rucker, Lindsay.
68. Rucker, Henry.
69. Shiner, David H.
70. Stokes, William C.
71. Stone, John W.
72. Stewett, Mayor D.
73. Turner, Daniel M.
74. Thomas, Lewis.
75. Tarver, Ben J.
76. Taylor, William E.
77. Terry, Thomas B.
78. Thompson, John S.
79. Thompson, William E.
80. Ursory, Edward G.
81. Vaughn, Turner P.
82. Wrenn, Theodore J.
83. Whallon, Daniel.

Copied from the original Muster Roll of the Magnolia Cadets, owned by Henry R. Dawson, son of N. H. R. Dawson.

CHAPTER II.

THE WAR RECORD OF DEKALB COUNTY.

DeKalb county, Georgia, of which Decatur is the county site, was among the first to enroll troops for Confederate service. The first volunteers from Decatur were James L. George, Hardy Randall, L. J. Winn and Beattie Wilson, who went with the Atlanta Greys the last of May, 1861.

The first company from DeKalb county was that of Captain John W. Fowler. It was called the DeKalb Light Infantry, and was mustered into service in Atlanta, as part of the 7th Georgia Volunteers, and left for Virginia on the 1st of June, 1861. Those going from DeKalb county in this company were: First Lieutenant, John J. Powell; Second Lieutenant, John M. Hawkins; Third Lieutenant, James L. Wilson; First Sergeant, M. L. Brown; Second Sergeant, D. C. Morgan; Third Sergeant, D. E. Jackson; Fourth Sergeant, John W. Fowler, jr.; Corporals—H. H. Norman, R. F. Davis, C. W. L. Powell; Privates—W. W. Bradbury (afterwards captain), E. M. Chamberlain, W. W. Morgan, W. L. Herron, P. H. Pate, C. E. McCulloch, James W. McCulloch, L. C. Powell, H. G. Woodall, J. S. Woodall, A. W. Mashburn, V. A. Wilson, W. J. Mason, J. V. Austin, W. M. Austin, John Eads, E. A. Davis, Dr. A. S. Mason, John W. Norman, E. L. Morton, Henry Gentry,

W. M. Cochran, J. B. Cochran, James Hunter (promoted captain), W. W. Brimm, William Carroll, C.
W. McAllister, J. O. McAllister, and many others from
the county, making it a full company.

The second company from DeKalb was the Steph-
ens Rifles, captain, L. J. Glenn. They went into
Cobb's Legion about August, 1861. Dr. Liddell,
Frank Herron, Norman Adams, John McCulloch, John
J. McKoy, and some others, went from Decatur in
this company.

The third company was the Murphey Guards, captain, John Y. Flowers. They came from the upper
part of the county, near Doraville. This company
was named in memory of Hon. Charles Murphey, of
DeKalb county, a prominent lawyer and member of
Congress, but then recently deceased. The company
had been uniformed by the people of the county, a
large sharge being contributed by Mr. and Mrs. Milton A. Candler, and Mr. and Mrs. Ezekiel Mason.
Mrs. Candler, whose maiden name was Eliza Murphey, the only child of Charles Murphey, gave the
banner, upon which was inscribed, "The God of Jacob
is with us."

The Fourth Company was The Bartow Avengers,
Captain William Wright, from the lower part of the
county about South River. The Fifth Company, Captain Rankin, was from Stone Mountain. These three
last mentioned companies went into the 38th Georgia
Regiment, in September, 1861, and belonged to the
Virginia Army. The Sixth Company, Captain E. L.
Morton's, entered service the last of August, 1861, in
the 36th Georgia Regiment, and was with the

Western Army under Johnston. The Seventh Company, the Fowler Guards, Captain Clay, went into the 42nd Georgia Regiment in the early part of 1862, and was also i: 'he Western Army.

There were several companies, mostly composed of DeKalb County men, that were made up and went from the camp of instruction near Decatur. Moses L. Brown was Captain of one, and L. D. Belisle of another. Besides the companies already named, all of which went into the infantry, there were many soldiers from DeKalb that went into the Cavalry and Artillery service of the regular army.

In the year 1863, when Georgia was threatened by Rosecrans coming into the State on its northern border, special troops were raised for its defence. Major General Howell Cobb commanded the division; General Henry R. Jackson one of the brigades. In Jackson's Brigade, in the 10th Georgia Regiment State Guards (Col. John J. Glenn and Lieutenant-Colonel J. N. Glenn), we find Company A of Cavalry troops. Of this company Milton A. Candler had command. These troops served through 1863 and 1864.

In April, 1863, Paul P. Winn, now a Presbyterian minister, then a mere youth, went into the army in the 45th Georgia Regiment, commanded by Col. Thomas J. Simmons. Other Decatur boys went into the service from other sections where the war found them located. Among these were Dr. James J. Winn, who enlisted at Clayton, Alabama, with the Barker Greys, and was in the battle of Bull Run. After a year or two he received a surgeon's commission, being the youngest surgeon in the army.

John C. Kirkpatrick, just eighteen, went into the service from Augusta with the Oglethorpe Infantry. With him were his cousin, William Dabney (now a Presbyterian minister in Virginia), and his friend, Frank Stone. This was in 1862, and John remained in the service until the close of the war, having been in severe battles (for he was in Cleburne's Division), including that of Jonesboro. In this engagement were other Decatur boys in other commands. Mr. John B. Swanton, but seventeen years old, was in that battle, and says that by his side stood, when mortally wounded, Franklin Williams, the brother of Mr. Hiram J. Williams. Says Mr. Swanton : "He was so near me I could have touched him with my hand." Three sons of Mrs. Martha Morgan, and cousins of DeWitt Morgan, were all in the service, Henry, Daniel, and Joseph Morgan. Jesse Chewning and Samuel Mann were in the 64th Georgia.

Josiah J. Willard, the only son of Mr. Levi Willard, while a sprightly, active youth, was nearsighted. He had a position in the commissary department at Camp Randolph, near Decatur, and went with it to Macon, July 11th, 1864, and remained there until the place surrendered after the fall of Richmond. He, also, is mentioned in other sketches.

There were also several companies of old men and boys who went into the State service when the last call for troops was made by the Confederate government.

Before the DeKalb soldiers go to meet the fortunes of war, let us recall some incidents that preceded their departure. On the northern side of the court-house

square there stood a large building, the residence of
Mr. Ezekiel Mason.   Here, day after day, a band of
devoted women met to make the uniforms for the
DeKalb Light Infantry.   These uniforms had been
cut by a tailor, but they were to be made by women's
hands.   Among the leading and directing spirits in
this work were Mrs. Jonathan B. Wilson, Mrs. Jane
Morgan, Mrs. Ezekiel Mason, Mrs. Levi Willard, Miss
Anna Davis, Mrs. James McCulloch, and Miss Lou
Fowler.   The most of this sewing was done by hand.

To the DeKalb Light Infantry, the day before its
departure, a beautiful silken banner was given.   The
ladies of the village furnished the material.   The address of presentation was made by Miss Mollie G.
Brown.   In September, of that same year, my sister
was invited to present a banner to Captain William
Wright's Company.   Her modest little address was
responded to in behalf of the company by Rev. Mr.
Mashburn, of the Methodist Church.   In March, 1862,
there was another banner presented from the piazza
of "the Mason Corner"—this time to the Fowler
Guards, by Miss Georgia Hoyle.   This banner was
made by the fair hands of Miss Anna E. Davis.   By
this time the spirit of independence of the outside
world had begun to show itself in the Southern-made
grey jeans of the soldiers, and in the homespun dress
of Miss Hoyle.

This banner, so skillfully made by Miss Anna
Davis, had a circle of white stars upon a field of blue,
and the usual bars of red and white—two broad red
bars with a white one between.   The banner of this
pattern was known as the "stars and bars," and was

the first kind used by the Confederate States. In May, 1863, the Confederate Congress adopted a National Flag, which had a crimson field with white stars in a blue-grounded diagonal cross, the remainder of the flag being white. But, when falling limp around the staff, and only the white showing, it could easily be mistaken for a flag of truce; therefore in March, 1865, the final change was made by putting a red bar across the end of the flag.

But what of the fate of these gallant young men, going forth so full of hope and courage, with tender and loving farewells lingering in their hearts?

Soon, ah! so soon, some of them fell upon the crimson fields of Virginia. James L. George ("Jimmie," as his friends lovingly called him) was killed in the first battle of Manassas. "Billy" Morgan died soon after the battle, and was buried with military honors in a private cemetery near Manassas. Two years after, his brother, De Witt Morgan, worn out in the siege of Vicksburg, was buried on an island in Mobile Bay. At the second battle of Manassas, James W. McCulloch and James L. Davis were both killed. Later on W. J. Mason, William Carroll, John M. Eads, H. H. Norman, Billy Wilson, and Norman Adams, were numbered among the slain. Among the wounded were Henry Gentry, Mose Brown, John McCulloch, W. W. Brimm, Dave Chandler, Riley Lawhorn, and Bill Herring.

A volume could easily be written concerning the bravery and the sufferings of the DeKalb county troops; but I must forbear. Concerning Warren Morton, of the 36th Georgia Regiment, who went

into the service at the age of fifteen, and suffered so
severely, I will refer my readers to a sketch in the
latter part of this book. Of William M. Durham, so
young, so gallant, who enlisted in Company K., 42nd
Georgia Regiment, much of interest will be found in
another chapter.

Among the Decatur members of Cobb's Legion
was Mr. John J. McKoy, who went out in the
Stephens Rifles when not more than nineteen years
old. He was in the battle of Yorktown, Seven Pines,
and in the Seven Days Fight around Richmond.
Owing to illness, and to business arising from the
attainment of his majority, he came home in 1863,
and, hiring a substitute when the conscript law was
passed, went to work at the Passport Office in Atlanta. In this same year he was married to Miss
Laura Williams of Decatur. Having raised Company
A., for the 64th Georgia Regiment, Mr. McKoy was
with it when it was sent to Florida, and was in the
battle of Olustee or Ocean Pond, in February 1864,
where General Alfred H. Colquitt won the title of
"The Hero of Olustee." Mr. McKoy remembers to
have seen on that eventful day, Col. George W. Scott,
then of Florida, but now of Decatur. At the battle
of Olustee, Col. Scott was in command of a regiment
of Cavalry. The banner of the regiment is now in
possession of his daughter, Mrs. Thomas Cooper.

The 64th Georgia was then sent to Virginia in
General Wright's brigade. A few days after "The
Mine Explosion," or undermining of the Confederate
works, an engagement occurred at Deep Bottom.
Here, General Girardy, of Augusta, was killed, and

several hundred of the Confederates were captured, among the number being Mr. McKoy. This was in July, 1864. He was sent to Fort Delaware, where he remained in prison until the close of the war. Here he spent a whole winter without a fire, and was subject to all that Fort Delaware meant. To escape the horrors of that prison, many of the two thousand officers there confined, took the oath not to fight against the United States. But Mr. McKoy and thirty-four others remained in prision, firm and loyal, even after the surrender, believing and hoping, up to July, 1865, that the war would be carried on west of the Mississippi river.

The soldiers who went to Virginia knew from their own experience the scenes of Manassas, Malvern Hill, Fort Harrison, Sharpsburg, Fredericksburg, Gettysburg and the Wilderness. Yet some of them were left to be surrendered by Lee at Appomatox Court House. The companies which were in the Western Army were in the leading battles of that Division, and were equally brave and abiding in their devotion to the cause.

For many of the foregoing facts concerning the troops from DeKalb, I am greatly indebted to Mr. Robert F. Davis, who went with DeKalb's first company, and who, after braving the perils of the war, came off unscathed. He still lives near Decatur, and is an elder in the Presbyterian Church.

I greatly regret my inability, even if I had the space, to give the names of all the soldiers who went from DeKalb, and to tell of their deeds of bravery and endurance. It has not been intentional that many are wholly omitted. It has been my privilege to see but one muster-roll of our county troops—that of Company K, 38th Georgia Regiment, kindly furnished by Mr. F. L. Hudgins, of Clarkston, a brave soldier who was in command of the Company when Lee surrendered. This muster-roll shows that out of the 118 names, forty-six were killed (or died), and seventeen were wounded ; that its first Captain, William Wright, resigned, and that three other Captains by promotion were all killed, *i. e.*, Gustin E. Goodwin, George W. Stubbs and R. H. Fletcher. Indeed, in nearly every instance, promotion in this Company meant death upon the battle field. And can we wonder that both the commissioned and the noncommissioned fell, when some of the principal battles in which they were engaged bore such names as Cold Harbor, Malvern Hill, Second Manassas, Sharpsburg, Fredericksburg, Chancellorsville, Winchester, Gettysburg, The Wilderness, Spottsylvania Courthouse, Mechanicsville, Fisher's Hill, Cedar Creek, Louise Courthouse and High Bridge ?

In memory of the dead, for the sake of the living and for the descendants of all mentioned therein, I copy the muster-roll of this company :

Company K., 38th Georgia Regiment:

Captain William Wright—resigned July, 1862.

1st Lieutenant Julius J. Gober—Died July 26th, 1862.

2nd Lieutenant Gustin E. Goodwin—Promoted captain ; killed August 28th, 1862.

3rd Lieutenant George W. Stubbs—Promoted captain; killed July 24th, 1864.

1st Sergeant John S. Johnston—Killed June 27th, 1862.

2nd Sergeant W. R. Henry—Promoted to 1st Lieutenant; lost a leg December 13th, 1862.

3rd Sergeant J. A. Maddox—Killed at Wilderness, May 5th, 1864.

4th Sergeant F. L. Hudgins—Promoted 1st Sergeant; wounded at Malvern Hill; shot through the body at Gettysburg.

5th Sergeant E. H. C. Morris—Promoted 3rd Lieutenant; killed at Second Manassas, August, 1862.

1st Corporal F. M. Gassaway—Killed at Second Manassas, August, 1862.

2nd Corporal J. M. Walker—Died in camp.

3rd Corporal W. A. Ward—Died in camp.

4th Corporal James L. Anderson—Wounded at Manassas and Spottsylvania court house.

John H. Akers—Killed at Second Manassas, 1862.

A. W. Allman—Killed at Cedar Creek, October 19th, 1864.

John Adams—Died in camp.

Enos Adams—

Isaac W. Awtry—

W. A. Awtry—

H. V. Bayne—Disabled by gunshot wound. Still living.

Allen Brown—

Lewis Brown—

Killis Brown—

William M. Brooks—

H. M. Burdett—

J. S. Burdett—
John S. Boyd—
James E. Ball—Killed at Gettysburg, July, 1863.
W. H. Brisendine—
L. R. Bailey—Transferred to Cobb's Legion.
John E. J. Collier—
James Collier—Died at Charlottesville, Va., 1862.
Z. J. Cowan—
J. J. Cowan—
G. G. Cook—
James E. Chandler—Killed at Sharpsburg, Md.,
    September 17th, 1862.
W. B. Chandler—Died in camp, May 31st, 1863.
John W. Chandler—Killed at Second Manassas, Au
    gust, 1862.
W. A. Childress—A physician in Atlanta.
J. H. Childers—
J. M. Dowis—Killed at Coal Harbor, June, 27th,
    1862.
W. H. Ellis—
John Eunis—
R. H. Fletcher—Promoted Captain ; killed in 1865.
A. M. Gentry—Died at Savannah in 1862.
W. F. Goodwin—Promoted 3rd Lieutenant; killed at
    Gettysburg in 1863.
C. H. Goodwin—Killed at Coal Harbor.
Joseph Grogan—
J. H. Grogan—
J. D. Grogan—Killed at Sharpsburg, Maryland, Sep-
    tember 17th, 1862.
Gideon Grogan—Killed at Sharpsburg, Maryland,
    September 17th, 1862.

James H. Gasaway—Disabled by gunshot.
William Gasaway—Disabled by gunshot.
John Gasaway—Discharged.
W. L. Goss—
F. L. Guess—Transferred to the 9th Georgia Artillery
    Battalion.
H. L. Head—
J. L. Henry—Killed at Coal Harbor, June 27th, 1862.
W. B. Heldebrand—Died recently.
H. H. Hornbuckle—Killed at Coal Harbor, June 27th,
    1862.
Joshua Hammond—Killed at Sharpsburg, September
    17th, 1862.
R. F. Jones—Killed at Coal Harbor.
J. W. Jones—Disabled by gunshot.
C. S. Jones—Killed in Richmond.
R. D. F. Jones—Disabled by gunshot.
J. M. Jones—
J. H. Jones—Disabled by gunshot.
James Jones—
John F. Kelley—
John H. Kelley—
James Kelley—
W. J. Little—Disabled by gunshot.
George Lee—Died in camp.
A. J. Lee—Discharged.
Wiley Manghon—
J. R. Mitchell—Killed December 13th, 1862, at Fred-
    ericksburg.
W. G. Mitchell—Disabled by gunshot.
E. J. Mitchell—

W. R. Maguire—Disabled by gunshot.

W. A. Morgan—

B. S. McClain—Died in camp.

John W. Nash—Killed December 13th, 1862, at Fredericksburg.

David N. Fair—Killed at Coal Harbor, June 27th, 1862.

W. B. Owen—

J. J. Pruett—Discharged.

John W. Phillips—Killed at Coal Harbor, June 27th, 1862.

John B. Thompson—

Will Thompson—

W. M. Richardson—Disabled at Second Manassas.

J. S. Richardson—Killed at Coal Harbor, June 27th, 1862.

D. D. Richardson—Died at Hanover Junction, 1862.

A. W. Stowers—

W. A. Smith—

J. M. Summey—Shot through at Coal Harbor.

S. J. Summey—Killed at Winchester, Va., June 13th, 1863.

James Toney—Musician.

C. W. Toney—Musician.

M. J. Tweedle—Wounded at Winchester, Va., September 19th, 1864.

S. J. Thomas—

R. L. Vaughn—Died at Savannah, Ga.

J. S. Vaughn—Wounded eight times at Coal Harbor.

W. T. Vaughn—Had both hands blown off.

J. C. Wiggins—Promoted Second Lieutenant; killed in June, 1864.

J. M. Wiggins—

R. W. Wiggins—Killed at Petersburg, Va., March 27th, 1865.

E. W. Wiggins—Killed at Sharpsburg, Maryland, September 17th, 1862.

G. W. Wiggins—

M. O. Wiggins—Disabled at Cedar Creek, October 19th, 1864.

G. W. Wade—Musician.

E. D. Wade—

F. M. Wade—

B. L. Wilson—Killed at Marie's Heights, May 4th, 1863.

W. A. Wright—

W. R. Wood—

Amos Wheeler—Killed at Spottsylvania, May 12th, 1864.

J. H. Wilson—Killed at Gettysburg, July 1st, 1863.

Jordan Wilson—Killed at Coal Harbor, June 27th, 1862.

CHAPTER III.

LABORS OF LOVE.

Musical—Decatur.

To a woman who lives and moves and has her being in the past, an invocation to time to "turn backward in its flight," would seem surperfluous. The scenes of other years being ever present, it would also seem that time, as a loving father, would linger fondly around her with panaceas for decay, mental and physical ; that her heart would never grow old, and her person never lose the attractions of youth ; but, in the economy of Him who doeth all things well, such is not the decree regarding aught that is mortal. And when the ravages incident to one's career have destroyed personal charm, and divested the mind of sparkling gem, the soul yearns for the protection of childhood and the companionship of youth. Scenes of the past, though dyed with "the blood of martyrs," are ever passing in kaleidoscopic beauty before the mind's eye, and tones too sweet for mortal ear are ever thrilling the heart with strange, sweet, expectant pleasure. This train of reflection, only far more elaborate, seizes for its guiding star, on this occasion, a scene which at the time of its enactment was indelibly impressed upon my mind, and left living, glowing tints, illuming my pathway through subsequent life ; a scene in which lovely girlhood, arrayed in pure white robes, lent a helping hand in the important work of supplying our soldiers with comforts, all the more appreciated because of the source from which emanating. With closed eyes, I see it now and listen to its enchanting melody. To render it more realistic than could be done by any description of mine, I subjoin a copy of the "Programme," the original of which I have preserved :

GRAND MUSICAL ENTERTAINMENT !

RELIEF FUND

FOR OUR SOLDIERS,

THURSDAY, MAY 15, 1862,

AT THE COURTHOUSE.

By the ladies of Decatur, Georgia, assisted by William H. Barnes, Colonel Thomas F. Lowe, Professor Hanlon, W. A. Haynes, R. O. Haynes, Dr. Geutebruck and Dr. Warmouth, of Atlanta.

PROGRAMME.

Part I.

1. Opening Chorus—Company.
2. Piano Duet—"March from Norma"—Miss Georgia Hoyle and Miss Missouri Stokes.
3. Solo—"Roy Neil"—Mrs. Robert Alston.
4. Quartette—Atlanta Amateurs.
5. "Tell Me, Ye Winged Winds"—Company.
6. "Our Way Across the Sea"—Miss G. Hoyle and Professor Hanlon.

7. March—Piano Duet—Miss Laura Williams and Miss Fredonia Hoyle.

8. Solo—Professor Hanlon.

9. Comic Song—W. H. Barnes.

10. Violin Solo—Colonel Thomas F. Lowe.

11. Solo—Dr. Warmouth.

12. "When Night Comes O'er the Plain"—Miss M. Stokes and Professor Hanlon.

13. "The Mother's Farewell"—Mrs. Maggie Benedict.

Part II.

1. Chorus—"Away to the Prairie"—Company.

2. Piano Solo—Miss G. Hoyle.

3. Song—Atlanta Amateurs.

4. Coquette Polka—Misses Hoyle and Stokes.

5. Chorus—"Let us Live with a Hope"—Company.

6. "Mountain Bugle"—Miss M. Stokes and Company.

7. "Mazurka des Traineaux"—Piano Duet—Misses Hoyle and Stokes.

8. Shiloh Retreat—Violin—Colonel Thomas F. Lowe.

Concluding with the Battle Song: "Cheer, Boys, Cheer"—W. H. Barnes.

Tickets, 50c. Children and Servants, half price.

Doors open 7:30 o'clock. Commence at 8:15 o'clock.

Atlanta Intelligencer Power Print.

LABORS OF LOVE.

Musical—Atlanta.

The citizens of Decatur were always invited to entertainments, social, literary, and musical, in Atlanta, that had in view the interest, pleasure or comfort of our soldiers ; therefore the invitation accompanying the following programme received ready response :

TWELFTH MUSICAL SOIREE

—of the—

ATLANTA AMATEURS,

Monday evening, June 24, 1861,

For the Benefit of

ATLANTA VOLUNTEERS,

Captain Woddail,

and the

CONFEDERATE CONTINENTALS,

Captain Seago,

Who Are Going to Defend Our Land.

Let all attend and pay a parting tribute to our brave soldiers.

PROGRAMME.

Part I.

1. We Come Again—(Original)—Company.
2. Dreams—(A Reverie)—Miss J. E. Whitney.
3. Violin Solo—(Hash)—Colonel Thomas F. Lowe.
4. "Not for Gold or Precious Stones"—Miss R. J. Hale.

5. Yankee Doodle—According to W. A. Haynes.

6. Dixie Variations—Mrs. W. T. Farrar.

7. "Two Merry Alpine Maids"—Misses M. F. and J. E. Whitney.

8. "When I Saw Sweet Nellie Home"—Misses Sasseen and Judson.

9. "Root Hog or Die"—W. H. Barnes.

Instrumental Trio, "La Fille du Regiment"—Messrs. Schoen and Heindl.   Vermicelli, (Variations)—W. H. Barnes and Openheimer.

Part II.

1. "Our Southern Land"—C. P. Haynes and Company.

2. "Through Meadows Green"—Miss M. F. Whitney.*

3. Solo—Thomas D. Wright.

4. "Home, Sweet Home"—Miss R. J. Hale.

5. Violin Exemplification—Col. Thomas F. Lowe.

6. "Happy Days of Yore"—Mrs. Hibler.

7. Quartette—(original)—Misses Whitney, Messrs. Barnes and Haynes.

8. "Rocked in the Cradle of the Deep"—Prof. Hanlon.   Encore—Ballad.

9. "I Come, I Come"—Misses Sasseen, Westmoreland and Sims.

The whole to conclude with the grand original.

---

*This lady, Miss "Frank" Whitney, is now the wife of Mr. Charles W. Hubner, the well-known Atlanta poet.

TABLEAU,

(In Two Parts).

The Women and Children of Dixie Rejoicing Over the Success of the Confederate Banner.

Scene 1. The Children of Dixie.

Scene 2. The Women—The Soldiers—Our Flag—Brilliant Illumination.

Doors open at half past 7 o'clock. Curtain will rise at half past 8 o'clock.

Tickets, Fifty Cents. Ushers will be on hand to seat audience.

W. H. BARNES, Manager.

CHAPTER IV.

LABORS OF LOVE.

Knitting and Sewing, and Writing Letters to " Our Soldiers."

A patriotic co-operation between the citizens of Decatur and Atlanta soon sprang up, and in that, as in all things else, a social and friendly interchange of thought and feeling and deed existed ; and we were never so pleased as when aiding each other in the preparation of clothing and edibles for "our soldiers," or in some way contributing to their comfort.

Many of us who had never learned to sew became expert handlers of the needle, and vied with each other in producing well-made garments ; and I became a veritable knitting machine. Besides the discharge of many duties incident to the times and tending to useful results, I knitted a sock a day, long and large, and not coarse, many days in succession. At the midnight hour the weird click of knitting needles chasing each other round and round in the formation of these useful garments for the nether limbs of "our boys," was no unusual sound ; and tears and orisons blended with woof and warp and melancholy sighs. For at that dark hour, when other sounds were shut out, we dared to listen with bated breath to "the still, small voice" that whispered in no unmistakable language suggestions which would have been rebuked in the glare of the noonday sun.

No mother nor sister nor wife nor aunt of a Confederate soldier, need be told what were the depressing suggestions of that "still, small voice" on divers occasions.

When the knitting of a dozen pairs of socks was completed, they were washed, ironed and neatly folded by one of our faithful negro women, and I then resumed the work of preparing them for their destination. Each pair formed a distinct package. Usually a pretty necktie, a pair of gloves, a handkerchief and letter, deposited in one of the socks, enlarged the package. When all was ready, a card bearing the name of the giver, and a request to "inquire within," was tacked on to each package. And then these twelve packages were formed into a bundle, and addressed to an officer in command of some company chosen to be the recipient of the contents.

I will give a glimpse of the interior of my letters to our boys. These letters were written for their spiritual edification, their mental improvement and their amusement.

"Never saw I the righteous forsaken."

"Full many a gem of purest ray serene,
 The dark unfathomed caves of ocean bear;
Full many a flower is born to blush unseen,
 And waste its sweetness on the desert air."

P. S.—"Apples are good but peaches are better;
 If you love me, you will write me a letter."—M.

"Remember now thy Creator in the days of thy youth.

> " If in the early morn of life,
>   You give yourself to God,
> He'll stand by you 'mid earthly strife,
>   And spare the chast'ning rod."—

P. S.—" Roses are red and violets blue,
    Sugar is sweet and so are you."—M.

" Love thy neighbor as thyself."

> " May every joy that earth can give
>   Around thee brightly shine;
> Remote from sorrow may you live,
>   And all of heaven be thine."—

P. S.—Remember me when this you see,
    Though many miles apart we be.—M

" Love worketh no ill to his neighbor ; therefore love is the fulfillment of the law."

> " This above all—to thine own self be true,
>   And it must follow as night the day,
> Thou canst not then be false to any one."

P. S.—"Sure as the vine twines round the stump,
    You are my darling sugar lump."—**M**.

" The night is far spent, the day is at hand ; let us, therefore, cast off the works of darkness and let us put on the armour of light."

> " As for my life, it is but short,
>   When I shall be no more ;
> To part with life I am content,
>   As any heretofore.
> Therefore, good people, all take heed,
>   This warning take by me—
> According to the lives you lead,
>   Rewarded you shall be."

P. S.—" My pen is bad, my ink is pale,
My love for you shall never fail."—M.

"Blessed are the peacemakers ; for they shall be called the children of God."

" The harp that once through Tara's halls
The soul of music shed,
Now hangs as mute on Tara's wall,
As if that soul were fled.
So sleeps the pride of former days,
So glory's thrill is o'er ;
And hearts that once beat high for praise
Now feel that pulse no more.
No more to chiefs and ladies bright
The harp of Tara swells ;
The chord alone that breaks at night
Its tale of ruin tells.
Thus Freedom, now so seldom wakes,
The only throb she gives
Is when some heart indignant breaks
To show that still she lives."—

P. S.—" My love for you will ever flow,
Like water down a cotton row."—M

"'The earth is the Lord's and the fullness thereof ; the world and they that dwell therein.

" For He hath founded it upon the seas, and established it upon the floods.

"Who shall ascend into the hill of the Lord, or who shall stand in his holy place ?

" He that hath clean hands and a pure heart ; who hath not lifted up his soul unto vanity nor sworn deceitfully."

" Know thyself, presume not God to scan.
The proper study of mankind is man."

P. S.—"Round as the ring that has no end,
　　Is my love for you, my own sweet friend."—M.

"God is love."

"Poor soul, the centre of my sinful earth,
　　Fooled by those rebel powers that there array,
Why dost thou pine within and suffer dearth,
　　Painting thy outward walls so costly gay?
Why so large cost, having so short a lease,
　　Dost thou upon thy fading mansion spend?
Shall worms, inheritors of this excess,
　　Eat up thy charge? Is this thy body's end?"

P. S.—"If you love me as I love you,
　　No knife can cut our love in two."—M.

"But this I say, He that soweth sparingly shall reap also sparingly; and he which soweth bountifully, shall reap also bountifully. Every man according as he purposeth in his heart, so let him give, not grudgingly, or of necessity; for God loveth a cheerful giver."

"Before Jehovah's awful throne
　　Ye nations bow with sacred joy;
Know that the Lord is God alone;
　　He can create and He destroy."

P. S.—"Above, below, in ocean, earth and skies,
　　Nothing's so pretty as your blue eyes."—M.

"I am come a light into the world, that whosoever believeth on Me should not abide in darkness."

"And neither the angels in heaven above,
　　Nor the demons down under the sea,
Can ever dissever my soul from the soul
　　Of the beautiful Annabel Lee."

P. S.—"Remember me! Remember me!
　　When this you see—Remember me!"—M.

" The Lord shall command the blessing upon thee in the storehouses, and in all that thou settest thine hand unto."

> " Lives of great men all remind us,
>   We can make our lives sublime,
> And departing, leave behind us,
>   Footprints on the sands of Time."

> P. S.—" Remember well and bear in mind,
>   A pretty girl's not hard to find ;
>   But when you find one nice and Gay
>   Hold on to her both night and day.—M.

" He that covereth his sins shall not prosper ; but whoso confesseth and forsaketh them shall have mercy."

> " I'd give my life to know thy art,
>   Sweet, simple, and divine ;
> I'd give this world to melt one heart,
>   As thou hast melted mine."—Mary.

> P. S.—" As the earth trots round the sun,
>   My love for you will ever run."—M.

CHAPTER V.

THE THIRD MARYLAND ARTILLERY.

Some Old Songs.

At some time in 1863, it was my privilege to meet a gallant band of men whose faith in the justice of our cause was so strong that they were constrained to turn their faces Southward and imperil their lives in its defence. These men represented the highest type of manhood in Maryland.

Sickness entered their camp, and the good ladies of Decatur insisted upon providing the comforts of home for the sick and wounded. Those to whom it was my privilege to minister belonged to the Third Maryland Artillery, under command of Captain John B. Rowan.*

Among them was one whose appreciation of kindness shown him ripened into an undying friendship, Captain W. L. Ritter, a devoted Christian gentleman, and now an elder in Doctor LeFevre's Church, Baltimore.

His fondness for that beautiful Southern song, by James R. Randall, entitled "Maryland, My Maryland!" was truly pathetic.

I subjoin the words to stir up the souls of our people by way of remembrance.

---

*This brave officer was killed near Nashville, Tennessee, Dec. 16th, 1864.

MARYLAND, MY MARYLAND.

The despot's heel is on thy shore,
  Maryland, My Maryland!
His touch is on thy temple door,
  Maryland, My Maryland.
Avenge the patriotic gore,
That flowed the streets of Baltimore,
And be the battle-queen of yore,
  Maryland, My Maryland.

Hark to a wand'ring son's appeal,
  Maryland, My Maryland!
My mother state, to thee I kneel,
  Maryland, My Maryland!
For life and death, for woe and weal,
Thy peerless chivalry reveal,
And gird thy beauteous limbs with steel,
  Maryland, My Maryland.

Thou wilt not cower in the dust,
  Maryland, My Maryland!
Thy beaming sword shall never rust,
  Maryland, My Maryland.
Remember Carroll's sacred trust,
Remember Howard's warlike thrust,
And all thy slumberers with the just,
  Maryland, My Maryland.

Come, 'tis the red dawn of the day,
  Maryland, My Maryland!
Come with thy panoplied array,
  Maryland, My Maryland.
With Ringold's spirit for the fray,
With Watson's blood at Monterey,
With fearless Lowe and dashing May ;
  Maryland, My Maryland.

Dear Mother! burst thy tyrant's chain,
  Maryland, My Maryland!
Virginia should not call in vain,

Maryland, My Maryland.
She meets her sisters on the plain,
"Sic Semper," 'tis the proud refrain
That baffles minions back again,
    Maryland, My Maryland.

Come! for thy shield is bright and strong,
    Maryland, My Maryland!
Come! for thy dalliance does thee wrong,
    Maryland, My Maryland.
Come to thy own heroic throng,
That stalks with liberty along,
And give a new Key to thy song,
    Maryland, My Maryland.

I see the blush upon thy cheek,
    Maryland, My Maryland!
But thou wast ever bravely meek,
    Maryland, My Maryland.
But, lo! there surges forth a shriek,
From hill to hill, from creek to creek,
Potomac calls to Chesapeake,
    Maryland, My Maryland.

Thou wilt not yield the vandal toll,
    Maryland, My Maryland!
Thou wilt not crook to his control,
    Maryland, My Maryland.
Better the fire upon thee roll,
Better the shot, the blade, the bowl,
Than crucifixion of the soul,
    Maryland, My Maryland.

I hear the distant thunder hum,
    Maryland, My Maryland!
The Old Line bugle, fife and drum,
    Maryland, My Maryland.
She is not dead, nor deaf, nor dumb—
Huzza! she spurns the Northern scum;
She breathes! She burns! She'll come, she'll come!
    Maryland, My Maryland.

An additional verse as sung by Mrs. Jessie Clark, of Crisp's Co., Friday night, Sept. 12th, 1862.

> Hark! tis the cannon's deaf'ning roar,
> Maryland, My Maryland!
> Old Stonewall's on thy hallow'd shore,
> Maryland, My Maryland.
> Methinks I hear the loud huzza
> Ring through the streets of Baltimore—
> Slaves no longer—free once more
> Maryland, My Maryland.

There were other songs sung in those days. Some of the most popular were "Bonnie Blue Flag," "Dixie," "Bob Roebuck is my Soldier Boy," "Who will Care for Mother Now?" "Her Bright Smile Haunts me Still," "Let me Kiss Him for his Mother," "All Quiet Along the Potomac To-Night," "Rock me to Sleep, Mother," "When I Saw Sweet Nellie Home," "Just Before the Battle, Mother." In a collection of old music, now never played, there lie before me copies of these songs. They were published in various Southern cities on paper not firm and smooth, but rather thin and coarse, but quite presentable. What memories these songs awake! Where, oh where, are those who sang them over thirty years ago! Who of the singers are now living? How many have gone to the Eternal Shore?

CHAPTER VI.

A DARING AND UNIQUE CHASE.

The Capture and Re-capture of the Railroad Engine, "The "General."

In the early spring of 1862, there occurred an episode of the war which, up to that date, was the most exciting that had happened in our immediate section. The story has often been told ; but instead of relying upon my memory, I will condense from the written statement of Mr. Anthony Murphy, of Atlanta, Georgia, who was one of the principal actors in the chase.

Mr. Murphy begins his narrative by saying : "On Saturday morning, April 12th, 1862, about 4 o'clock, I went aboard a passenger train that started then for Chattanooga, Tennessee. My business that day was to examine an engine that furnished power to cut wood and pump water for the locomotives at Allatoona, a station forty miles from Atlanta. As foreman of machine and motive power, it became my duty to go that morning. This train was in charge of Engineer Jeff Cain, and Conductor W. A. Fuller. It was known as a freight and passenger train. The train arrived in Marietta, twenty miles from Atlanta, shortly after daylight. I stepped from the coach and noticed a number of men getting on the car forward of the one I rode in. They were dressed like citizens from the country, and I supposed they were volunteers for the

army, going to Big Shanty, now known as Kennesaw,
a station about eighteen miles from Marietta, where
troops were organized and forwarded to the Confederate army in Virginia and other points. At this station the train stopped for breakfast, and, as the engineer, conductor, myself and other passengers went
to get our meals, no one was left in charge of the locomotive. I had about finished, when I heard a noise
as if steam were escaping. Looking through a window I saw the cars move, saw the engineer and fireman at the table, and said to them : 'Some one is
moving your engine.' By this time I was at the front
door, and saw that the train was divided and passing
out of sight."

Mr. Murphy, the conductor, and the engineer then
held a brief consultation. He asked about the men
who got on at Marietta (who afterwards proved to be
a Federal raiding party, Andrews and his men), and
remarked : " They were the men who took the engine
and three cars." At the time he thought they were
Confederate deserters, who would run the engine as
far as it would have steam to run, and then abandon
it. Mr. Murphy and his two comrades concluded that
it was their duty to proceed after them. A Mr. Ken-
drick, connected with the railroad, coming up, they
requested him to go on horseback to Marietta, the
nearest telegraph station, and communicate with the
superintendent at Atlanta, while they "put out on
foot after a locomotive under steam." Knowing they
would reach a squad of track-hands somewhere on the
line, they had some hope, and they did, in a few miles,
meet a car and hands near Moon's Station, about two

miles from Big Shanty. They pressed the car, and
two hands to propel it, which propelling was done by
poles pressed against the ties or ground, and not by a
crank. Soon they reached a pile of cross-ties on the
track, and found the telegraph wire cut. Clearing off
the ties, they pressed on until they reached Acworth
Station, six miles from Big Shanty. There they
learned that the train they were pursuing had stopped
some distance from the depot, and having been carefully examined by its engineer, had moved off at
a rapid rate. This satisfied the pursuers that the
capturers of the engine "meant something more than
deserters would attempt ;" and then they "thought of
enemies from the Federal army." Says the narrator :
"We moved on to Allatoona. At this place we received two old guns, one for Fuller, and one for the
writer. I really did not know how long they had been
loaded, nor do I yet, for we never fired them. These
were the only arms on our engine during our chase.
Two citizens went along from here, which made about
seven men on our little pole-car. As we proceeded
toward Etowah, we moved rapidly, being down grade,
when suddenly we beheld an open place in the track.
A piece of rail had been taken up by the raiders. Having no brake, we could not hold our car in check, and
plunged into this gap, turning over with all hands
except Fuller and myself, who jumped before the car
left the track. The little car was put on again, and
the poling man sent back to the next track-gang to
have repairs made for following trains."

Arriving at Etowah, the pursuers found the engine
"Yonah," used by the Cooper Iron Company, and

pressed it into service. They got an open car, and stocked it with rails, spikes and tools, and moved on to Cartersville. Passing on to Rogers' Station, they learned that the raiders had stopped there for wood and water, telling Mr. Rogers that they were under military orders, and that the engine crew proper were coming on behind. At Kingston the raiders had told that they were carrying ammunition to General Beauregard, on the line of the Memphis and Charleston Railroad, near Huntsville, Alabama. At this point the "Yonah" was sent back to Etowah, and the supply car of the pursuers coupled to the engine "New York." But at Kingston the Rome Railroad connects with the Western & Atlantic road, and the Rome engine and train were in the way. Instead of clearing the track for the "New York," the crowd at the Kingston depot, having learned the news, took possession of the Rome engine and some cars attached, and pulled out for the chase, which compelled Mr. Murphy and his friends to abandon their outfit and run to get on the same train. A few miles were made, when they found a pile of cross-ties on the rails, and the telegraph wires cut. Clearing the track they moved on, when they encountered another gap. Here Messrs. Murphy and Fuller, believing that they would meet the engine "Texas" with a freight train, left the obstructed train and pressed on again on foot, advising the crowd to return, which they did. The pursuers met the "Texas" two miles from Adairsville, and, motioning the engineer to stop, they went aboard and turned him back. At Adairsville they learned that Andrews had not been long gone. Says the narrator : "About three miles from Calhoun we came in sight for the first time of the captured engine, and three freight cars. They had stopped to remove another rail, and were in the act of trying to get it out when we came in sight. * * * As we reached them, they cut loose one car and started again. We coupled this car to our engine, and moved after them. * * * From Resaca to Tilton the road was very crooked, and we had to move cautiously. The distance between us was short. * * * I feared ambushing by Andrews—reversing the engine and starting it back under an open throttle valve. * * * To prevent us closing in on them, the end of the box car was broken out, and from this they threw cross-ties on the track to check our speed and probably derail us. * * * I had a long bar fastened to the brake wheel of the tender to give power so that four men could use it to help check and stop the engine suddenly. I also stood by the reverse lever to aid the engineer to reverse his engine, which he had to do many times to avoid the cross-ties.

"Passing through and beyond Tilton, we again came in sight. At this point the road has a straight stretch of over a mile. A short distance from Tilton and just as we rounded the curve, 'The General' with the raiders was rounding another curve, leaving the straight line, giving us a fine view for some distance across the angle. * * * The fastest run was made at this point. * * * I imagine now, as I write this, I see the two great locomotives with their human freight speeding on, one trying to escape, the other endeavoring to overtake, and if such had happened none might

have been left to give the particulars of that exciting
and daring undertaking. The chances of battle were
certainly against us if Andrews had attempted fight."

Just beyond Dalton the pursuers found the telegraph wire cut. On reaching the "tunnel," they
were satisfied that Andrews was short of wood, or the
tunnel would not have been so clear of smoke. Passing through the tunnel they kept on, and beyond
Ringgold, about two miles, the captors left "The
General" and made for the woods. The pursuers
were in sight of them. Mr. Fuller and others started
after the raiders. Mr. Murphy went on the engine to
examine the cause of the stop. He found no wood in
the furnace, but plenty of water in the boiler. Says
Mr. Murphy: "I took charge of the engine, 'General,'
had it placed on the side-track, and waited for the
first train from Chattanooga to Atlanta. I reached
Ringgold about dark. I went aboard, and reaching
Dalton, the first telegraph station, I sent the first
news of our chase and re-capture of the 'General' to
Atlanta."

5

CHAPTER VII.

Coming Home from Camp Chase—The Faithful Servant's
Gift—A Glimpse of Confederate Braves.

"A letter from Marse Thomie," said our mail carrier, Toby, as he got in speaking distance on his return from the post office.

"What makes you think so ?" I said, excitedly.

"I know his hand-write, and this is it," selecting a
letter from a large package and handing it to me. The
very first glimpse of the superscription assured me of
his confident assertion.

The letter was addressed to our mother, and bore a
United States postage stamp, and the beloved signa-
ture of her only son, Thomas J. Stokes. A thrill of
gratitude and joy filled our hearts too full for utterance, as we read :

"MY DEAR MOTHER : I have learned that the soldiers of the 10th Texas Infantry will be exchanged
for the United States troops very soon, perhaps to-
morrow; and then, what happiness will be mine ! I
can scarcely wait its realization. A visit home, a
mother's embrace and kiss, the heart-felt manifestations of the love of two sisters, and the joy and glad
expression of faithful servants. I may bring several
friends with me, whom I know you will welcome, both
for my sake and theirs—they are valiant defenders of
the cause we love. Adieu, dear mother, and sisters,
until I see you at home, 'home, sweet home.' "

"Thomie is coming home!" "Thomie Stokes is coming home!" was the glad announcement of mother, sisters, and friends; and the servants took up the intelligence, and told everybody that Marse Thomie was coming home, and was going to bring some soldiers with him.

Another day dawned and love's labor commenced in earnest. Doors were opened, and rooms ventilated : bed-clothing aired and sunned, and dusting brushes and brooms in willing hands removed every particle of that much dreaded material of which man in all his glory, or ignominy, was created. Furniture and picture frames were polished and artistically arranged. And we beheld the work of the first day, and it was good.

When another day dawned we were up with the lark, and his matin notes found responsive melody in our hearts, the sweet refrain of which was, "Thomie is coming"—the soldier son and brother. Light bread and rolls, rusks and pies, cakes, etc., etc., were baked, and sweetmeats prepared, and another day's work was ended and pronounced satisfactory.

The third day, for a generous bonus, "Uncle Mack's" services were secured, and a fine pig was slaughtered and prepared for the oven, and also a couple of young hens, and many other luxuries too numerous to mention.

When all was ready for the feast of thanksgiving for the return of the loved one, the waiting seemed interminable. There was pathos in every look, tone, and act of our mother—the lingering look at the calendar, the frequent glance at the clock, told that the days were counted, yea, that the hours were numbered. At length the weary waiting ended, and the joyous meeting came of mother and son, of sisters and brother, after a separation of four years of health and sickness, of joy and anguish, of hope and fear.

As we stood upon the platform of the Decatur depot, and saw him step from the train, which we had been told by telegram would bring him to us, our hearts were filled with consternation and pity, and tears unbidden coursed down our cheeks, as we looked upon the brave and gallant brother, who had now given three years of his early manhood to a cause rendered dear by inheritance and the highest principles of patriotism, and, in doing so, had himself become a physical wreck. He was lean to emaciation, and in his pale face was not a suggestion of the ruddy color he had carried away. A constant cough, which he tried in vain to repress, betrayed the deep inroads which prison life had made upon his system; and in this respect he represented his friends—in describing his appearance, we leave nothing untold about theirs. In war-worn pants and faded grey coats, they presented a spectacle never to be forgotten.

Joy and grief contended for the supremacy. We did not realize that even a brief period of good nursing and feeding would work a great change in the physical being of men just out of the prison pens of the frigid North, and wept to think that disease, apparently so deeply rooted, could not be cured, and that they were restored to us but to die. Perceiving our grief and divining the cause, our Thomie took us, our mother first, into his arms and kissed us, and said in his old-time way, "I'll be all right soon."

And Toby and Telitha, the house servants, came in for their share of kindly greeting.

Thomie then introduced us to Captain Lauderdale, Captain Formwalt, and Lieutenant McMurray, his Texas friends and comrades in arms. Our cordial, heart-felt welcome was appreciated by this trio of gentlemen, and to this day we receive from them messages of abiding friendship. Captain Lauderdale was one of the most perfect gentlemen I ever saw—tall, graceful, erect, and finely formed. His face, of Grecian mould, was faultless; and his hair, black as a raven's plumage, and interspersed with grey, would have adorned the head of a king. His bearing was dignified and yet affable, and so polished and easy in manner as to invite most friendly intercourse.

Captain Formwalt was also a fine specimen of manhood—free and easy, gay and rollicking. He seemed to think his mission on earth was to bring cheerfulness and glee into every household he entered.

Lieutenant McMurray was unlike either of his friends. Apparently cold, apathetic and reserved, he repelled all advances tending to cordial relations, until well acquainted, after which he was metamorphosed into a kind and genial gentleman.

Thomie, dear Thomie, was a boy again, and while our guests were refreshing themselves preparatory to

dinner, he was going all over the house, for every
nook and corner was endeared by association.   He
opened the piano, and running his fingers over the
keys with the grace and ease of his boyhood, he
played accompaniments to his favorite songs, "Home
Again," and "Way Down Upon the Suwanee River,"
trying to sing, but prevented by the irrepressible
coughing.   Then, with nervous hand, he essayed
"When this Cruel War is Over."   Turning away from
the piano, he went to the library and handled with
tender care the books he had read in boyhood.   Shake-
speare, Milton, Byron and Moore possessed no interest for him now; and Blackstone and Chitty were
equally ignored.   The books his mother and sister
read to him in his childhood were, as if by intuition,
selected, and fondly conned and handled.   His own
name was written in them, and his tearful eyes lingered long and lovingly upon these reminders of boyhood's happy hours.   With a sigh he left the library,
and espying Toby, who kept where he could see as
much as possible of "Marse Thomie," he called the
boy and held an encouraging little conversation with
him.

Dinner being ready, our mother led the way to the
dining room.   Our guests having taken the seats assigned them, Thomie took his near his mother—his
boyhood's seat at table.   By request, Captain Lauderdale asked the blessing.   And, oh, what a blessing
he invoked upon the "dear ones, who, with loving
hands, prepared this feast for the son and brother
of the household, and for his friends in peace and comrades in war."   Pleasant conversation ensued, and all

enjoyed the repast. But the gentlemen seemed to us to eat very little, and, in reply to our expression of disappointment, they explained the importance of limiting themselves for several days in this respect.

As there was no trunk to send for, and no valise to carry, we rightly surmised that the clothing of these good men was limited to the apparel in which they were clad, and it was decided by my mother and myself that I should go to Atlanta and get material for a suit of clothes for Thomie, and good warm underclothing for them all. Arrived at Atlanta, I was irresistibly led by that mystic power, which has often controlled for good results the acts of man, to go to Dr. Taylor's drug store. Here I found King, our faithful negro man, as busy as a bee, labeling and packing medicine for shipment. I approached him and said :

" King, Thomie has come."

" Marse Thomie ?"

" Yes."

" Thank God," he said, with fervor.

When I was about leaving the store, he said :

" Miss Mary, just wait a minute, please, and I will get something that I want you to take to Marse Thomie, and tell him I don't want him to be hurt with me for sending it to him. I just send it because I love him—me and him was boys together, you know, and I always thought he ought to 'er took me with him to the war."

" What is it, King ?"

" Just a little article I got in trade, Miss Mary," was all the satisfaction he vouchsafed.

When he handed it to me, knowing by the sense of touch that it was a package of dry goods, I took it to Mrs. O'Connor's millinery establishment, and asked the privilege of opening it there. Imagine my astonishment and delight, when I beheld a pattern of fine grey cassimere. I felt of it, and held it up between my eyes and the light. There was nothing shoddy about it. It was indeed a piece of fine cassimere, finer and better than anything I could have procured in Atlanta at that time. The circumstance was suggestive of Elijah and the ravens, and I thanked God for the gift so opportune, and lost no time in returning to the drug store, and thanking King, the raven employed by the Lord to clothe one of His little ones. Nor did I lose any time in adding to the package other articles of necessity, flannel and the best Georgia-made homespun I could procure, and was then ready to take the return train to Decatur. Thomie was deeply touched by the opportune gift, and said that King was a great boy, and that he must see him.

After supper I clandestinely left the house, and ran around to Todd McAllister's and begged him to take the job of making the suit. He agreed to cut the coat, vest and pantaloons by measure, and for that purpose went home with me, shears and tape measure in hand. Having finished this important part of the job, he told me he could not make the suit himself, but he thought if I would " talk right pretty to the old lady," she would do it. Next morning I lost no time in "talking pretty" to the old lady, and, having secured her promise to undertake the work, it was soon in her hands. With the help of faithful, efficient women, and I suspect of her husband, too, the job was executed surprisingly soon. In the meantime the making of flannel garments, and homespun shirts with bosoms made of linen pillow-cases, was progressing with remarkable celerity.

When all was finished, and Thomie was arrayed in his new suit, which set admirably well notwithstanding the room allowed for increasing dimensions, which we doubted not under good treatment he would attain—King Solomon, in purple and fine linen, was not looked upon with more admiration than was he by his loving mother and sisters. His cough had in a measure yielded to remedies, and his cheeks bore the tinge of better blood.

Good Mr. Levi Willard, his wife and children, had already been to see Thomie and the strangers within our gates, and many others had sent kind messages and substantial tokens of regard. And the young people of Decatur, young ladies and little boys, were planning to give him a surprise party. And among these loving attentions was a visit from King, the faithful.

The flowers bloomed prettier, the birds sang sweeter, because of their presence; but time waits for no man, and we were admonished by low conversations and suggestive looks that these men, officers in the army of the Confederacy, were planning their departure.

Many amusing incidents, as well as those of a horrible character, were told of their prison life in Camp Chase. To illustrate the patriotism of Southern men, Colonel Deshler, as a prisoner of war, figured conspicuously; and many anecdotes, ludicrous and pathetic, quaint and original, revealed the deep devotion of his love for the South. In one of these word-paintings, he was represented as sitting on his legs, darning the seat of his pantaloons, when a feminine curiosity seeker came along. When she perceived his occupation, she said with a leer that would have done credit to Lucifer :

"You rebels find it pretty hard work to keep your gray duds in order, don't you?"

Without looking at her, he whistled in musical cadence the contempt he felt for her and her ilk ; and the imprecations, he would not have expressed in words, were so distinct and well modulated as to leave no doubt as to their meaning.

The time had come for the nature of the low-toned conversations referred to, to be revealed, and Thomie was chosen to make the revelation. Planning to have mother and sisters present, he discussed the duties of patriotism, and the odium men brought upon themselves by not discharging those duties. Making the matter personal, he referred to himself and friends, to the great pleasure and personal benefit derived from a week's sojourn at home; of the love for us that would ever linger in their hearts; of the pleasant memories that would nerve them in future conflicts ; and in conclusion told us that to-morrow they would leave us to join their command at Tullahoma, where the decimated regiment was to stay until its numbers were sufficiently recruited for service.

Instead of yielding to grief, we repressed every evidence of it, and spoke only words of encouragement to these noble men who had never shirked a duty, or sought bomb-poof positions in the army of the Confederacy. After this interview, Thomie abandoned himself to cheerfulness, to almost boyish .gaiety. He kept very close to his mother. She had grown old so rapidly since the troubles began, that she needed all the support that could be given her in this ordeal. This he perceived without seeming to do so, and left nothing within his power undone for her encouragement. He even discussed with perfect equanimity the probability, yea, the more than probability, of his getting killed in battle ; for, said he, "he that taketh up the sword, by the sword shall he perish." And, he added, "strong, irrepressible convictions constrained me to enter the army in defense of mother, home, and country. My vote was cast for the secession of my state from the union of states which existed only in name, and I would not have accepted any position tendered me which would have secured me from the dangers involved by that step. I was willing to give my life if need be, for the cause which should be dear to every Southern heart."

Every one present responded to these noble sentiments, for were we not soldiers, too, working for the same noble cause, and aiding and abetting those who fought its battles?

Before retiring to our rooms, Captain Lauderdale, as usual, led in prayer, fervent, deep and soul supporting, more for our mother and ourselves than for himself and his comrades in their perilous positions. And dear Thomie, whom I had never heard pray since his cradle invocation,

" Now I lay me down to sleep,
I pray the Lord my soul to keep,"

finished in words thrilling and beautiful. The effect was electrical. Tears and sobs were no longer repressed, and all found relief from long pent-up feelings. O, the blessedness of tears!

Morning came, clear as crystal, and cool and exhilarating. The household were up at early dawn. A strong decoction of coffee was prepared, and fresh cream toast and boiled eggs, meat relishes being served cold. Knapsacks—there were knapsacks now—were packed, and blankets rolled and buckled in straps, and our ebony Confederates, Toby and Telitha, stood ready to convey them to the depot. In order to meet the morning train at seven o'clock we started, but the services of Toby and Telitha were not accepted. The gentlemen said it would never do for soldiers to start off to report for service with negroes carrying their knapsacks and blankets. They had no muskets to shoulder, for of these they had been divested at Arkansas Post, months ago, when captured by the enemy.

Lieutenant McMurray, who was in feeble health, announced himself unable to report for duty, and remained with us several weeks longer.

The parting at the depot did not betray the grief, almost without earthly hope, that was rankling in our hearts, and the "good-bye's" and "God bless you's" were uttered with a composure we little thought at our command.

As the time of his departure had drawn near, Thomie had sought opportunities to tell me much of the young girl in Texas, who had healed the lacerations of his youthful heart, and won the admiration of

his manhood, and whom he had made his wife. Upon
her devotion he dwelt with peculiar pathos and gratitude ; and he concluded these conversations with the
request that under any and all circumstances I would
be a sister to her. On one occasion we were standing near the piano, and, when we ceased to talk,
Thomie opened it, and in tones that came from the
heart, and that were tremulous with emotion, he
sang, "When this Cruel War is Over."

> Why sings the swan its sweetest notes,
> When life is near its close ?

Since writing the foregoing, I have had access to a
journal kept during the war by my half sister, Missouri Stokes, in which are the following entries of historic value : "On the 11th of January, 1868, Arkansas Post, the fort where Thomie was stationed, fell
into the hands of Yankees. General Churchhill's
whole command, numbering about four thousand,
were captured, a few being killed aud wounded. We
knew that Thomie, if alive, must be a prisoner, but
could hear no tidings from him. Our suspense continued until the latter part of March, when ma received
a letter from our loved one, written at Camp Chase
(military prison), Ohio, February 10th. This letter
she forwarded to me, and I received it March 21st,
with heart-felt emotions of gratitude to Him who had
preserved his life. A few weeks afterwards another
letter came, saying he expected to be exchanged in a
few days, and then for several weeks we heard no
more."

From this journal I learn that the date of Thomie's
arrival was May 16th, 1863. My sister wrote of him :

" He seemed much changed, although only four years and a half had elapsed since we parted. He looked older, thinner, and more careworn, and gray hairs are sprinkled among his dark brown curls. His health had been poor in the army, and then, when he left Camp Chase, he, as well as the other prisoners, was stripped by the Yankees of nearly all his warm clothing. He left the prison in April, and was exchanged at City Point. How strange the dealings of Providence. Truly was he led by a way he knew not. He went out to Texas by way of the West, and returned home from the East. God be thanked for preserving his life, when so many of his comrades have died. He is a miracle of mercy. After their capture, they were put on boats from which Yankee small-pox patients had been taken. Some died of small-pox, but Thomie has had varioloid and so escaped. He was crowded on a boat with twenty-two hundred, and scarcely had standing room. Many died on the passage up the river, one poor fellow with his head in Thomie's lap. May he never go through similar scenes again !"

From this same journal I take the following, written after Missouri's return to the school she was teaching in Bartow county :

"Sabbath morning, June 14th. Went to Cartersville to church. Some time elapsed before preaching commenced. A soldier came in, sat down rather behind me, then, rising, approached me. *It was Thomie.* I soon found (for we did talk in church) that he had an order to join Kirby Smith, with a recommendation from Bragg that he be allowed to recruit for his regiment. Fortunately there was a vacant seat in the carriage, so he went out home with us. Monday 15th, Thomie left. I rode with him a little beyond the school-house, then took my books and basket, and with one kiss, and, on my part, a tearful good-bye, we parted. As I walked slowly back, I felt so lonely. He had been with me just long enough for me to real·ize a brother's kind protection, and now he's torn away, and I'm again alone. I turned and looked. He was driving slowly along—he turned a corner and was hidden from my view. Shall I see him no more? Or shall we meet again? God only knows. After a fit of weeping, and one earnest prayer for him, I turned my steps to my little school."

And thus our brother went back to Texas, and gladly, too, for was not his Mary there?

Of Thomie's recall to join his command at Dalton; of his arrival at home the next February, on his way to "the front;" of his participation in the hard-fought battles that contested the way to Atlanta; and of his untimely death at the fatal battle of Franklin, Tennessee, I may speak hereafter.

Even in the spring and summer of 1863, the shadows began to deepen, and to hearts less sanguine than mine, affairs were assuming a gloomy aspect. I notice in this same journal from which I have quoted the foregoing extracts, the following:

"Our fallen braves, how numerous! Among our generals, Zollicoffer, Ben McCulloch, Albert Sidney Johnston, and the saintly, dauntless Stonewall Jackson, are numbered with the dead; while scarcely a household in our land does not mourn the loss of a brave husband and father, son or brother."

CHAPTER VIII.

SOME SOCIAL FEATURES.

Morgan's Men Rendezvous near Decatur—Waddell's Artillery
—Visits from the Texans—Surgeon Haynie and his Song.

In the winter of 1864 there seems to have been a
lull of hostilities between the armies at "the front."
Morgan's men were rendezvousing near Decatur.
Their brave and dashing chief had been captured, but
had made his escape from the Ohio penitentiary, and
was daily expected. Some artillery companies were
camping near, among them Waddell's. There was
also a conscript camp within a mile or two; so it is
not to be wondered at that the young ladies of Decatur
availed themselves in a quiet way of the social enjoyment the times afforded, and that there were little
gatherings at private houses at which "Morgan's
men" and the other soldiers were frequently represented.

Our brother was absent in Texas, where he had
been assigned to duty, but my sister was at home, and
many an hour's entertainment her music gave that
winter to the soldiers and to the young people of Decatur. My mother's hospitality was proverbial, and
much of our time these wintry months was spent in
entertaining our soldier guests, and in ministering to
the sick in the Atlanta hospitals, and in the camps
and temporary hospitals about Decatur.

So near were we now to "the front" (about a hundred miles distant), that several of my brother's Texas comrades obtained furloughs and came to see us. Among these were Lieutenants Prendergast and Jewell, Captain Leonard and Lieutenant Collins, Captain Bennett and Lieutenant Donathan. They usually had substantial boots made while here, by Smith, the Decatur boot and shoe maker, which cost less than those they could have bought in Atlanta. We received some very pleasant calls from Morgan's men and Waddell's Artillery. Among the latter we have always remembered a young man from Alabama, James Duncan Calhoun, of remarkable intellectual ability, refreshing candor and refinement of manner. Ever since the war Mr. Calhoun has devoted himself to journalism. Among the former we recall Lieutenant Adams, Messrs. Gill, Dupries, Clinkinbeard, Steele, Miller, Fortune, Rowland, Baker, and Dr. Lewis. These gentlemen were courteous and intelligent, and evidently came of excellent Kentucky and Tennessee families. One evening several of these gentlemen had taken tea with us, and after supper the number of our guests was augmented by the coming of Dr. Ruth, of Kentucky, and Dr. H. B. Haynie, surgeon of the 14th Tennessee Cavalry. Dr. Haynie was an elderly, gray-haired man, of fine presence, and with the courtly manners of the old school. On being unanimously requested, he sang us a song entitled: "The Wailings at Fort Delaware," which he had composed when an inmate of that wretched prison. As one of the gentlemen remarked, "there is more truth than poetry in it;" yet there are in it some indi-

6

cations of poetic genius, and Dr. Haynie sang it with
fine effect.

"THE WAILINGS AT FORT DELAWARE."

By B. H. HAYNIE, Surgeon 14th Tennessee Cavalry (Morgan's Division).

Oh! here we are confined at Fort Delaware,
With nothing to drink but a little lager beer,
Infested by vermin as much as we can bear;
Oh Jeff, can't you help us to get away from here ?

CHORUS—

And it's home, dearest home, the place I ought to be,
Home, sweet home, way down in Tennessee,
Where the ash and the oak and the bonny willow tree,
Are all growing green way down in Tennessee.

The Island itself will do well enough,
But the flat-footed Dutch are filthy and rough,
Oh! take us away from the vandal clan,
Down into Dixie among the gentlemen.

CHORUS—And its home, dearest home, etc.

Spoiled beef and bad soup is our daily fare,
And to complain is more than any dare ;
They will buck us and gag us, and cast us in a cell,
There to bear the anguish and torments of hell.

CHORUS —

The den for our eating is anything but clean,
And the filth upon the tables is plainly to be seen,
And the smell of putrefaction rises on the air,
" To fill out the bill " of our daily fare.

CHORUS—

*" The sick are well treated," as Southern surgeons say,
" And the losses by death are scarcely four per day ;"
It's diarrhœa mixture for scurvy and small-pox,
And every other disease of Pandora's box!

CHORUS—

Oh! look at the graveyard on the Jersey shore,
At the hundreds and the thousands who'll return no more;
Oh ! could they come back to testify
Against the lying devils, and live to see them die !

CHORUS—

* "Our kindness to prisoners you cannot deny,
For we have the proof at hand upon which you can rely ;
It's no Dutch falsehood, nor a Yankee trick,
But from Southern surgeons who daily see the sick."

CHORUS—

Our chaplain, whose heart was filled with heavenly joys,
Asked leave to pray and preach to Southern boys ;
"Oh, no !" says the General, "you are not the man,
You are a Southern rebel, the vilest of your clan !"

CHORUS—

Oh ! speak out, young soldier, and let your country hear,
All about your treatment at Fort Delaware ;
How they worked you in their wagons when weary and sad,
With only half rations, when plenty they had.

CHORUS—

The barracks were crowded to an overflow,
Without a single comfort on the soldier to bestow ;
Oh, there they stood shivering in hopeless despair,
With insufficient diet or clothing to wear !

CHORUS—

The mother stood weeping in sorrows of woe,
Mingling her tears with the waters that flow ;
Her son was expiring at Fort Delaware,
Which could have been avoided with prudence and care.

CHORUS—

Oh ! take off my fetters and let me go free,
To roam o'er the mountains of old Tennessee ;
To bathe in her waters and breathe her balmy air,
And look upon her daughters so lovely and fair.

CHORUS—

Then, cheer up, my brave boys, your country will be free,
Your battles will be fought by Generals Bragg and Lee ;
And the Yankees will fly with trembling and fear,
And we'll return to our wives and sweethearts so dear.

CHORUS—

And it's home, dearest home, the place where I ought to be,
Home, sweet home way down in Tennessee,
Where the ash and the oak, and the bonny willow tree,
Are all growing green way down in Tennessee.

---

* The fifth and seventh verses are criticisms upon four Southern surgeons. who gave the Federal authorities a certificate that our prisoners were well treated, and our sick well cared for, and that the average loss by death was only four per day.

CHAPTER IX.

THOMIE'S SECOND HOME COMING.

He Leaves for "The Front"—His Christian Labors in Camp—
He Describes the Battle of New Hope Church—The Great
Revival in Johnston's Army.

Early one morning in the February of the winter just referred to (that of 1864), as my sister lay awake, she heard some one step upon the portico and knock. As Toby opened the door, she heard him exclaim : "Why howd'y, Marse Thomie !" Her first thought was, "now he is back just in time to be in the battle !" for a resumption of hostilities was daily looked for near Dalton. We were all greatly surprised at Thomie's arrival on this side of the Mississippi, as only a few days before we had received a letter from him, written, it is true, so long as the November before, saying he had been assigned to duty out in Texas by General Henry McCulloch. But the consolidation of the regiments in Granbury's brigade having been broken up, he had been ordered back to join his old command. He had left Marshall, Texas, the 28th of January, having made the trip in one month, and having walked four hundred miles of the way. Under the circumstances, we were both glad and sorrowful at his return. After a stay of three days, he left us for "the front." In the early morning of February 29th, we went with him to the depot, the last time we four were ever together. Parting from him was a bitter trial to our mother, who wept silently as we walked back to the desolate home, no longer gladdened by the sunny presence of the only son and brother. Perhaps nothing will give a more graphic impression of some phases of army life at this time, nor a clearer insight into our brother's character, than a few extracts from his letters written at this period to his sister Missouri, and preserved by her to this day:

"Dalton, Ga., March 15th, 1864.— * * * Our regiment takes its old organization as the 10th Texas, and Colonel Young has been dispatched to Texas to gather all the balance, under an order from the war department. We are now in Dalton doing provost duty (our regiment), which is a very unpleasant duty. It is my business to examine all papers whenever the cars arrive, and it is very disagreeable to have to arrest persons who haven't proper papers. The regulations about the town are very strict. No one under a brigadier-general can pass without approval papers. My guard arrested General Johnston himself, day before yesterday. Not knowing him they wouldn't take his word for it, but demanded his papers. The old General, very good-humoredly showed them some orders he had issued himself, and, being satisfied, they let him pass. He took it good-humoredly, while little colonels and majors become very indignant and wrathy under such circumstances. From which we learn, first, the want of good common sense, and, secondly, that a great man is an humble man, and does not look with contempt upon his inferiors in rank, whatsoever that rank may be.

"There is a very interesting meeting in progress here. I get to go every other night. I have seen several baptized since I have been here. There are in attendance every evening from six to seven hundred soldiers. There are many who go to the anxious seat. Three made a profession of religion night before last. I am going to-night. There seems to be a deep interest taken, and God grant the good work may go on until the whole army may be made to feel where they stand before their Maker. Write soon.

Your affectionate brother,

Tom Stokes."

From another letter we take the following:

"Near Dalton, April 5th, 1864.—We have had for some weeks back very unsettled weather, which has rendered it very disagreeable, though we haven't suffered; we have an old tent which affords a good deal of protection from the weather. It has also interfered some with our meetings, though there is preaching nearly every night that there is not rain. Brother Hughes came up and preached for us last Friday night and seemed to give general satisfaction. He was plain and practical, which is the only kind of preaching that does good in the army. He promised to come back again. I like him very much. Another old brother, named Campbell, whom I heard when I was a boy, preached for us on Sabbath evening. There was much feeling, and at the close of the services he invited mourners to the anxious seat, and I shall never forget that blessed half-hour that followed; from every part of that great congregation they came, many with streaming eyes; and, as they gave that old patriarch their hands, asked that God's people would pray for them. Yes, men who never shrank in battle from any responsibility, came forward weeping. Such is the power of the Gospel of Christ when preached in its purity. Oh, that all ministers of Christ could, or would, realize the great responsibility resting upon them as His ambassadors.

"Sabbath night we had services again, and also last night, both well attended, and to-night, weather permitting, I will preach. God help me and give me grace from on high, that I may be enabled, as an humble instrument in His hands, to speak the truth as it is in Jesus, for 'none but Jesus can do helpless sinners good.' I preached last Sabbath was two weeks ago to a large and attentive congregation. There seemed to be much seriousness, and although much embarrassed, yet I tried, under God, to feel that I was but in the discharge of my duty; and may I ever be found battling for my Savior. Yes, my sister, I had rather be an humble follower of Christ than to wear the crown of a monarch. Remember me at all times at a Throne of Grace, that my life may be spared to become a useful minister of Christ.

"Since my return we have established a prayer-meeting in our company, or, rather, a kind of family service, every night after roll call. There is one other company which has prayer every night. Captain F. is very zealous. There are four in our company who pray in public—one sergeant, a private, Captain F. and myself. We take it time about. We have cleared up a space, fixed a stand and seats, and have a regular preaching place. I have never seen

such a spirit as there is now in the army. Religion is
the theme. Everywhere, you hear around the camp-
fires at night the sweet songs of Zion. This spirit
pervades the whole army. God is doing a glorious
work, and I believe it is but the beautiful prelude to
peace. I feel confident that if the enemy should
attempt to advance, that God will fight our battles for
us, and the boastful foe be scattered and severely
rebuked.

"I witnessed a scene the other evening, which did
my heart good—the baptism of three men in the creek
near the encampment. To see those hardy soldiers
taking up their cross and following their Master in
His ordinance, being buried with Him in baptism,
was indeed a beautiful sight. I really believe, Missouri, that there is more religion now in the army
than among the thousands of skulkers, exempts and
speculators at home. There are but few now but who
will talk freely with you upon the subject of their
soul's salvation. What a change, what a change!
when one year ago card playing and profane language
seemed to be the order of the day. Now, what is the
cause of this change? Manifestly the working of
God's spirit. He has chastened His people, and this
manifestation of His love seems to be an earnest of
the good things in store for us in not a far away
future. 'Whom the Lord loveth He chasteneth, and
scourgeth every son whom He receiveth.' Let all the
people at home now, in unison with the army, hum-
bly bow, acknowledge the afflicting hand of the
Almighty, ask Him to remove the curse upon His own
terms, and soon we will hear, so far as our Nation is

concerned, 'Glory to God in the highest, on earth peace, good will toward men!'

"I received the articles ma sent by Brother Hughes, which were much relished on the top of the coarse fare of the army. * * * Write me often. God bless you in your labors to do good.

Your affectionate brother,

T. J. STOKES."

From another of those time-stained, but precious letters, we cull the following, under the heading of:

"In Camp, Near Dalton, Ga., April 18, 1864.— * * * The good work still goes on here. Thirty-one men were baptized at the creek below our brigade yesterday, and I have heard from several other brigades in which the proportion is equally large (though the thirty-one were not all members of this brigade). Taking the proportion in the whole army as heard from (and I have only heard from a part of one corps), there must have been baptized yesterday 150 persons —maybe 200. This revival spirit is not confined to a part only, but pervades the whole army. * * * * Brother Hughes was with us the other night, but left again the next morning. The old man seemed to have much more influence in the army than young men. I have preached twice since writing to you, and the Spirit seemed to be with me. The second sermon was upon the crucifixion of Christ: text in the 53d chapter of Isaiah: 'He was wounded for our transgressions and bruised for our iniquities.' It was the first time in my life, that is, in public speaking, that my feelings got so much the mastery of me as to make me weep like a child. In the conclusion I asked all who felt an interest in the prayers of God's people to come to the anxious seat. Many presented themselves, and I could hear many among them, with sobs and groans, imploring God to have mercy upon them; and I think the Lord did have mercy upon them, for when we opened the door of the church six united with us. Every Sabbath you may see the multitude wending their way to the creek to see the solemn ordinance typical of the death, burial and resurrection of our Savior. Strange to say that a large number of those joining the pedo-Baptist branches prefer being immersed; though in the preaching you cannot tell to which denomination a man belongs. This is as it should be; Christ and Him crucified should be the theme. It is time enough, I think, after one is converted, to choose his church rule of faith.

"If this state of things should continue for any considerable length of time, we will have in the Army of Tennessee an army of believers. Does the history of the world record anywhere the like? Even Cromwell's time sinks into insignificance. A revival so vast in its proportions, and under all the difficulties attending camp life, the bad weather this spring, and innumerable difficulties, is certainly an earnest of better, brighter times not far in the future."

To the believer in Jesus, we feel sure that these extracts concerning this remarkable work of grace, will prove of deep interest; so we make no apologies for quoting in continuation the following from another of those letters of our soldier brother, to whom the conquests of the cross were the sweetest of all themes:

"Near Dalton, April 28th, 1864.—My Dear Sister:
I should have written sooner but have been very much
engaged, and when not engaged have felt more like
resting than writing, and, to add to this, Sister Mary
very agreeably surprised me by coming up on last
Saturday. She left on Tuesday morning for home.
While she was at Dalton, I went down on each day
and remained until evening. I fear ma and sister are
too much concerned about me, and therefore render
themselves unhappy. Would that they could trust
God calmly for the issue. And I fear, too, that they
deny themselves of many comforts, that they may furnish me with what I could do (as many have to do)
without.

    *   *   *   *   *   *   *

" The great unexampled revival is fast increasing
in interest. I have just returned from the creek,
where I saw thirty-three buried with Christ in baptism, acknowledging there before two thousand persons that they were not ashamed to follow Jesus in
His ordinance. My soul was made happy in witnessing the solemn scene. In that vast audience everything was as quiet and respectful as in a village
chapel ; and, by the way, I have seen village congre-
gations who might come here and learn to behave.
General Lowry baptized about thirteen of them who
were from his brigade. He is a Christian, a soldier
and a zealous preacher, and his influence is great. It
was truly a beautiful sight to see a general baptizing
his men. He preaches for our brigade next Sabbath.
I preached for General Polk's brigade night before
last, and we had a very interesting meeting. They

have just begun there, yet I had a congregation of some 400. At the conclusion of the services, I invited those who desired an interest in our prayers to manifest their desire by coming to the altar. A goodly number presented themselves, and we prayed with them. I shall preach for them again very soon. The revival in our brigade has continued now for four weeks, nearly, and many have found peace with their Savior. If we could remain stationary a few weeks longer, I believe the greater portion of the army would be converted. This is all the doings of the Lord, and is surely the earnest of the great deliverance in store for us. It is the belief of many, that this is the 'beginning of the end.' From all parts of the army the glad tidings comes that a great revival is in progress. I wish I had time to write to you at length. One instance of the power of His spirit : A lieutenant of our regiment, and heretofore very wild, became interested, and for nearly three weeks seemed groaning in agony. The other day he came around to see me, and, with a face beaming with love, told me he had found Christ, and that his only regret now was that he had not been a Christian all his life. It is growing dark. I must close. More anon.

Affectionately,

YOUR BROTHER."

We take up the next letter in the order of time. It is numbered 25. The envelope is of brown wrapping paper, but neatly made, and has a blue Confederate 10 cent postage stamp. It is addressed to my sister, who was then teaching at Corinth, Heard county, Georgia. It is dated :

"Near Dalton, May 5th, 1864." After speaking of having to take charge early the next morning of the brigade picket guard, Thomie goes on to say:

"The sun's most down, but I think I can fill these little pages before dark. Captain F., coming in at this time, tells me a dispatch has just been received to the effect that the Yankees are advancing in the direction of Tunnel Hill, but they have made so many feints in that direction lately that we have become used to them, so don't become uneasy.

"The great revival is going on with widening and deepening interest. Last Sabbath I saw eighty-three immersed at the creek below our brigade. Four were sprinkled at the stand before going down to the creek, and two down there, making an aggregate within this vicinity of eighty-nine, while the same proportion, I suppose, are turning to God in other parts of the army, making the grand aggregate of many hundreds. Yesterday I saw sixty-five more baptized, forty more who were to have been there failing to come because of an order to be ready to move at any moment. They belong to a more distant brigade. * * If we do not move before Monday, Sabbath will be a day long to be remembered—'the water will,' indeed, 'be troubled.' Should we remain three weeks longer, the glad tidings may go forth that the Army of Tennessee is the army of the Lord. But He knoweth best what is for our good, and if He sees proper can so order His providence as to keep us here. His will be done."

The next letter is addressed to me, but was sent to

my sister at my request, and is dated "Allatoona
Mountains, Near Night, May 22nd." He writes :

"Oh, it grieved my very soul when coming through
the beautiful Oothcaloga valley, to think of the sad
fate which awaited it when the foul invader should
occupy that 'vale of beauty.' We formed line of battle
at the creek, at the old Eads place ; our brigade was
to the left as you go up to Mr. Law's old place on the
hill, where we stayed once when pa was sick. Right
here, with a thousand dear recollections of by-gone
days crowding my mind, in the valley of my boyhood,
I felt as if I could hurl a host back. We fought them
and whipped them, until, being flanked, we were compelled to fall back. We fought them again at Cass
Station, driving them in our front, but, as before, and
for the same reason, we were compelled to retreat.

    *   *   *   *   *   *

"As I am requested to hold prayer-meeting this
evening at sunset, I must close."

Thomie's next letter in this collection is addressed
to his sister Missouri, who had returned home, and is
headed, simply, "Army of Tennessee, May 31st." It
is written in a round, legible, but somewhat delicate
hand, and gives no evidence of nervousness or hurry.
To those fond of war history, it will be of special interest :

"Our brigade, in fact our division, is in a more quiet
place now than since the commencement of this campaign. We were ordered from the battlefield on Sunday morning to go and take position in supporting
distance of the left wing of the army, where we arrived about the middle of the forenoon, and remained

there until yesterday evening, when our division was ordered back in rear of the left centre, where we are now. Contrary to all expectations, we have remained here perfectly quiet, there being no heavy demonstration by the enemy on either wing. We were very tired, and this rest has been a great help to us; for being a reserve and flanking division, we have had to trot from one end of the wing of the army to the other, and support other troops.

*   *   *   *   *   *

"Well, perhaps you would like to hear something from me of the battle of New Hope Church, on Friday evening, 27th inst. We had been, since the day before, supporting some other troops about the centre of the right wing, when, I suppose about 2 o'clock, we were hurried off to the extreme right to meet a heavy force of the enemy trying to turn our right. A few minutes later the whole army might now have been in the vicinity of Atlanta, but, as it was, we arrived in the nick of time, for before we were properly formed the enemy were firing into us rapidly. We fronted to them, however, and then commenced one of the hottest engagements, so far, of this campaign. We had no support, and just one single line against a whole corps of the enemy, and a lieutenant of the 19th Arkansas, wounded and captured by them, and subsequently retaken by our brigade, stated that another corps of the enemy came up about sundown. The fighting of our men, to those who admire warfare, was magnificent. You could see a pleasant smile playing upon the countenances of many of the men, as they would cry out to the Yankees. 'Come on, we are demoralized!'

"One little incident right here, so characteristic of the man. Major Kennard (of whom I have told you often, lately promoted), was, as usual, encouraging the men by his battle-cry of, 'Put your trust in God, men, for He is with us,' but concluding to talk to the Yankees awhile, sang out to them, 'Come on, we are demoralized,' when the Major was pretty severely wounded in the head, though not seriously; raising himself up, he said:

" 'Boys, I told them a lie, and I believe that is the reason I got shot.'

"The fighting was very close and desperate, and lasted until after dark. About 11 o'clock at night, three regiments of our brigade charged the enemy, our regiment among them. We went over ravines, rocks, almost precipices, running the enemy entirely off the field. We captured many prisoners, and all of their dead and many of their wounded fell into our hands. This charge was a desperate and reckless thing, and if the enemy had made any resistance they could have cut us all to pieces. I hurt my leg slightly in falling down a cliff of rocks, and when we started back to our original line of battle I thought I would go back alone and pick my way; so I bore off to the left, got lost, and completely bewildered between two armies. I copy from my journal:

" 'Here I was, alone in the darkness of midnight, with the wounded, the dying, the dead. What an hour of horror! I hope never again to experience such. I am not superstitious, but the great excitement of seven hours of fierce conflict, ending with a bold, and I might say reckless, charge—for we knew not what

7

was in our front—and then left entirely alone, causes
a mental and physical depression that for one to fully
appreciate he must be surrounded by the same circumstances. My feelings in battle were nothing to compare to this hour. After going first one way and then
another, and not bettering my case, I heard some one
slipping along in the bushes. I commanded him to
halt, and inquired what regiment he belonged to, and
was answered, '15th Wisconsin,' so I took Mr. Wisconsin in, and ordered him to march before me—a nice
pickle for me then, had a prisoner and did not know
where to go. Moved on, however, and finally heard
some more men walking, hailed them, for I had become
desperate, and was answered, 'Mississippians.' Oh,
how glad I was! The moon at this time was just rising,
and, casting her pale silvery rays through the dense
woods, made every tree and shrub look like a spectre.
I saw a tall, muscular Federal lying dead and the
moonlight shining in his face. His eyes were open
and seemed to be riveted on me. I could not help but
shudder. I soon found my regiment, and 'Richard
was himself again.'

"I went out again to see if I could do anything for
their wounded. Soon found one with his leg shot
through, whom I told we would take care of. Another, shot in the head, was crying out continually;
'Oh, my God! oh, my God!!' I asked him if we could
do anything for him, but he replied that it would be
of no use. I told him God would have mercy upon
him, but his mind seemed to be wandering. I could
not have him taken care of that night, and, poor fellow, there he lay all night.

"The next morning I had the privilege of walking over the whole ground, and such a scene! Here lay the wounded, the dying, and the dead, hundreds upon hundreds, in every conceivable position; some with contorted features, showing the agony of death, others as if quietly sleeping. I noticed some soft beardless faces which ill comported with the savage warfare in which they had been engaged. Hundreds of letters from mothers, sisters, and friends were found upon them, and ambrotypes, taken singly and in groups. Though they had been my enemies, my heart bled at the sickening scene. The wounded nearly all expressed themselves tired of the war.

"For the numbers engaged upon our side, it is said to be the greatest slaughter of the enemy of any recent battle. Captain Hearne, the old adjutant of our regiment, was killed. Eight of our regiment were instantly killed; two mortally wounded, since dead.

"I did not think of writing so much when I began, but it is the first opportunity of writing anything like a letter that I have had. Lieutenant McMurray is now in charge of the Texas hospital at Auburn, Alabama.

*　　*　　*　　*　　*　　*

"Well, you are now Aunt Missouri. Oh, that I could see my boy! Heaven has protected me thus far and I hope that God will consider me through this dreadful ordeal, and protect me for Christ's sake; not that there is any merit that I can offer, but I do hope to live that I may be an humble instrument in the hands of my God to lead others to Him. I hold prayer in our company nearly every night when circumstances will permit, and the men don't go to sleep before we are quiet. Poor fellows, they are ever willing to join me, but often are so wearied I dislike to interrupt them.

"My sister, let our trust be confidently in God. He can save or He can destroy. Let us pray Him for peace. He can give it us ; not pray as if we were making an experiment, but pray believing God will answer our prayers, for we have much to pray for."

My sister subsequently copied into her journal the following extract, taken from his, and written soon after the Battle of New Hope Church :

"May 31st, 1864.—Here we rest by a little murmuring brook, singing along as if the whole world was at peace. I lay down last night and gazed away up in the peaceful heavens. All was quiet and serene up there, and the stars seemed to vie with each other in brightness and were fulfilling their allotted destiny. My comrades all asleep ; nothing breaks the silence. I leave earth for a time, and soar upon 'imagination's wings' far away from this war-accursed land to where bright angels sing their everlasting songs of peace and strike their harps along the golden streets of the New Jerusalem, and the swelling music bursts with sweet accord throughout vast Heaven's eternal space !'"

*   *   *   *   *   *

Again on Sabbath, June 5th, he writes: "No music of church bells is heard today summoning God's people to worship where the gospel is wont to be heard. We are near a large log church called Gilgal. What a different scene is presented to-day from a Sabbath four years ago when the aged minister of God read to a large and attentive congregation : "The

Lord is my shepherd, I shall not want. He maketh
me to lie down in green pastures, He leadeth me
beside the still waters." O, God, wilt thou not inter-
pose Thy strong arm to stop the bloody strife? Wilt
Thou not hear the prayers of Thy people who daily
say, Lord, give us peace? The Lord will answer,
and soon white-robed peace will smile upon our
unhappy country. O God, hasten the day, for we are
sorely vexed; and thine shall be all the glory."

Ere peace was to dawn upon his beloved country,
his own soul was to find it through the portals of
death ; but ere that time, save a brief interval of enforced rest, weary marchings and heart-breaking
scenes and sorrows were to intervene.

Thomie's next letter is dated " In the Field, near
Lost Mountain, June 14th," and the next "In the
Ditches, June 22nd, 1864." The next, "Near Chattahoochee River, July 6th, 1864," tells of the retreat of
the army from Kennesaw Mountain to Smyrna
Church, and of his coming off safely from another
"small fight" the day before, in which several of his
comrades were killed.

Owing to nervous prostration, and other illness,
Thomie was soon after sent to the hospital at Macon,
transferred from there to Augusta, and from the latter
point given leave of absence to visit his sister, who
had found refuge with her cousin, Mrs. T. J. Hillsman, a daughter of Rev. Wm. H. Stokes of blessed
memory. Here, with his father's kindred, cheered by
beautiful hospitality and cousinly affection, our
darling brother enjoyed the last sweet rest and quiet
earth was e'er to give him before he slept beneath its sod.

CHAPTER X.

A visit to Dalton—The fidelity of an old-time slave.

"From Atlanta to Dalton, $7.75. From the 23d to the 26th of April, 1864, to Mrs. John Reynolds, for board, $20.00. From Dalton to Decatur, $8.00."

The above statement of the expense attending a round trip to Dalton, Georgia, is an excerpt from a book which contains a record of every item of my expenditures for the year 1864.

This trip was taken for the purpose of carrying provisions and articles of clothing to my brother and his comrades in General Joseph E. Johnston's command. In vain had our mother tried to send appetizing baskets of food to her son, whose soldier rations consisted of salty bacon and hard tack; some disaster, real or imaginary, always occurred to prevent them from reaching their destination, and it was, therefore, determined at home that I should carry the next consignment.

After several days' preparation, jugs were filled with good sorghum syrup, and baskets with bread, pies, cakes and other edibles at our command, and sacks of potatoes, onions and peppers were included. My fond and loving mother and I, and our faithful aid-de-camps of African descent, conveyed them to the depot. In those days the depot was a favorite resort with the ladies and children of Decatur. There they always heard something from the front—wherever that might be. The obliging agent had a way, all his own, of acquiring information from the army in all its varied commands, and dealt it out galore to the encouragement or discouragement of his auditors, as his prejudices or partialities prompted. On this occasion many had gone there, who, like myself, were going to take the train for Atlanta, and in the interim were eager to hear everything of a hopeful character, even though reason urged that it was hoping against hope.

I was the cynosure of all eyes, as I was going to "the front;" and every mother who had a darling son in that branch of the army hoped that he would be the first to greet me on my arrival there, and give me a message for her. And I am sure, if the love consigned to me for transmission could have assumed tangible form and weight, it would have been more than fourteen tons to the square inch.

Helpful, willing hands deposited with care my well-labeled jugs, baskets, etc., and I deposited myself with equal care in an already well-filled coach on the Georgia Railroad. Arrived in Atlanta I surreptitiously stowed the jugs in the car with me, and then asked the baggage-master to transfer the provisions to a Dalton freight train. Without seeming to do so, I watched his every movement until I saw the last article safely placed in the car, and then I went aboard myself. Surrounded by jugs and packages, I again became an object of interest, and soon found myself on familiar terms with all on board ; for were we not friends and kindred bound to each other by the closest ties? Every age and condition of Southern life was represented in that long train of living, anxious freight. Young wives, with wee bit tots chaperoned by their mothers and sometimes by their grandmothers, were going to see their husbands, for, perhaps, the last time on earth; and mothers, feeling that another fond embrace of their sons would palliate the sting of final separation. The poor man and the rich man, fathers alike of men fighting the same battles in defense of the grandest principle that ever inspired mortal man to combat, on their way to see those men and leave their benedictions with them; and sisters, solitary and alone, going to see their beloved brothers and assure them once more of the purest and most disinterested love that ever found lodgment in the human heart. Many and pleasant were the brief conversations between those dissimilar in manners, habits and conditions in life; the great bond connecting them rendered every other consideration subordinate, and the rich and poor, the educated and ignorant, met and mingled in harmonious intercourse.

Those were days of slow travel in the South. The roads were literally blockaded with chartered cars, which contained the household goods of refugees who had fled from the wrath and vandalism of the enemy, and not unfrequently refugees themselves inhabited cars that seemed in fearful proximity to danger. Ample opportunity of observation on either side was furnished by this slow travel, and never did the fine, arable lands bordering the Western & Atlantic road from the Chattahoochee river to Dalton give greater promise of cereals, and trees in large variety were literally abloom with embryo fruit. Alas! that such a land should be destined to fall into the hands of despoilers.

At Dalton I went immediately to the agent at the depot, whom I found to be my old friend, John Reynolds, for the purpose of getting information regarding boarding houses. He told me his wife was in that line and would accommodate me, and, to render the application more easy, he gave me a note of introduction to her.

A beautiful, well-furnished room was given me, and a luscious supper possessed exhilarating properties.

In the meantime, Mr. Reynolds had, at my request, notified my brother, whom he knew, of my presence in his house, and I awaited his coming anxiously; but I was disappointed. A soldier's time is not his own, even in seasons of tranquility, and he was on duty and could not come then, but he assured me on a small scrap of paper, torn from his note-book, that he would come as soon as he could get off "tomorrow morning."

The waiting seemed very long, and yet it had its ending. The night was succeeded by a typical April day, replete with sunshine and shower, and the hopes and fears of a people struggling for right over wrong.

At length the cheery voice of him, who always had a pleasant word for every one, greeted me, and I hastened to meet him. That we might be quiet and undisturbed, I conducted him to my room, and a long and pleasant conversation ensued. I wish I had time and space to recapitulate the conversation; for its every word and intonation are preserved in the archives of memory, and will enter the grand eternities with me as free from discord as when first uttered. Our mother's failing health gave him concern, but his firm reliance in Him who doeth all things well, quieted his sad forebodings and led the way to pleasanter themes.

He loved to dwell upon the quaint and innocent peculiarities of his younger sister, and, as for his older one, it was very evident that he regarded her fully strong enough to "tote her own skillet," and "paddle her own canoe." A rap upon the door indicated that some one wished to see either one or the other of us. I responded, and was met by a negro boy bearing a huge waiter, evidently well-filled, and covered over with a snow-white cloth. The aroma from that waiter would have made a mummy smile. I had it put upon a table, and then I removed the cover, and saw with gratification the squab pie which I had ordered for dear Thomie, and a greater gratification awaited me, *i. e.*, seeing him eat it with a relish. Nor was the pie the only luxury in that waiter. Fresh butter and buttermilk, and a pone of good corn bread, etc., etc., supplemented by baked apples and cream and sugar.

"Come, dear Thomie, and let us eat together once more," was my invitation to that dinner, and radiant with thanks he took the seat I offered him. I did not have the Christian courage to ask him to invoke a blessing upon this excellent food, but I saw that one was asked in silence, nevertheless, and I am sure that an invocation went up from my own heart none the less sincere.

"Sister, I appreciate this compliment," he said.

"I could do nothing that would compliment you, Thomie," I answered, and added, "I hope you will enjoy your dinner as a love offering from me."

We lingered long around that little table, and many topics were touched upon during that period.

After dinner I asked Thomie to lie down and rest awhile. He thanked me, and said that the bed would tempt an anchorite to peaceful slumber, and he could not resist its wooings. A few minutes after he lay down he was sound asleep. He slept as a child—calm and peaceful. That a fly might not disturb him, I improvised a brush—my handkerchief and a tender twig from a tree near by being the component parts. As I sat by him and studied his manly young face, and read its expression of good will to all mankind, I wept to think that God had possibly required him as our sacrifice upon the altar of our country.

The slanting rays of the Western sun fell full and radiant upon his placid face, and awakened him from this long and quiet slumber. With a smile he arose and said :

"This won't do for me."

Hasty good-byes and a fervent "God bless you" were uttered, and another one of the few partings that remained to be taken took place between the soldier and his sister.

*　　*　　*　　*　　*　　*

The day was bright and exhilarating, in the month of June, 1864. Gay laughing Flora had tripped over woodland and lawn and scattered with prodigal hands flowers of every hue and fragrance, and the balmy

atmosphere of early summer was redolent with their
sweet perfume; and all nature, animate and inanimate,
seemed imbued with the spirit of adoration towards
the Giver of these perfect works. Although many
hearts had been saddened by the mighty conflict being
waged for the supremacy of Constitutional rights,
there were yet in Decatur a large number to whom
personal sorrow for personal bereavement had not
come, and they were in sympathy with this beautiful
scene, whose brilliant tints were but the reflection of
divine glory, and whose faintest odor was distilled in
the alchemy of heaven.

I was contemplating this scene in grateful admiration, and blended with my thoughts came the memory
of my brother, who was in the foremost ranks of the
contest. He, too, loved the beautiful and the good,
and "looked from nature up to nature's God." All
unconsciously I found myself plucking his favorite
flowers, and arranging a choice boquet, a spirit offering to him who might even then be hovering over me
and preparing my mind for the sad denouement. With
these reflections, I ascended the steps of my cottage
home, and turned to take another look upon the enchanting scene, when I saw, approaching, one of my
mother's faithful servants, who was hired to Dr.
Taylor, a well-known druggist of Atlanta. Ever apprehensive of evil tidings from "the front," and "the
front" being the portion of the army that embraced
my brother, I was almost paralyzed. I stood as if riveted to the floor, and awaited developments. King, for
that was the name of the ebony-hued and faithful
servant whose unexpected appearance had caused such

a heart-flutter, came nearer and nearer. On his approach I asked in husky voice, "Have you heard anything from your Marse Thomie, King ?"

" No, ma'am ; have you ?"

The light of heaven seemed to dispel the dark
clouds which had gathered over and around my horizon, and I remembered my duty to one, who, though
in a menial position, had doubtless come on some kind
errand.

"Come in, King, and sit down and rest yourself,"
I said, pointing to an easy chair on the portico.

" I am not tired, Miss Mary, and would rather
stand," he replied.

And he did stand, with his hat in his hand ; and I
thought for the first time in my life, probably, that
he evinced a true manhood, worthy of Caucasian lin-
eage ; not that there was a drop of Caucasian blood
in his veins, for he was a perfect specimen of the African race and as black as Erebus.

The suspense was becoming painful, when it was
broken by King asking :

"Miss Mary, is Miss Polly at home ?"

" Yes, King, and I will tell her you are here."

" Miss Polly," my mother and King's mistress,
soon appeared and gave him a genuine welcome.

King now lost no time in making known the object
of his visit, and thus announced it :

"Miss Polly, don't you want to sell me ?"

" No ; why do you ask ?"

"Because, Miss Polly, Mr. Johnson wants to buy
me, and he got me to come to see you and ask you if
you would sell me."

"Do you want me to sell you, King? Would you rather belong to Mr. Johnson than me?"

"Now, Miss Polly, you come to the point, and I am going to try to answer it. I love you, and you have always been a good mistuss to us all, and I don't think there is one of us that would rather belong to some one else; but I tell you how it is, Miss Polly, and you musn't get mad with me for saying it; when this war is over none of us are going to belong to you. We'll all be free, and I would a great deal rather Mr. Johnson would lose me than you. He is always bragging about what he will do; hear him talk, you would think he was a bigger man than Mr. Lincoln is, and had more to back him; but I think he's a mighty little man myself, and I want him to lose me. He says he'll give you his little old store on Peachtree street for me. It don't mean much, I know, but, much or little, it's going to be more than me after the war."

And thus this unlettered man, who in the ordinary acceptation of the term had never known what it was to be free, argued with his mistress the importance of the exchange of property of which he himself was a part, for her benefit and that of her children.

"Remember, Miss Polly," he said, "that when Marse Thomie comes out of the war, it will be mighty nice for him to have a store of his own to commence business in, and if I was in your place I would take it for me, for I tell you again, Miss Polly, when the war's over we'll all be free."

But the good mistress, who had listened in silence to these arguments, was unmoved. She saw before her a man who had been born a slave in her family,

and who had grown to man's estate under the fostering care of slavery, whose high sense of honor and
gratitude constrained him to give advice intelligently,
which, if followed, would rescue her and her children
from impending adversity ; but she determined not to
take it. She preferred rather to trust their future
well-being into the hands of Providence. Her beautiful faith found expression in this consoling passage of
Scripture : " The Lord is my shepherd, I shall not
want." And this blessed assurance must have determined her to pursue the course she did, else it would
have been reckless and improvident. She told King
that when our people became convinced that the troubles between the South and North had to be settled by
the sword, that she, in common with all good citizens,
staked her all upon the issues of the war, and that
she would not now, like a coward, flee from them, or
seek to avert them by selling a man, or men and
women who had endeared themselves to her by service and fidelity.

CHAPTER XI.

A PERILOUS TRUST.

"It is most time to go to the post-office, ain't it, Miss Mary ? We are going to get a letter from Marse Thomie this morning."

"What makes you so certain of it, Toby ?"

"I don't know'm, but I am ; and every time I feels this way, I gets one ; so I'll just take my two little black calves and trot off to the office and get it ;" and suiting the action to the word he struck a pretty brisk gait and was soon around the corner and out of sight.

Then Decatur received but two mails per day—one from an easterly direction and the other from a westerly direction. The northern, northwestern, southern and southwestern, all coming in on the morning's Georgia Railroad train. Therefore ever since Thomie's return to his command, the western mail was the one around which our hopes and fears daily clustered.

General Joseph E. Johnston's army was, at the time of this incident, at Dalton, obstructing the advance of Sherman's " three hundred thousand men " on destruction bent. And though there had been no regular line of battle formed for some time by the Confederate and Federal forces, there were frequent skirmishes, disastrous alike to both sides. Hence the daily alternation of hopes and fears in the hearts of those whose principal occupation was waiting and watching for "news from the front."

The team of which Toby was the proud possessor did its work quickly, and in less time than it takes to tell it he appeared in sight, returning from the post-office—one hand clasping a package of papers and letters, and the other, raised high above his head, holding a letter. I could not wait, and ran to meet him.

"I've got a whole lot of letters, and every one of them is from Dalton, and this one is from Marse Thomie!"

Toby had read the Dalton post-mark, and had made a correct statement. The well-known chirography of my brother had become so familiar to him that he never mistook it for another, and was unerring in his declarations regarding it. On this occasion Thomie's letter thus read:

"MY DEAR SISTER:—Those acquainted with army tactics know that General Johnston is on the eve of an important move, or change of base; and that it should be the effort of the men, officers and privates, to be prepared to make the change, whatever it may be, with as little loss of army paraphernalia as possible. As the Confederate army has no repository secure from the approach of the enemy, several of our friends suggest that you might be willing to take care of anything which we might send to you, that would be of future use to us—heavy overcoats, extra blankets, etc., etc. Consider well the proposition before you consent. Should they be found in your possession, by the enemy, then our home might be demolished, and

8

you perhaps imprisoned, or killed upon the spot. Are you willing to take the risk, trusting to your ingenuity and bravery to meet the consequences? Let me know as soon as possible, as war times admit of little delay. General Granbury, Colonel Bob Young, and others may make known to you their wishes by personal correspondence. Love to my mother and sister, and to yourself, brave heart.

Affectionately, your brother

T. J. STOKES."

This letter was read aloud to my mother, and the faithful mail carrier was not excluded. She listened and weighed every word of its contents. For several moments a silence reigned, which was broken by her asking me what I was going to do in the matter.

"What would you have me do?" I asked in reply.

"What would they do, Mary, in very cold weather, if they should lose their winter clothing, overcoats and blankets, now that supplies are so difficult to obtain?"

This question, evasive as it was, convinced me that my mother's patriotism was fully adequate to the occasion, and, fraught with peril as it might be, she was willing to bear her part of the consequences of taking care of the soldiers' clothes.

The return mail bore the following letter addressed jointly to General Granbury, Colonel Robert Young, Captains Lauderdale and Formwalt, Lieutenant Stokes, and Major John Y. Rankin;

"MY DEAR BROTHER AND FRIENDS :—I thank you for the estimate you have placed upon my character and patriotism, as indicated by your request that I

should take care of your overcoats, blankets, etc., until you need them. If I were willing to enjoy the fruits of your valor and sacrifices without also being willing to share your perils, I would be unworthy indeed. Yes, if I knew that for taking care of those things, I would subject myself to real danger, I would essay the duty. Send them on. I will meet them in Atlanta, and see that they continue their journey to Decatur without delay.   Your friend,
                              M. A. H. G."

Another mail brought intelligence of the shipment of the goods, and I lost no time in going to Atlanta and having them re-shipped to Decatur. There were nine large dry goods boxes, and I went, immediately on their arrival, to Mr. E. Mason's and engaged his two-horse wagon and driver to carry them from the depot to our home. When they were brought, we had them placed in our company dining-room. This room, by a sort of tacit understanding, had become a store-room for the army before this important lot of goods came, and, as a dining-room, much incongruity of furniture existed, among which was a large, high wardrobe. The blinds were now closed and secured, the sash put down and fastened, the doors shut and locked, and this room given up to the occupancy of Confederate articles; and thus it remained during the eventful period intervening between the departure of General Joseph E. Johnston's army from Dalton, and Sherman's infamous order to the people of Atlanta and vicinity to leave their homes, that they might be destroyed by his vandal hordes.

CHAPTER XII.

A SCENE IN AN ATLANTA CONFEDERATE HOSPITAL.

"Well, my boy, our patients are all getting along nicely in the Fair Ground hospital," was the comforting assurance I gave to Toby, who was my faithful co-worker in all that pertained to the comfort of our soldiers. "Suppose we go to the Empire hospital and see what we can do there." ·

"Yes'm, I have always wanted to go there."

Taking one of the baskets we had brought with us from Decatur, and which contained biscuits, rusk, broiled and fried chicken, ground coffee and blackberry wine, I handed it to him and we wended our way to the hospital. Things were not in as good shape there as at the Fair Ground hospital. I perceived this at a glance, and, upon asking and receiving permission from the superintendent, I soon tidied up things considerably. Toby brought pails of fresh water, and aided in bathing the faces, hands and arms of the convalescing soldiers, while I hunted up the soldier lads who ought to have been at home with their mothers, and bestowed the tender loving service that woman only can give to the sick and suffering.

Entering one of the wards I perceived a youth, or one I took to be a youth, from his slender fragile figure, and his beardless face, lean and swarthy in sickness, but beautiful in its fine texture and the marblelike whiteness of the brow. That he was of French extraction there could be no doubt. Quietly kneeling by the side of his cot, I contemplated his face, his head, his figure—I listened to his breathing, and watched the pulsations of his heart, and knew that his days, yea, his hours were numbered. Taking his hand in mine, I perceived that the little vitality that remained was fast burning up with fever. Putting back the beautiful rings of raven hair that lay in disheveled clusters over his classic head, and partly concealed his white brow, I thought of his mother, and imprinted upon his forehead a kiss for her sake. The deep slumber induced by anodynes was broken by that touch, and a dazed awakening ensued. " Mother," was his pathetic and only utterance.

"What can I do for you, my dear child ?"

There are looks and tones which are never forgotten, and never shall I forget the utter despair in the eyes, lustrous and beautiful enough to look upon the glory of heaven, and the anguish of the voice, musical enough to sing the songs of everlasting bliss, as he said in tremulous tone and broken sentences:

" I want to see a Catholic priest. I have paid several men to go for me. They have gone off and never returned. I have no money with which to pay any one else."

In silence I listened and wept. At length I said :

" My dear young friend, can you not make confession to ' our Father which art in Heaven,' and ask Him for Christ's sake to absolve you from all sins of which you may think yourself guilty ? He

will do it without the intervention of a priest, if you
will only believe on Him and trust Him.   Can you not
do this ?"

The pencil of Raphael would fail to depict the anguish of his face ; all hope left it, and, as he turned
his despairing look upon the wall, tear drops glisten-
ed in his eyes and filled the sunken hollows beneath
them.   Again I took his passive hand in mine, and
with the other hand upon his white forehead, I told
him he should see a priest—that I myself would go
for one, and just as soon as he could be found I would
return with him.   Before leaving, however, I went to
the ward where I had left Toby and the basket, and
filling a little glass with wine, I brought it to the
sinking youth.   He could not be induced to taste it.
In vain I plead with him, and told him that it would
strengthen him for the interview with the priest.   " I
am going now, and will come back, too, as soon as I
can," I said to the dying youth, for to all intents and
purposes he was dying then.   Seeing the other
patients watching my every movement with pathetic
interest, I was reminded to give the rejected wine to
the weakest looking one of them.

Leaving Toby either to wait on, or amuse the
soldiers of the ward first entered (where I found him
playing the latter role, much to their delight), with
hasty steps I went to the Catholic parsonage on
Hunter street.   In response to my ring the door was
opened by an Irish woman from whom I learned that
the priest was not in, and would not be until he came
to luncheon at 12 o'clock M.   It was then 11 o'clock,
and I asked the privilege of waiting in·the sitting

room until he came. This being granted, I entered the room consecrated to celibacy, and perhaps to holy thoughts, judging from the pictures upon the walls and the other ornaments. These things furnished food for reflection, and the waiting would not have seemed so long but for the thought of the poor suffering one who had given his young life for our cause. Intuitively I knew the sound of clerical footsteps as they entered the hall, and hastening to meet him I asked, "Is this Father O'Riley?" Receiving an affirmative answer, I told him of the youth at the Empire hospital who refused to be comforted other than by a Catholic priest, and of my promise to bring one to him. Father O'Riley said he had been out since early morning, visiting the sick, and would be obliged to refresh himself, both by food and repose, but that I could say to the young man that he would be there by 3 o'clock. "O, sir, you don't realize the importance of haste. Please let me remain in your sitting room until you have eaten your luncheon, and then I know you will go with me. I, too, have been out ever since early morning engaged in the same Christ-like labors as yourself, and I do not require either food or repose."

My earnestness prevailed, and in a short while we were at our destination. At my request, Father O'Riley waited in the passage-way leading to the ward until I went in to prepare the young man for his coming. I found him in that restless condition, neither awake nor asleep, which often precedes the deep sleep that knows no waking. Wetting my handkerchief with cold water, I bathed his face and hands, and spoke gently to him, and, when he seemed sufficiently aroused to understand me, I told him in cheerful tones that he could not guess who had come to see him. Catching his look of inquiry, I told him it was Father O'Riley, and that I would bring him in. Opening the door, I motioned to Father O'Riley to follow me. The dying youth and the Catholic priest needed no introduction by me. There was a mystic tie between them that I recognized as sacred, and I left them alone. Telling Father O'Riley that I consigned my charge to him, and that I would come back to-morrow, I bade them good-bye and left.

The contents of the basket had been gratefully received and devoured by those who deserved the best in the land, because they were the land's defenders.

To-morrow Toby and I, and the basket, were at the Empire hospital in due time, but the poor suffering youth was not there. The emancipated spirit had taken its flight to Heaven, and all that was mortal of that brave young soldier had been consigned by the ceremonies of the church he loved so well to the protecting care of mother earth.

CHAPTER XIII.

Concealing Confederate Clothing—Valuables Carried to Atlanta—Toby Taken Ill.

On the way to the post-office early one morning in the sultry month of July, 1864, to mail a number of letters which I deemed too important to be entrusted to other hands, I was accosted as follows by "Uncle Mack," the good negro blacksmith, whose shop was situated immediately upon the route :

"Did you know, Miss Mary, that the Yankees have crossed the river, and are now this side of the Chattahoochee."

"Why, no !" I said, and added with as much calmness as I could affect, "I do not know why I should be surprised—there is nothing to prevent them from coming into Decatur."

With an imprecation more expressive than elegant, that evil should overtake them before getting here, he resumed hammering at the anvil, and I my walk to the post-office. Nor was Uncle Mack the only one who volunteered the information that "The Yankees are coming—they are this side the river."

The time had come to devise means and methods of concealing the winter clothing and other accoutrements entrusted to my care by our dear soldiers. In order to save them, what should I do with them ?—was a question which I found myself unable to an-

swer. An attempt to retain and defend them would
be futile indeed. And I have no right to jeopardize
my mother's home by a rash effort to accomplish an
impossibilty. But what shall I do with these precious
things, is the question. A happy thought struck me,
and I pursued it only to find it delusive. The near approach of Sherman's army developed the astounding
fact that Dr. A. Holmes, of Decatur, a Baptist minister of some prominence, claimed to be a Union man,
in full sympathy with any means that would soonest
quell the rebellion. This I had not heard, and in my
dilemma I went to him to impart my plans and ask
advice. He was morose and reticent, and I hesitated ;
but, driven by desperation, I finally said : "Dr.
Holmes, as a minister of the gospel, are you not safe ?
All civilized nations respect clerical robes, do they
not ?"

"I think so," he said, and continued by saying, "I
have other claims upon the Federal army which will
secure me from molestation."

A look of surprise and inquiry being my only
answer, he said, "Amid the secession craze, I have
never given up my allegiance to the United States."

"Why, Dr. Holmes!" I said, in unfeigned surprise.

"I repeat most emphatically that I have remained
unshaken in my allegiance to the United States. I
have no respect for a little contemptible Southern
Confederacy, whose flag will never be recognized on
land or on sea."

This was a sad revelation to me. On more than
one occasion I had heard Dr. Holmes pray fervently
for the success of the Southern cause, and to hear

such changed utterances from him now, pained me exceedingly. Heartsore and discouraged, I turned from him, and was leaving without the usual ceremony, when he said :

"What can I do for you?"

"I came, sir, to ask a great favor of you, but after hearing you express yourself as you have, I deem it useless to make known my wishes. Good morning."

This interview with Dr. Holmes was very brief ; it did not consume as much time as it has done to tell it.

I did not walk in those days, but ran, and it required only a few moments to transfer the scene of action from Dr. Holmes' to my mother's residence. A hurried, whispered conversation acquainted her with the situation; and at my request, and upon a plausible pretense, she took Toby to the depot where she remained until I sent for her. My confidence in Toby had not in the least diminished, but, being a boy, I feared that he might have his price, or be intimidated by threats into the betrayal of our secret; hence the management as above related to get him off the place while I consummated a plan, which, if successful, would be a great achievement, but, if a failure, would be fraught with disaster. In those days "the depot" was a place of popular resort—it was the emporium of news; and either from the agent, or from the Confederate scouts that were ever and anon dashing through Decatur with cheerful messages and words of hope, the anxious mothers and sisters of the soldiers often wended their way there in hope of hearing something from their loved ones. Therefore no suspicion was aroused by this going to the depot.

Watching the receding form of my mother until she had passed out of the gate, and Toby had closed it after her, I then went to the rear·door and motioned to Telitha, who chanced to be in the right place, to come into the house. After seeing that every outside door was thoroughly secure, I took her into the dining room where the boxes were which contained the winter clothing, blankets, etc., already mentioned as having been sent for storage by our soldier friends at Dalton, and told her in pantomime that the Yankees were coming, and if they saw these things they would kill us and burn the house. She fully understood and repeated the pantomime illustrative of possible—yea, probable—coming events, with pathetic effect. I showed her that I wanted a hammer and chisel with which to take off the lids of the boxes, and she brought them. The lids removed, each article was carefully lifted from its repository and placed on chairs. This important step being taken towards the concealment of the goods, I raised the sash and opened the shutters of the window nearest the cellar, which was unlocked and open, and Telitha, climbing out the window, received the boxes as I handed them to her, and carried them into the cellar. Old and soiled as the boxes were, they were not in a condition to create suspicion of recent use, so from that source we had nothing to fear. Telitha again in the house, shutters closed, and sash down, preparation was resumed for the enactment of a feat dangerous and rash, the thought of which, even at this remote period, almost produces a tremor. The wardrobe mentioned in a former sketch as an incongruity in a dining room, was emptied of its contents, and inch by inch placed as near the center of the room as possible ; then a large table was placed beside it, and a chair upon that; and then with the help of another chair, which served as a step, I got upon the table and then upon the chair that was upon the table. As I went up, Telitha followed ; standing upon the table she grasped the wardrobe with her strong hands and held it securely. I ascended from the chair to the top of it, stood up and steadied myself, and waited, immovable as a statue, until she got down and brought the chisel and hammer and placed them at my feet, and resumed her hold upon the wardrobe. I stooped and picked up the utensils with which I had to work, and straightened and steadied myself again. The chisel touched the plastered ceiling and the hammering began. Very slow work it was at first, as the licks had to be upward instead of downward, and the plastering was very thick. Finally the chisel went through and was withdrawn and moved to another place, and by repeated efforts I secured an aperture large enough to insert my fingers, and a few well-directed licks round and about so cracked and weakened the plastering that I was enabled to pull of some large pieces. A new difficulty presented itself. The laths were long, much longer than those of the present day, and I not only had to make a large opening in the ceiling, but to take off the plastering without breaking the laths. More than once the wardrobe had to be moved that I might pull off the plastering, and then with the greatest care prize off the laths. At length the feat was accomplished, and I laid the lids of the boxes, which had been reserved for this purpose, across the joists, and made a floor upon which to lay the goods more than once specified in these sketches. When the last article had been laid on this improvised shelf, I gazed upon them in silent anguish and wept. Telitha caught the melancholy inspiration and also wept. Each lath was restored to its place and the perilous work was completed, and how I thanked the Lord for the steady nerve and level head that enabled me to do this service for those who were fighting the battles of my country.

But the debris must be removed. While the doors were yet closed and fastened, we pounded and broke the plastering into very small pieces and filled every vessel and basket in the house. I then went out and walked very leisurely over the yard and lot, and lingered over every lowly flower that sweetened the atmosphere by its fragrance, and when I was fully persuaded that no spy was lurking nigh I re-entered the house and locked the door. Picking up the largest vessel, and motioning Telitha to follow suit, I led the way through a back door to a huge old ash hopper, and emptied the pulverized plastering into it. In this way we soon had every trace of it removed from the floor. The dust that had settled upon everything was not so easily removed, but the frequent use of dusting brushes and flannel cloths disposed of the most of it.

I now wrote a note to my mother, inviting her to come home, and to bring Toby with her. We kept the doors of the dining room closed, as had been our wont for some time, and if Toby ever discovered the change, he never betrayed the knowledge of it by

word or look. After a light breakfast, and the excitement of the day, I felt that we ought to have a good,
luscious dinner, and, with the help at my command,
went to work preparing it, and, as was my custom of
late, I did not forget to provide for others who might
come in. More than once during the day Confederate scouts had ·galloped in and spoken a few words of
encouragement ; and after taking a drink of water
from the old oaken bucket, had galloped out again,
so I hoped they would come back when the biscuit
and tea-cakes were done, that I might fill their
pockets.

After the last meal of the day had been eaten, I
held another whispered consultation with my mother,
and in pursuance of the course agreed upon I
emptied several trunks, and with her help filled one
with quilts and blankets, and other bedding ; another
with china and cut glass, well packed ; and another
with important papers, treasured relics, etc., and
locked and strapped them ready for shipment next
morning.

A night of unbroken rest and sleep prepared me for
another day of surprises and toil, and before dawn I
was up, dressed, waiting for daylight enough to
justify me in the effort to see Mr. Ezekiel Mason, and
beg him to hire me his team and driver to carry
the trunks to the depot. After my ready compliance
with his terms, he agreed to send them as soon as
possible. The delay caused me to go on a freight
train to Atlanta, but I congratulated myself upon
that privilege, as the trunks and Toby went on the
same train. There was unusual commotion and activ-

ity about the depot in Atlanta, and a superficial
observer would have been impressed with the business-
like appearance of the little city at that important
locality. Men, women, and children moved about as
if they meant business. Trains came in rapidly, and
received their complement of freight, either animate
or inanimate, and screamed themselves hoarse and
departed, giving place to others that went through
with the same routine. Drays and every manner of
vehicles blocked the streets, and endangered life, limb,
and property of all who could not vie with them in
push, vim, and dare-deviltry. In vain did I appeal to
scores of draymen, white and black, to carry my trunks
to the home of Mr. McArthur, on Pryor street—money
was offered with liberality, but to no avail. Despairing of aid, I bade Toby follow me, and went to Mr.
McArthur's. He and his good wife were willing to
receive the trunks and give them storage room, but
could extend no aid in bringing them there. At length,
as a last resort, it was decided that Toby should take
their wheelbarrow and bring one trunk at a time. I
returned with him to the depot and had the most valuable trunk placed upon the wheelbarrow, and, with my
occasional aid, Toby got it to its destination. A
second trip was made in like manner, and the third
was not a failure, although I saw that Toby was very
tired. Thanking my good friends for the favor they
were extending, I hurried back to the depot, myself and
Toby, to take the first train to Decatur. Imagine our
consternation on learning that the Yankees had dashed
in and torn up the Georgia Railroad track from Atlanta to Decatur, and were pursuing their destructive

work towards Augusta. Neither for love nor money could a seat in any kind of vehicle going in that direction be obtained, nor were I and my attendant the only ones thus cut off from home; and I soon discovered that a spirit of independence pervaded the crowd. Many were the proud possessors of elegant spans of "little white ponies" which they did not deem too good to propel them homeward. Seeking to infuse a little more life and animation into Toby, I said:

"Well, my boy, what do you think of bringing out your little black ponies and running a race with my white ones to Decatur? Do you think you can beat in the race?"

"I don't know'm," he said, without his usual smile, when I essayed a little fun with him, and I evidently heard him sigh. But knowing there was no alternative, I started in a brisk walk towards Decatur, and said to him, "Come on, or I'll get home before you do." He rallied and kept very close to me, and we made pretty good time. The gloaming was upon us, the period of all others auspicious to thought, and to thought I abandoned myself. The strife between the sections of a once glorious country was a prolific theme, and I dwelt upon it in all of its ramifications, and failed to find cause for blame in my peculiar people; and my step became prouder, and my willingness to endure all things for their sakes and mine was more confirmed. In the midst of these inspiring reflections, Toby, who had somewhat lagged behind, came running up to me and said:

"Oh! Miss Mary, just look at the soldiers. And they are ours, too!"

9

To my dying day I shall never forget the scene to which he called my attention. In the weird stillness it appeared as if the Lord had raised up of the stones a mighty host to fight our battles. Not a sound was heard, nor a word spoken, as those in the van passed opposite me, on and on, and on, in the direction of Decatur, in what seemed to me an interminable line of soldiery. Toby and I kept the track of the destroyed railroad, and were somewhere between General Gartrell's residence and Mr. Pitts', the midway station between Atlanta and Decatur, when the first of these soldiers passed us, and we were at Kirkwood when that spectre-like band had fully gone. Once the moon revealed me so plainly that a cheer, somewhat repressed, but nevertheless hearty, resounded through the woods, and I asked :

"Whose command? "

"Wheeler's Cavalry," was the simultaneous response of many who heard my inquiry.

"Don't you know me ? I am the one you gave the best breakfast I ever ate, that morning we dashed into Decatur before sun-up."

"And I'm the one too."

"O, don't mention it," I said. "You are giving your lives for me, and the little I can do for you is nothing in comparison. May God be with you and shield you from harm until this cruel war is over."

I missed Toby, and looking back, saw him sitting down. I hurried to him, saying, "What is it, my boy?"

"O, Miss Mary, I am so sick. I can't go any further. You can go on home, and let me stay here—when I feel better I'll go too."

"No, my boy, I'll not leave you." And sitting by him I told him to rest his head upon my lap, and maybe after awhile he would feel better, and then we would go on. In the course of a half hour he vomited copiously, and soon after he told me he felt better, and would try to go on. More than once his steps were unsteady and he looked dazed; but under my patient guidance and encouraging words he kept up and we pursued our lonely walk until we reached Decatur.

As soon as we entered the town, we perceived that we had overtaken Wheeler's Cavalry. They were lying on the ground, asleep, all over the place; and in most instances their horses were lying by them, sleeping too. And I noticed that the soldiers, even though asleep, never released their hold upon the bridles. At home I found my mother almost frantic. She knew nothing of the causes detaining me, and supposed that some disaster had befallen me individually. A good supper, including a strong cup of tea prepared by her hands, awaited us, and I attested my appreciation of it by eating heartily. Toby drank a cup of tea only, and said he "was very tired and hurt all over."

CHAPTER XIV.

The advance guard of the Yankee army—I am ordered out—A
noble Federal.

The day clear, bright and beautiful, in July, 1864,
and though a midsummer's sun cast its vertical rays
upon the richly-carpeted earth, refreshing showers
tempered the heat and preserved in freshness and
beauty the vernal robes of May and kept the atmosphere pure and delightful. Blossoms of every hue
and fragrance decked the landscape, and Ceres and
Pomona had been as lavish with their grains and fruits
as Flora had been with flowers.

And I, assisted by Toby and Telitha, had gathered
from the best of these rich offerings, and prepared a
feast for Wheeler's Cavalry. By the way, strive
against it as I would, I was more than once disturbed
by the mental inquiry: "What has become of Wheeler's Cavalry? I saw it enter Decatur last night, and
now there is not a soldier to be seen. It is true a
large number of scouts came in this morning, and
spoke comforting words to my mother, and reconnoi-
tered around town fearlessly, but what has become of
them?" Hope whispered: "Some strategic movement that will culminate in the capture of the entire
Yankee army, no doubt is engaging its attention."
Yielding to these delusive reflections, and the seduc-

tive influence of earth, air and sky, I became quite exhilarated and hummed little snatches of the songs I used to sing in the happy days of childhood, before a hope had been disappointed or a shadow cast over my pathway.

These scenes and these songs were not in keeping with the impending disasters even then at our portals. Crapen draperies and funeral dirges would have been far more in keeping with the developments of the day.

Distant roar of cannon and sharp report of musketry spoke in language unmistakable the approach of the enemy, and the rapidity of that approach was becoming fearfully alarming. Decatur offered many advantages as headquarters to an invading, devastating foe, "and three hundred thousand men" under the guidance of a merciless foe ought to have entered it long before they did—and would have done so if their bravery had been commensurate with their vandalism.

"Yank! Yank!" exclaimed our deaf negro girl, Telitha, as she stroked her face as if stroking beard, and ran to get a blue garment to indicate the color of their apparel, and this was our first intimation of their appearance in Decatur. If all the evil spirits had been loosed from Hades, and Satan himself had been turned loose upon us, a more terrfic, revolting scene could not have been enacted.

Advance guards, composed of every species of criminals ever incarcerated in the prisons of the Northern States of America, swooped down upon us, and every species of deviltry followed in their footsteps. My poor mother, frightened and trembling,

and myself, having locked the doors of the house, took
our stand with the servants in the yard, and witnessed
the grand *entre* of the menagerie.   One of the beasts
got down upon his all-fours and pawed up the dust
and bellowed like an infuriated bull.   And another
asked me if I did not expect to see them with hoofs
and horns.   I told him, "No, I had expected to see
some gentlemen among them, and was sorry I should
be disappointed."

My entire exemption from fear on that occasion
must have been our safeguard, as no personal
violence was attempted.   He who personated a bull
must have been the king's fool, and was acting in
collusion with the house pillagers sent in advance
of the main army to do their dirty work, and to
reduce the people to destitution and dependence.
While he thought he was entertaining us with his
quadrupedal didos, a horde of thieves were rummaging
the house, and everything of value they could get
their hands upon they stole—locks and bolts having
proved ineffectual barriers to this nefarious work.   By
this time the outside marauders had killed every
chicken and other fowl upon the place, except one set-
ting hen.   A fine cow, and two calves, and twelve
hogs shared a similar fate.

Several hours had passed since the coming of the
first installment of the G. A. R., and a few scattering
officers were perambulating the streets, and an occasional cavalryman reconnoitering.   Having surveyed the situation, and discovered that only women
and children and a few faithful negroes occupied the
town, the main army came in like an avalanche.

Yea, if an avalanche and a simoon had blended their fury and expended it upon that defenceless locality, a greater change could scarcely have been wrought.

The morning's sun had shone upon a scene of luxuriant beauty, and heightened its midsummer loveliness, but the same sun, only a few hours later, witnessed a complete transformation, and blight and desolation reigned supreme. My mother and myself, afraid to go in the house, still maintained our outdoor position, and our two faithful servants clung very close to us, notwithstanding repeated efforts to induce them to leave. Our group had received addition. Emmeline, a negro girl whom we had hired out in Decatur, had been discharged, and had now come home. She was not so faithful as her kith and kin, and was soon on familiar terms with the bummers. Toby complained of being very tired, and when we all came to think about it, we discovered that we, too, were tired, and without being asked took seats upon the capacious lap of mother earth. As we were not overly particular about the position we assumed, we must have presented quite an aboriginal appearance. But what mattered it—we were only rebels. Notwithstanding the insignia of the conqueror was displayed on every hand, we felt to a certain degree more protected by the presence of commissioned officers, and ventured to go into the house. I will not attempt a description of the change that had taken place since we had locked the door, and, for better protection, had taken our stand in the yard,

Garrard's Cavalry selected our lot, consisting of several acres, for headquarters, and soon what appeared to us to be an immense army train of wagons commenced rolling into it. In less than two hours our barn was demolished and converted into tents, which were occupied by privates and non-commissioned officers, and to the balusters of our portico and other portions of the house were tied a number of large ropes, which, the other ends being secured to trees and shrubbery, answered as a railing to which at short intervals apart a number of smaller ropes were tied, and to these were attached horses and mules, which were eating corn and oats out of troughs improvised for the occasion out of bureau, washstand, and wardrobe drawers.

Men in groups were playing cards on tables of every size and shape; and whisky and profanity held high carnival. Thus surrounded we could but be apprehensive of danger; and, to assure ourselves of as much safety as possible, we barricaded the doors and windows, and arranged to sit up all night, that is, my mother and myself.

Toby complained of being very tired, and "hurting all over," as he expressed it. We assisted him in making the very best pallet that could be made of the material at our command, and he lay down completely prostrated. Telitha was wide awake, and whenever she could secure a listener chattered like a magpie in unintelligible language, accompanied by unmistakable gestures—gestures which an accomplished elocutionist might adopt with effect—and the burden of her heart was for Emmeline. Emmeline having repudiated our protection, had sought shelter, the Lord only knows where. Alas, poor girl!

As we sat on a lounge, every chair having been taken to the camps, we heard the sound of footsteps entering the piazza, and in a moment, loud rapping, which meant business. Going to the window nearest the door, I removed the fastenings, raised the sash, and opened the blinds. Perceiving by the light of a brilliant moon that at least a half-dozen men in uniforms were on the piazza, I asked:

"Who is there?"

"Gentlemen," was the laconic reply.

"If so, you will not persist in your effort to come into the house. There is only a widow and one of her daughters, and two faithful servants in it," I said.

"We have orders from headquarters to interview Miss Gay. Is she the daughter of whom you speak?"

"She is, and I am she."

"Well, Miss Gay, we demand seeing you, without intervening barriers. Our orders are imperative," said he who seemed to be the spokesman of the delegation.

"Then wait a moment," I amiably responded. Going to my mother I repeated in substance the above colloquy, and asked her if she would go with me out of one of the back doors and around the house into the front yard. Although greatly agitated and trembling, she readily assented, and we noiselessly went out. In a few moments we announced our presence, and our visitors descended the steps and joined us. And those men, occupying a belligerent attitude towards ourselves and all that was dear to us, stood face to face and in silence contemplated each other. When the silence was broken the aforesaid officer

introduced himself as Major Campbell, a member of
General Schofield's staff.   He also introduced the
accompanying officers each by name and title.   This
ceremony over, Major Campbell said :

"Miss Gay, our mission is a painful one, and yet
we will have to carry it out unless you satisfactorily
explain acts reported to us."

"What is the nature of those acts ?"

"We have been told that it is your proudest boast
that you are a rebel, and that you are ever on duty to
aid and abet in every possible way the would-be
destroyers of the United States government.   If this
be so, we cannot permit you to remain within our
lines.   Until Atlanta surrenders, Decatur will be our
headquarters, and every consideration of interest to
our cause requires that no one inimical to it should
remain within our boundaries established by conquest."

In reply to these charges, I said :

"Gentlemen, I have not been misrepresented, so
far as the charges you mention are concerned.   If I
were a man, I should be in the foremost ranks of those
who are fighting for rights guaranteed by the Constitution of the United States.   The Southern people
have never broken that compact, nor infringed upon
it in any way.   They have never organized mobs to
assassinate any portion of the people sharing the priv-
ileges granted by that compact.   They have constructed no underground railroads to bring into our
midst incendiaries and destroyers of the peace, and
to carry off stolen property.   They have never sought
to array the subordinate element of the North in

deadly hostility to the controlling element. No class of the women of the South have ever sought positions at the North which secured entrance into good households, and then betrayed the confidence reposed by corrupting the servants and alienating the relations between the master and the servant. No class of the women of the South have ever mounted the rostrum and proclaimed falsehoods against the women of the North—falsehoods which must have crimsoned with shame the very cheeks of Beelzebub.

"No class of the men of the South have ever tramped over the North with humbugs, extorting money either through sympathy or credulity, and engaged at the same time in the nefarious work of exciting the subordinate class to insurrection, arson, rapine and murder. If the South is in rebellion, a well-organized mob at the North has brought it about. Long years of patient endurance accomplished nothing. The party founded on falsehood and hate strengthened and grew to enormous proportions. And, by the way, mark the cunning of that party. Finding that the Abolition party made slow progress and had to work in the dark, it changed its name and took in new issues, and by a systematic course of lying in its institutions of learning, from the lowly school-house to Yale College, and from its pulpits and rostrums, it inculcated lessons of hate towards the Southern people whom it would hurl into the crater of Vesuvius if endowed with the power. What was left us to do but to try to relieve that portion of the country which had permitted this sentiment of hate to predominate, of all connection with us, and of all responsibility for the sins of which it proclaimed us guilty? This effort the South has made, and I have aided and abetted in every possible manner, and will continue to do so just as long as there is an armed man in the Southern ranks. If this be sufficient cause to expel me from my home, I await your orders. I have no favors to ask."

Imagine my astonishment, admiration and gratitude, when that group of Federal officers, with unanimity said:

"I glory in your spunk, and am proud of you as my countrywoman; and so far from banishing you from your home, we will vote for your retention within our lines."

Thus the truth prevailed; but a new phase of the conflict was inaugurated, as proved by subsequent developments.

Turning to my mother, Major Campbell said:

"Mother, how did our advance guards treat you?"

A quivering of the lips, and a tearful effort to speak, was all the response she could make. The aggravation of already extreme nervousness was doing its work.

"Would you like to see?" I said. He indicated rather than expressed an affirmative answer.

I went around and entered the house, and, opening the front door, invited him and his friends to come in. A hindrance to the exhibit I was anxious to make presented itself—we had neither candle nor lamp, and this I told to the officers. Calling to a man in the nearest camp, Major Campbell asked him to bring a light. This being done, I led the way into the front room, and there our distinguished guests were confronted by a huge pallet occupied by a sixteen-year-old negro boy. A thrill of amusement evidently passed through this group of western men, and electrical glances conveyed messages of distrust when I told them of my walk yesterday afternoon, accompanied by this boy, and his exhaustion before we got home, and his complaints of "hurting all over" before he lay down an hour ago.

A low consultation was held, and one of the officers left and soon returned with another who proved to be a physician. He aroused the boy, asked several questions, and examined his pulse and tongue.

"That will do," said he, and turning to the others, he said :

"He is a very sick boy, and needs medical treatment at once. I will prescribe and go for the medicine, which I wish given according to directions."

Having received a statement of the boy's condition from a trusted source, we were evidently re-instated into the good opinion of Major Campbell and his friends. Telitha had retired from them to as great a distance as the boundaries of the room would permit, and every time she caught my eye she looked and acted what she could not express in words—utter aversion for the "Yank."

We now resumed our inspection of the interior of the house. The contents of every drawer were on the floor, every article of value having been abstracted. Crockery scattered all over the room, suggested to the eye that it had been used to pelt the ghosts of the witches burned in Massachusetts a century or two ago. Outrages and indignities too revolting to mention met the eye at every turn. And the state of affairs in the parlor baffled description. Not an article had escaped the destroyer's touch bnt the piano, and circumstances which followed proved that that was regarded as a trophy and only waited removal.

"Vandals! Vandals!" Major Campbell sorrowfully exclaimed, and all his friends echoed the opinion, and said :

" If the parties who did this work could be identified, we would hang them as high as Haman."

But these parties were never identified. They were important adjuncts in the process of subjugation.

After wishing that the worst was over with us, these gentlemen, who had come in no friendly mood, bade us good night and took their leave. Thus the Lord of Hosts, in his infinite mercy, furnished a just tribunal to pass judgment upon my acts as a Southern woman, and that judgment, influenced by facts and surroundings, was just and the verdict humane.

CHAPTER XV.

The Battle of the 22d of July, 1864—The Death of Toby.

The excitement incident to the morning and evening of yesterday left my mother and myself in no frame of mind for repose, and we spent the night in suspense and painful apprehension of trouble yet to come greater and more dreadful than that through which we had passed. The medicine left for Toby by the physician summoned last night was faithfully administered according to direction, and the morning found him better, though able to sit up only for a short while at a time. Measles had developed, and we felt hopeful that it would prove to be a very slight attack ; and such it might have been could we have controlled him properly, but the excitement and ever-varying scenes in the yard, and as far as vision extended, were so new and strange to him that, when unobserved, he spent much of his time at a window commanding the best view of the scene, and, thus exposed to a current of air, the disease ceased to appear on the surface and a troublesome cough ensued.

Having been without food since the preceding morning, our thoughts turned to the usual preparation for breakfast, but alas, those preparations had to be dispensed of, as we had nothing to prepare. This state of affairs furnished food for at least serious reflection, and the inquiry, " What are we to do ?"

found audible expression. The inexorable demands of hunger could not be stifled, and we knew that the sick boy needed hot tea and the nourishment which food alone could give, and yet we had nothing for ourselves or for him—so complete had been the robbery of the "advance guards" of the Grand Army of the Republic that not a thing, animate or inanimate, remained with which to appease our hunger. "What are we to do?" was iterated and reiterated, and no solution of the question presented itself. Even then appetizing odors from the camp-fires were diffusing themselves upon the air and entering our house, but aliens were preparing the food and we had no part in it. We debated this question, and finally resolved not to expose ourselves to the jeers and insults of the enemy by an act of ours that would seem to ask for food ; but that we would go to our Southern citizens in the war-stricken and almost deserted town, and, if they were not completely robbed, ask them to share their supplies with us until we could procure aid from outside of the lines so arbitrarily drawn.

In this dilemma an unexpected relief came to us, and convinced us that there was good even in Nazareth. A large tray, evidently well-filled, and covered with a snow-white cloth, was brought in by an Irishman, who handed a card to my mother containing these words :

"To Mrs. Stokes and daughter, Miss Gay, with compliments of   (MAJOR) CAMPBELL.

"Please accept this small testimonial of regard and respectful sympathy."

The latter part of the brief message was the

sesame that secured acceptance of this offering, and
my mother and myself jointly acknowledged it with
sincere thanks, and again we thought of Elijah and
the ravens. The contents of the tray—coffee, sugar,
and tea, sliced ham and a variety of canned relishes,
butter, potatoes, and oatmeal and bread, were removed
and the tray returned. That tray on its humane mission, having found its way into our house, more than
once opportunely reappeared. We enjoyed the repast
thus furnished, although briny tears were mingled
with it.

The day passed without any immediate adventure.
Great activity prevailed in army ranks. The coming
and going of cavalry ; the clatter of sabre and spur ;
the constant booming of cannon and report of musketry, all convinced us that the surrender of Atlanta
by the Confederates was quite a matter of time. A
few thousand men, however brave and gallant, could
not cope successfully with " three hundred thousand "
who ignored every usage of civilized warfare, and
fought only for conquest.

I cannot say how long this state of affairs lasted
before Wheeler's Cavalry, supported by Confederate
infantry, stole a march upon the Yankees and put
them to flight. Garrard and his staff officers were in
our parlor—their parlor *pro tem.*—holding a council ;
the teamsters and army followers were lounging about
promiscuously, cursing and swearing and playing
cards, and seeming not to notice the approaching artillery until their attention was called to it, and then
they contended that it was their men firing off blank
cartridges. I intuitively felt that a conflict was on

10

hand.   Ma and I held whispered conversations and went from one window to another, and finally rushed into the yard.   Men in the camps observed our excitement and said, "Don't be alarmed, it is only our men firing off their blank cartridges."

The irony of fate was never more signally illustrated than on this occasion.   I would have laid down my life, yea, a thousand breathing, pulsing lives of my own, to have witnessed the overthrow of the Yankee army, and yet, I may have been the means of saving a large portion of it on that occasion.   Dreading for my mother's sake and for the sake of the deaf girl and the sick boy, an attack upon the forces which covered our grounds, I ran to one of the parlor doors and knocked heavily and excitedly.   An officer unlocked the door and opening it said:

"What is it?"

"Our men must be nearly here," I replied.

"Impossible," he said, and yet, with a bound he was in the yard, followed in quick succession by each member of the conclave.

A signal, long, loud, and shrill, awakened the drowsy, and scattered to the four winds of heaven cards, books and papers; and, in a few minutes, horses and mules were hitched to wagons, and the mules, wagons and men were fairly flying from the approach of the Confederates.   Women and children came pouring in from every direction, and the house was soon filled.   Before Garrard's wagon train was three hundred yards away, our yard was full of our men—our own dear "Johnnie Rebs."   Oothcaloga Valley boys, whom I had known from babyhood, kissed, in passing, the hand that waved the handkerchief. An officer, ah, how grand he looked in gray uniform, came dashing up and said :

"Go in your cellar and lie down; the Federals are forming a line of battle, and we, too, will form one that will reach across the grounds, and your house will be between the two lines. Go at once."

My mother ran and got Toby's shoes and put them on for him, and told him to get up and come with her, and as he went out of the house, tottering, I threw a blanket over him, and he and Telitha went with ma to our near neighbor, Mrs. Williams, her cellar being considered safer than ours. I remained in our house for the twofold purpose of taking care of it, if possible, and of protecting, to the best of my ability, the precious women and children who had fled to us for protection. Without thought of myself I got them all into the room that I thought would be safest, and urged them to lie down upon the floor and not to move during the battle. Shot and shell flew in every direction, and the shingles on the roof were following suit, and the leaves, and the limbs, and the bark of the trees were descending in showers so heavy as almost to obscure the view of the contending forces. The roaring of cannon and the sound of musketry blended in harmony so full and so grand, and the scene was so absorbing, that I thought not of personal danger, and more than once found myself outside of the portals ready to rush into the conflict— for was not I a soldier, enlisted for the war? Nor was I the only restless, intrepid person in the house on that occasion. An old lady, in whose veins flowed the blood of the Washingtons, was there, and it was with the greatest difficulty that I restrained her from going out into the arena of warfare. The traditions of her ancestors were so interwoven with her life, that, at an age bordering on four score years and. ten, they could not relax their hold upon her ; and she and I might have gone in opposite directions had we fled to the ranks of the contending armies.

Mine was, no doubt, the only feminine eye that witnessed the complete rout of the Federals on that occasion. At first I could not realize what they were doing, and feared some strategic movement; but the "rebel yell" and the flying blue-coats brought me to a full realization of the situation, and I too joined in the loud acclaim of victory. And the women and children, until now panic-stricken and silent as death, joined in the rejoicing. All the discouragement of the past few weeks fled from me, and hope revived, and I was happy, oh, so happy ! I had seen a splendidly equipped army, Schofield's division, I think, ignominiously flee from a little band of lean, lank, hungry, poorly-clad Confederate soldiers, and I doubted not an over-ruling Providence would lead us to final victory.

When the smoke of the battle cleared away, my mother and her ebony charge returned home. Toby quickly sought his pallet, and burning fever soon rendered him delirious the greater part of the time. In one of his lucid intervals, he asked me to read the Bible to him, and he told me what he wanted me to read about, and said :

"Miss Missouri used to read it to me, and I thought it was so pretty." And I read to him the story of the cross—of Jesus' dying love, and he listened and believed. I said to him :

"My boy, do you think you are going to die ?"

"Yes'm, I think I am."

I bowed my head close to him and wept, oh, how bitterly.

"Miss Mary, don't you think I'll go to heaven ?" he anxiously asked.

"Toby, my boy, there is one thing I want to tell you; can you listen to me ?"

"Yes'm."

"I have not always been just to you. I have often accused you of doing things that I afterwards found you did not do, and then I was not good enough to acknowledge that I had done wrong. And when you did wrong, I was not forgiving enough ; and more than once I have punished you for little sins, when I, with all the light before me, was committing greater ones every day, and going unpunished, save by a guilty conscience. And now, my boy, I ask you to forgive me. Can you do it ?"

"Oh, yes'm !"

"Are you certain that you do ? Are you sure that there is no unforgiving spirit in you towards your poor Miss Mary, who is sorry for all she has ever done that was wrong towards you."

"Oh, yes'm !"

"Then, my boy, ask the Lord to forgive you for your sins just as I have asked you to forgive me, and He will do it for the sake of Jesus, who died on the cross that sinners might be redeemed from their sins and live with Him in heaven."

I can never forget the ineffable love, and faith, and gratitude, depicted in that poor boy's face, while I live; and as I held his soft black hand in mine, I thought of its willing service to "our boys," and wept to think I could do no more for him, and that his young life was going out before he knew the result of the cruel war that was waged by the Abolitionists! He noticed my grief, and begged me not to feel so badly, and added that he was willing to die.

I arose from my position by his bed and asked him if there was anything in the world I could do for him. In reply he said:

"I would like to have a drink of water from the Floyd spring."

"You shall have it, my boy, just as soon as I can go there and back," and I took a pitcher and ran to the spring and filled and refilled it several times, that it might be perfectly cool, and went back with it as quickly as possible. He drank a goblet full of this delicious water and said it was "so good," and then added:

"You drink some, too, Miss Mary, and give Miss Polly some."

I did so, and he was pleased. He coughed less and complained less than he had done since the change for the worse, and I deluded myself into the hope that he might yet recover. In a short while he went to sleep, and his breathing became very hard and his temperature indicated a high degree of fever. I urged my mother to lie down, and assured her that if I thought she could do anything for Toby at any time during the night I would call her.

I sat there alone by that dying boy. Not a movement on his part betrayed pain. His breathing was hard and at intervals spasmodic. With tender hands I changed the position of his head, and for a little while he seemed to breathe easier. But it was only for a little while, and then it was evident that soon he would cease to breathe at all. I went to my mother and waked her gently and told her I thought the end was near with Toby, and hurried back to him. I thought him dead even then; but, after an interval, he breathed again and again, and all was over. The life had gone back to the God who gave it, and I doubt not but that it will live with Him forever. The pathos of the scene can never be understood by those who have not witnessed one similar to it in all its details, and I will not attempt to describe it. No timepiece marked the hour, but it was about midnight, I ween, when death set the spirit of that youthful negro free. Not a kindred being nor a member of his own race was near to lay loving hand upon him, or prepare his little body for burial. We stood and gazed upon him as he lay in death in that desolated house, and thought of his fidelity and loving interest in our cause and its defenders, and of his faithful service in our efforts to save something from vandal hands; and the fountain of tears was broken up and we wept with a peculiar grief over that lifeless form.

My mother was the first to become calm, and she came very near me and said, as if afraid to trust her voice :

"Wouldn't it be well to ask Eliza Williams and others to come and 'lay him out?' "

Before acting on this suggestion I went into another room and waked Telitha and took her into the chamber of death. A dim and glimmering light prevented her from taking in the full import of the scene at first ; but I took her near the couch, and, pointing to him, I said :

" Dead!—Dead !"

She repeated interrogatively, and, when she fully realized that such was the case, her cries were pitiable, oh, so pitiable.

I sank down upon the floor and waited for the paroxysm of grief to subside, and then went to her and made her understand that I was going out and that she must stay with her mistress until I returned. An hour later, under the manipulation of good "Eliza Williams"—known thoughout Decatur as Mrs. Ammi Williams' faithful servant—and one or two others whom she brought with her, Toby was robed in a nice white suit of clothes prepared for the occasion by the faithful hands of his "Miss Polly," whom he had loved well and who had cared for him in his orphanage.

We had had intimation that the Federals would again occupy Decatur, and as soon as day dawned I went to see Mr. Robert Jones, Sen., and got him to make a coffin for Toby, and I then asked "Uncle Mack," and "Henry"—now known as Decatur's Henry Oliver—to dig the grave. Indeed, these two men agreed to attend to the matter of his burial. After consultation with my mother, it was agreed that that should take place as soon as all things were in readiness. Mr. Jones made a pretty, well-shaped

coffin out of good heart pine, and the two faithful
negro men already mentioned prepared with care the
grave. When all was in readiness, the dead boy was
placed in the coffin and borne to the grave by very
gentle hands.

Next to the pall-bearers my mother and myself
and Telitha fell in line, and then followed the few
negroes yet remaining in the town, and that funeral
cortege was complete.

At the grave an unexpected and most welcome
stranger appeared. "Uncle Mack" told me he was a
minister, and would perform the funeral service—and
grandly did he do it. The very soul of prayer seemed
embodied in this negro preacher's invocation ; nor did
he forget Toby's "nurses," and every consolation and
blessing was besought for them. And thus our Toby
received a Christian burial.

CHAPTER XVI.

EVERETT'S DESERTION.

During the early spring of that memorable year, 1864, it was announced to the citizens of Decatur that Judge Hook and family, including his accomplished daughter, Mrs. Whitesides, and her children, from Chattanooga, had arrived at the depot, and were domiciled, *pro tem.*, in cars which had been switched off the main track of the famous old Georgia Railroad. This novel mode of living, even in war times, by people in their monetary condition and social standing, naturally attracted much attention, and brought us to a full realization of approaching danger. That this family, accustomed to all the luxuries of an elegant home, should live in such an abode, with its attendant privations, was convincing proof that the home they had abandoned had become intolerable because of the proximity of the enemy ; and it was also fearfully suggestive that that ubiquitous enemy was extending his dominion and bringing the fiery, bloody conflict into the very heart of the "rebellion."

A rebellion, by way of parenthesis, which impartial historians will put on record as the grandest uprising of a long suffering people that was ever known in the annals of nations ; "a mutiny" (as that chief of Southern haters, John Lathrop Motley, whose superb egotism impressed him with the idea that his influence could change the political trend of Great Britain towards the South, has seen proper to denominate it) in the camp of American councils brought about by unceasing abuse of the Southern States by political tricksters, whose only hope of survival lay in the hatred for the South thus engendered.

The coming of Judge Hook's family was hailed with pleasure by all good and loyal citizens, and was a ligament connecting more closely states suffering in a common cause; and we all called upon them and soon numbered them with our intimate friends. Mrs. Whitesides and Miss Hook were effective workers in all that benefited our soldiers or their families.

Judge Hook was superintendent of the Government Iron Works, and literally brought the foundry as well as the operatives with him. Among the latter was a man by the name of Everett, who, with his family, consisting of his wife and five children, occupied an old one-room house near a corner of our home lot. Although a hearty, hale, and rather good-looking man, Everett was very poor, and the first time I ever saw his wife she came to borrow "a little flour." As my mother never turned away from a borrower, Mrs. Everett's vessel was filled to overflowing, and, besides, a pitcher of buttermilk and a plate of butter was given to her, for which she was extremely grateful.

An acquaintance thus begun continued during the spring and early summer months, and there was not a day during that period that my mother did not find it convenient to do something for this family. Mrs. Everett was more than ordinarily intelligent for a person in her position, and the blush which mantled

her pretty cheeks when she asked for anything betrayed her sensibility; and her children were pretty
and sweet-mannered.   I never saw Everett, only as I
met him going and coming from his work, and on those
occasions he showed the greatest respect for me by
taking off his hat as he approached me, and holding it
in his hand until he had fully passed.   He seemed to
be a steady worker, and if he ever lost a day I never
heard of it; and Mrs. Everett was industrious, but
much of the time unemployed for lack of material with
which to work, and she often begged for something to
do.   She was anxious to work for our soldiers, and
told me that all of her male relatives were in the Confederate army.   This circumstance endeared her very
much to me; and I made the support of his family
very much easier to Everett than it would have been
had he lived in a non-appreciative neighborhood.   And
when the village girls met at our house to practice for
concerts for the benefit of our soldiers, which they did
almost weekly, I never forgot that Mrs. Everett's
brothers were in our army fighting valiantly, no doubt,
for our cause, and I always asked her to come and
bring her children to my room and listen with me to
the sweet music and patriotic songs.

As time sped, many opportunities for witnessing
Mrs. Everett's devotion to her native land presented
themselves; and her service to its defenders, though
humble and unobtrusive, was valuable.   Her children,
too, always spoke lovingly of our soldiers, and were
never more happy than when doing something for
them.   At length the time came for another move of
the foundry, and quietly, as if by magic, it and its

appurtenants, under the judicious management of
Judge Hook, got on wheels and ran at the rate of
thirty-five miles an hour until it reached Augusta—
another haven of rest invested with heavenly beauty.
After the departure of this important adjunct to this
portion of the Confederacy, it was discovered that
Everett and his family remained in Decatur. And a
remarkable change came over them. Instead of the
free-spoken, unsophisticated woman that she had
always appeared to be, Mrs. Everett became reserved
and taciturn, and seldom left the enclosure by which
her humble dwelling was surrounded. And the children ceased to cheer us by their merry prattle and
daily trip for a pitcher of buttermilk, which, under
the changed and unexplained circumstances, my
mother sent to them.

On the never-to-be-forgotten 19th of July, 1864,
when a portion of Sherman's army dashed into Decatur, it obtained a recruit. In an incredibly short time,
Everett was arrayed in the uniform of a Yankee private, and was hustling around with the Yankees as if
" to the manner born."

On the 22d of July, when the Confederates ran
the Yankees out of the little village they had so
pompously occupied for a few days, Everett disappeared, and so did his family from the little house on
the corner. I supposed they had left Decatur, until
I went out in town to see if I could hear anything
from the victors—their losses, etc.—when by chance I
discovered that they had taken shelter in the old post-
office building on the northeast corner of the court-
house square.

The morning after the hurried evacuation of Decatur by the Federal troops, I arose, as was my custom, as day was dawning, and, as soon as I thought I could distinguish objects, I opened the front door and stepped out on the portico. As I stood looking upon the ruin and devastation of my war-stricken home, imagine my surprise and consternation when I saw a white handkerchief held by an invisible hand above a scuppernong grape arbor. My first impulse was to seek security within closed doors, but the thought occurred to me that some one might be in distress and needed aid. I therefore determined to investigate the case. In pursuance of this object I went down the steps, and advanced several yards in the direction of the waving signal, and asked :

" Who is there ?"

" Come a little nearer, please," was the distinct answer.

" I am near enough to hear you ; what can I do for you ?" I said, and did go a little nearer.

" Miss Mary, don't be afraid of me ; I would die for you and such as you, but I cannot die for a lost cause "—and through an opening in the foliage of the vines, which were more on the ground than on the scaffolding, a head protruded—handsome brown eyes and dark whiskers included—Everett's head, in all the naturalness of innocence.

I thought of his wife and of his children, and of his wife's brother in the Confederate army, and again asked with deliberation :

" What can I do for you ?"

" Bless me or curse me," was the startling answer, and he continued :

" Your kindness to my wife and children has nerved me to come to you and ask that you will aid me in seeing them, especially her. Will you do it ?"

" Yes, though I despise you for the steps you have taken, I will grant your request. Don't be afraid that I will betray you."

" Where shall I go ?" he asked, with a perceptible tremor in his voice.

" While I am out here seeming to prop up these shrubs, make your way to the kitchen and enter its front door, and don't close it after you, but let it remain wide open. But be still until I tell you to start."

As if going for something, I walked hastily around the house and kitchen, and entering the latter brought out an old hoe, and seemed to use it quite industriously in banking up earth around fallen shrubbery. Watching an opportunity—for in those war times all things, animate and inanimate, seemed to have ears —I said :

" When I go into the house, you must go into the kitchen, and be certain to let the doors remain open."

I never knew how Everett made his journey, whether upright as a man, or upon all-fours like a beast.

From sheer exhaustion my poor mother was sleeping still, and Toby's breathing and general appearance as he lay upon his pallet, plainly indicated the presence of deep seated disease. I looked around for Telitha, and not seeing her, went into the dining

room where I found her sitting by a window. By
unmistakable signs she made me understand that she
had witnessed the entire proceeding connected with
Everett through the window blinds.

Soon the loud tramping of horses' feet caused me
to run again to the front door, and I beheld a number
of our scouts approaching.   I went to meet them and
shook hands with every one of them.   No demonstration, however enthusiastic, could have been an
exaggeration of my joy on again seeing our men, our
dear Confederate soldiers, and yet I thought of Everett and trembled.

" Have you seen any Billy Yanks this morning ?"
was asked by several of them ; and I replied :

" No, I have not seen any since our men ran them
out of Decatur yesterday."

" How did they treat you while they were here ?"

" You see the devastation of the place," I replied.
"Personally we escaped violence ; but I would like
you to go into the house and see the condition of
affairs there."

Said they :

" It would not be new to us.   We have seen the
most wanton destruction of property and household
goods wherever they have gone."

" Do wait and let me have a pot of coffee made for
you.   The Yankees give our negro girl quite a good
deal of it, and not using it herself, she gave it to
my mother, and I want you to enjoy some of it," I
said.   They replied.

"Soldiers can't wait for luxuries."

" Good-bye and God bless you," was their parting

benediction. And then as if impelled by some strange inspiration they galloped round to the well. I ran into the house and got several tumblers and fairly flew out there with them, as there was no gourd at the well. The kitchen was in close proximity, and the door stood invitingly open. What if a bare suspicion should prompt these brave men to enter ? Alas ! All would be up with the poor miscreant who had thrown himself upon my mercy, and who was even then lurking there under my direction. But, thank the good Lord, they did not enter, and after again invoking God's blessings upon me, they galloped off in a southerly direction ; and never did retreating sounds give more relief.

I went into the house. My mother, thoroughly exhausted, and perhaps discouraged, chose to remain in bed, and as she lay gazing intently upon the wall above her, I doubt if she saw it, so intense was her meditation. As Telitha by this time had a fire made in the dining room, I prepared a pot of good strong coffee, and after partaking of the exhilarating beverage myself, and seeing that each of the household was supplied, I took the remainder with necessary adjuncts to Everett. Never will I forget his appearance as we stood face to face—he a miserable deserter from the cause I loved, and the recipient of favors I scorned myself for bestowing. I told him I would go at once for his wife, and that after seeing her he must make his way into the enemy's lines as soon as possible.

A few minutes sufficed to carry me to Mrs. Everett's retreat, already mentioned. I sat down on the front doorsteps and drew from my pocket a news-

11

paper, which chanced to be there, and commenced reading aloud. At length I saw that my presence had attracted the notice of the children, and I called them. One by one they came to me, and I shook hands with them and asked them about their mother. Hearing my voice and inquiries, she spoke to me most pleasantly. I asked her to come out and take a seat by me on the steps. She did so, blushingly and timidly. I wrote on the margin of the paper, " Send the children away," and handed it to her. She did so. Assured that they were not in hearing distance, I held the paper before me, and, as if reading, I told her the story of my early interview with her husband ; of his earnest desire to see her ; of my consent, on her account, to plan a meeting with her ; of his secretion in our kitchen ; and the necessity of the greatest caution in our movements. I told her that after walking around a little, and exchanging experiences with the brave ladies of the village, she would see me, by keeping watch, going home, and then she could take a little basket in her hand, as if going for something, and come on to our house. She implicitly followed my directions. My mother received her as if nothing of an unpleasant nature had transpired ; and, although it is a very difficult problem, and never solved without the aid of necromancy, I undertook to deduct something from nothing, and so far succeeded that I had several small packages to lay in her basket as she started. Knowing that she knew the way to the kitchen, I gave her a wish that all would end well, and bade her good-bye, never, doubtless, to meet her again on earth. The tears flowed plenteously down her cheeks, and her tongue refused to speak, but the pressure of her hand attested gratitude, and affection, and farewell. I got a glimpse of her as she went out of the alley gate ; but I never knew when he abandoned his hiding place. I heard that about dusk a Federal army wagon, under protection of a company of troops, came and took her and her little children out of Decatur.

CHAPTER XVII.

A visit to Confederate lines—A narrow escape—My return—
The fall of Atlanta.

No news from "the front;" no tidings from the
loved ones in gray; no friendly spirit whispering
words of cheer or consolation. Shut up within a
narrow space, and guarded by Federal bayonets! not
a ray of friendly light illuminated my environment.

The constant roaring of cannon and rattling of
musketry; the thousand, yea, tens of thousands of
shots blending into one grand continuous whole, and
reverberating in avalanchan volume over the hills of
Fulton, and the mountain heights of old DeKalb—
told in thunder tones of the fierce contest between
Federal and Confederate forces being waged without
intermission for the possession of Atlanta.

The haughty, insolent boast of the enemy, now
that Joe Johnston was removed from the command
of the Army of the Tennessee, that they would make
quick work of the rebellion, and of the complete subjugation of the South, had in no way a tendency to
mitigate anxiety or to encourage hope. Thus surrounded, I sought and obtained permission to read
Federal newspapers. The United States mail brought
daily papers to the officers in command of the forces
quartered in our yard; and through this medium I
kept posted, from a Northern standpoint, concerning

the situation of both armies. While there was little in these dispatches gratifying to me, there was much that I thought would be valuable to my people if I could only convey it to them; and I racked my brain day and night, devising ways and means by which to accomplish this feat. But the ways and means decided upon were, upon reflection, invariably abandoned as being impracticable.

In this dilemma, a most opportune circumstance offered an immediate solution of the difficult problem. In the midst of a deep study of the relative positions of the two armies, and of the hopes and fears animating both, a tall, lank, honest-faced Yankee came to the door of the portico and asked "if Miss Gay was in."

I responded that I was she, and he handed me a letter addressed to myself. I hastily tore it open and read the contents. It was written by a reverend gentleman whose wife was a distant relative of my mother, and told that she was very ill. "Indeed," wrote he, "I have but little hope of ever seeing her any better, and I beg you to come to see her, and spend several days."

I showed the letter to my mother, who was sitting near by, and, like myself, engaged in studying the situation. She strenuously objected to my going, and advanced many good reasons for my not doing so; but my reasons for going counteracted them all in my estimation, and I determined to go.

Taking Telitha with me, I carried the letter to the Provost Marshal, and asked him to read it and grant me the privilege of going. After reading the letter,

he asked me how I obtained it, and received my statement. He then asked me if I could refer him to the
party who brought it to me. Leaving the letter with
him, I ran home and soon returned with the desired
individual who had fortunately lingered in the yard
in anticipation of usefulness. Convinced that the invitation was genuine, and for a humane purpose, this
usually morose marshal granted me "a permit" to
visit those poor old sick people, for the husband was
almost as feeble as his wife. I told the obliging marshal that there was another favor I should like to ask
of him, if he would not think me too presumptuous.
"Name it," he said. I replied :

"Will you detail one or more of the soldiers to act
as an escort for me ? I am afraid to go with only
this girl."

To this he also assented, and said it was a wise
precaution. He asked when I wished to come home.

"Day after to-morrow afternoon," I told him, and
received assurance that an escort would be in waiting
for me at that time.

It now became necessary to make some important
preparations for the trip. A great deal was involved,
and if my plans were successful, important events
might accrue. A nice white petticoat was called into
requisition, and, when I got done with it, it was literally lined with Northern newspapers. "The Cincinnati Enquirer," and "The New York Daily
Times ;" "The Cincinnati Commercial Gazette," and
"The Philadelphia Evening Ledger," under the
manipulation of my fingers, took their places on the
inner sides and rear of the skirt, and served as a very

stylish " bustle," an article much in vogue in those days. This preparatory work having been accomplished, it required but a few moments to complete my toilet, and, under the auspices of a clear conscience and a mother's blessing, doubtless, I started on a perilous trip. The ever-faithful Telitha was by my side, and the military escort a few feet in advance.

After a walk of a mile and a half, I reached my destination for that day. I found the old lady in question much better than I had expected. Nervous and sick himself, her husband had greatly exaggerated her afflictions. By degrees, and under protest, I communicated to these aged people my intention of carrying information to Hood's headquarters, that might be of use to our army. I knew that these good old people would not betray me, even though they might not approve my course, and I confided to them my every plan. Both were troubled about the possible result if I should be detected ; but my plans were laid, and nothing could deter me from pursuing them.

The rising sun of another day saw Telitha and me starting on our way to run the gauntlet, so to speak, of Federal bayonets. These good old people had given me much valuable information regarding the way to Atlanta—information which enabled me to get there without conflict with either Confederate or Federal pickets. Knowing the topography of the country, I took a circuitous route to an old mill ; Cobb's, I believe, and from there I sought the Mc-Donough road. I didn't venture to keep that highway to the city, but I kept within sight of it, and under cover of breast-works and other obstructions, managed to evade videttes and pickets of both armies. After walking fourteen or fifteen miles, I entered Atlanta at the beautiful home of Mrs. L. P. Grant, at the southern boundary of the city. That estimable lady never lost an opportunity of doing good. The lessons of humanity and Christian grace impressed upon her youthful mind, and intensified by the life-long example of her devoted mother, Mrs. Ammi Williams, of Decatur, had called into action all that is ennobling in woman. On this occasion, as upon every other offering an opportunity, she remembered to do good. She ordered an appetizing lunch, including a cup of sure enough coffee, which refreshed and strengthened me after my long walk. Her butler having become a familiar personage on the streets of Atlanta, she sent him as a guide to important places. We entered the city unchallenged, and moved about at will. The force of habit, probably, led me to Mrs. McArthur's and to Mrs. Craig's on Pryor street ; and, by the way, these friends still own the same property, and occupy almost the same homes. The head of neither of these families was willing to accompany me to Confederate headquarters, and without a guide I started to hunt them for myself, What had seemed an easy task now seemed insurmountable. I knew not in what direction to go, and the few whom I asked seemed as ignorant as myself. Starting from Mrs. Craig's, I went towards the depot. I had not proceeded very far before I met Major John Y. Rankin. I could scarcely restrain tears of joy. He was a member of the very same command to which

my brother belonged. From Major Rankin I learned
that my brother, utterly prostrated, had been sent to
a hospital, either in Augusta or Madison. He told
me many other things of interest, which I cannot mention now, unless I was compiling a history instead of
a series of personal reminiscences. Preferring not to
stand upon the street, I asked Major Rankin to return
with me to Mrs. Craig's, which he did, and spent an
hour in pleasant conversation. Mrs. Craig was a
delightful conversationalist, and while she was entertaining the major with that fine art, I retired to a private apartment, and with the aid of a pair of scissors
ripped off the papers from my underskirt and smoothed
and folded them nicely, and after re-arranging my
toilet, took them into the parlor as a trophy of skill
in outwitting the Yankee. Telitha, too, had a trophy to which she had clung ever since we left home
with the tenacity of an eel, and which doubtless she
supposed to be an offering to "Marse Tom," and was
evidently anxious that he should receive it. Having
dismissed Mrs. Grant's butler as no longer necessary
to my convenience, Major Rankin, myself and
Telitha went direct to the headquarters of his command. The papers seemed to be most acceptable, but
I noticed that the gleanings from conversation seemed
far more so. The hopefulness and enthusiasm of our
soldiers were inspiring. But alas! how little they
knew of the situation, and how determined not to be
enlightened. Even then they believed that they
would hold Atlanta against Herculean odds, and
scorned the idea of its surrender. At length the opening of Telitha's package devolved on me. Shirts,

socks and soap, towels, gloves, etc., formed a compact bundle that my mother had sent to our soldiers. Many cheery words were said, and good-byes uttered, and I left them to meet once more under very different circumstances.

I now turned my thoughts to our negroes, who were hired in different parts of the city. Rachel, the mother of King, hired herself and rented a room from Mr. John Silvey, who lived upon the same lot on Marietta street upon which he has since erected his present elegant residence. In order that I might have an interview with Rachel without disturbing Mr. Silvey's family, I went to the side gate and called her. She answered and came immediately. I asked her if she realized the great danger to which she was continually exposed. Even then "shot and shell" were falling in every direction, and the roaring of cannon was an unceasing sound. She replied that she knew the danger, and thought I was doing wrong to be in Atlanta when I had a home to be at. I insisted that she had the same home, and a good vacant house was ready to receive her. But she was impervious to every argument, and preferred to await the coming of Sherman in her present quarters. Seeing that I had no influence over her, I bade her good-bye and left. Telitha and I had not gone farther than the First Presbyterian church (not a square away) from the gate upon which I had leaned during this interview with Rachel, before a bombshell fell by that gate and burst into a thousand fragments, literally tearing the gate into pieces. Had I remained there one minute longer, my mortal being would have been torn to atoms. After this fearfully impressive adventure, unfortified by any "permit" I struck a bee line to Mrs. Grant's, having promised her that I would go back that way and stop awhile. An old negro man belonging to Mrs. Williams, who had "come out" on a previous occasion, was there, and wanted to return under my protection to his home within the enemy's lines. Very earnest assurances from Mrs. Grant to that effect convinced me that I had nothing to fear from betrayal by him, and I consented that he should be a member of my company homeward bound. Two large packages were ready for the old man to take charge of, about which Mrs. Grant gave him directions, *sotto voce.* Putting one of them on the end of a walking cane he threw it over his right shoulder, and with his left hand picked up the other bundle. Telitha and I were unencumbered. With a good deal of trepidation I took the advance position in the line of march, and walked briskly. We had not proceeded very far before we encountered our pickets. No argument was weighty enough to secure for me the privilege of passing the lines without an official permit. Baffled in this effort, I approved the action of the pickets, and we turned and retraced our steps in the direction of Atlanta, until entirely out of sight of them, and then we turned southward and then eastward, verging a little northward. Constant vigilance enabled me to evade the Yankee pickets, and constant walking brought me safely to the home of my aged and afflicted friends, from which I had started early in the morning of that day. Not being tired, I could have gone home; but the policy of carrying out the original programme is too apparent to need explanation. These friends were conservative in every act and word, and, it may be, leaned a little out of the perpendicular towards that "flaunting lie," the United States flag; therefore they were favorites among the so-called defenders of the Union, and were kept supplied with many palatable articles of food that were entirely out of the reach of rebels who were avowed and "dyed in the wool."

A few minutes sufficed to furnish us with a fine pot of soup (and good bread was not lacking), of which we ate heartily. The old negro man was too anxious to get home to be willing to spend the night so near, just for the privilege of walking into Decatur under Yankee escort, and said he was "going home," and left me.

The next day my escort was promptly on hand, and in due time I was in Decatur, none the worse for having put into practice a favorite aphorism of the Yankees, that "all things are fair in war."

The old man had preceded me, and faithful to the behest of Mrs. Grant, had turned over a valuable package to my mother.

Not many mornings subsequent to the adventure just related, I discovered upon opening the door that the Yankee tents seemed to be vacant. Not a blue-coat was to be seen. What could it mean? Had they given up the contest and ignominiously fled? As if confirmatory of the gratifying suggestion, the booming of cannon in the direction of Atlanta was evidently decreasing. Then again I thought perhaps the wagon train had been sent out to forage upon the country,

and as it would now have to go forty-five and fifty miles
to get anything, it required an immense military escort to protect it from the dashing, sanguinary attacks
of the "rebels." The latter thought was soon dismissed and the former embraced, and how consoling
it was to me. Before the sun had attained its merid-
ian height, a number of our scouts appeared on the
abandoned grounds; and what joy their presence gave
us! But they left us as suddenly as they came, and
on reflection we could not think of a single encouraging word uttered by them during their stay. Suspense
became intolerable. With occasional lulls, the roaring of cannon was a continuous blending of ominous
sound.

In the midst of this awful suspense, an apparition,
glorious and bright, appeared in our presence. It was
my brother. He had left Madison a few days before,
where he had been allowed to spend a part of his fur-
lough, instead of remaining at the Augusta hospital,
and where he received the tender ministrations of his
estimable cousin, Mrs. Tom Hillsman, and her pretty
young daughters, and the loving care of his sister
Missouri, who was also at this time an inmate of her
cousin's household. How I wished he could have remained there until restored to health. One less patriotic and conscientious would have done so. His
mother's joy at meeting her beloved son, and under
such circumstances, was pathetic indeed, and I shall
never forget the effort she made to repress the tears
and steady the voice as she sought to nerve him for
the arduous and perilous duties before him. Much of
his conversation, though hurried, was regarding his

Mary, in Texas, and the dear little boy dropped down
from heaven, whom he had never seen.   The shades
of night came on, and darker grew until complete
blackness enveloped the face of the earth, and still the
low subdued tones of conversation between mother,
son and daughter, mingled with unabated interest.
Hark ! Hark ! An explosion ! An earthquake ? The angry bellowing sound rises in deafening grandeur, and
reverberates along the far-off valleys and distant hill-
tops.   What is it ?   This mighty thunder that never
ceases ?   The earth is ablaze—what can it be ?   This
illumination that reveals minutest objects ?   With
blanched face and tearful eye, the soldier said :

"Atlanta has surrendered to the enemy.   The
mighty reports are occasioned by the blowing up of
the magazines and arsenals."

Dumbfounded we stood, trying to realize the crushing fact.   Woman's heart could bear no more in
silence, and a wail over departed hopes mingled with
the angry sounds without.

Impelled by a stern resolve, and a spirit like to
that of martyred saints, our brother said :

"This is no place for me.   I must go."

And then he put an arm around each of us, and
kissed us with a fervor of love that knew no bounds,
and was quenching itself in unfathomable hopeless
tenderness.   The quiet fortitude and patriotism of his
mother gave way in that dread hour, and she cried
aloud in agonizing apprehension of never again clasping to her bosom her greatest earthly joy.   No pen
can describe the scene of that last parting between

mother and son, and in sheer impotency I drop the curtain.

As he walked away from his sobbing mother, through the war-illuminated village, I never beheld mortal man so handsome, so heroically grand. His great tender heart, which I had seen heave and sway under less trying circumstances, seemed to have ossified, and not an emotion was apparent.

CHAPTER XVIII.

THE TEN DAYS' ARMISTICE.

Going out with the Confederate clothes—Scenes at Atlanta
and at Lovejoy's Station—The visit to Granbury's Brigade—
The last interview with Thomie.

After every morsel of food had been taken from
the people, and every vestige of nutrition extracted
from the earth, the following order, in substance, was
proclaimed throughout the land held by the right of
conquest :

" All who cannot support themselves without ap-
plying to the United States Commissary for assistance, must go outside of our lines, either north or
south, within the period of time mentioned in this
order, etc., etc."

And by this order, and by others even more oppressive and diabolical, the Nero of the nineteenth century, alias William Tecumseh Sherman, was put upon
record as the born leader of the most ruthless, Godless
band of men ever organized in the name of patriotism
—a band which, but for a few noble spirits who, by
the power of mind over matter, exerted a restraining
influence, would not have left a Southerner to tell the
tale of fiendishness on its route to the sea.

And now, like Bill Nye, after one of his sententious
and doubtless truthful introductions to a Western

sketch, I feel easier in my mind, and will proceed with my reminiscences of that unholy period of this country, and tell the truth about it, without favor or prejudice, if it kills me. After this pronunciamento had been issued, all was bustle and rapid movement in every household within the boundaries of usurpation. Under the strong arm of military power, delay was not permitted. Homes were to be abandoned, and household goods and household gods to be left for the enemy, or destroyed ; and liberty under our own vine and fig tree was to be a thing of the past, and dependence upon strangers a thing of the future. In preparation for this enforced change, much that should have been done was left undone, but there was no time to correct mistakes—the armistice was only for ten days.

What were we to do, my mother and myself, was a question which presented itself with startling seriousness, and had to be answered without delay. Our farm in Gordon county had already been devastated by the invading army, and every improvement destroyed, and if we should lose our home in Decatur we would be poor indeed. But what were we to do ? If we left our home, we knew it would share the fate of all other " abandoned " property, and furnish material for a bonfire for Nero to fiddle by ; and if we remained, by grace of better men than he, what assurance had we that by any means within our grasp we could obtain even a scanty subsistence, or be protected from personal abuse and insult by an alien army whose gentlemen were vastly in the minority.

12

We learned that our neighbors and friends, Mrs. Ammi Williams and her estimable son, Mr. Frederick Williams, (an invalid from paralysis)—whose influence over General Schofield prevented my banishment from Decatur the very first night of its occupancy by the Federal army—and the venerable Mr. and Mrs. Buchanan (the latter a Bostonian and educated in Emerson's celebrated school for young ladies), and other families as true to the South as the needle to the pole, were going to remain and take their chances within the enemy's lines, and we determined to do so too.

The officers in command of the post, especially the provost marshal, interrogated us very closely regarding our plans and expectations during the occupancy of the place by Federal forces. Having satisfied them that our only remaining servant would do washing and ironing at reasonable prices, and that we would do darning and repairing, we were given a written permit to remain within the lines.

I, however, had a work to do, a feat to perform, which for audacity and courage, has seldom been surpassed, which would not admit of my staying at home until I had made a little trip to Dixie.

Knowing the value of his influence, I again went to Mr. Frederick Williams, and confiding my plans to him, asked his assistance in getting permission to go out and return during the armistice. I never knew what argument he employed for the accomplishment of this object. I only know by inference. But I received a letter from General Schofield, adjutant-general, of which the subjoined is an exact transcript:

"DECATUR, GA., Sept. 1, 1864.

"MISS GAY—It was hard for me to reconcile my conscience to giving the enclosed recommendation to one whose sentiments I cannot approve, but if I have committed an error it has been on the side of mercy, and I hope I'll be forgiven. Hereafter I hope you will not think of Yankees as all being bad, and beyond the pale of redemption.

"To-morrow I leave for my own home in the 'frozen North,' and when I return it will be to fight for my country, and against your friends, so that I suppose I shall not have the pleasure of again meeting you.   Very respectfully,

J. W. CAMPBELL."

And that Major Campbell's gallant act may be fully appreciated, I will add the letter which secured for me the great favor which I had the temerity to ask.

"HEADQUARTERS, ARMY OF OHIO,

DECATUR, GA., Sept. 14, 1864.

"MY DEAR COLONEL—I have the honor to introduce Miss Mary A. H. Gay, of this village, and I recommend her case to your favorable consideration. I do not know exactly what orders are now in force, but if you think you can grant her desires without detriment to the public service, I am confident the indulgence will not be abused.

Very respectfully your obedient servant,

J. W. CAMPBELL.

"To Colonel J. C. Parkhurst, Pro. Mar. Gen., Army of the Cumberland."

Thus recommended by one high in army ranks, Colonel Parkhurst granted me the privilege of going to see my young sister, then in Augusta, and carrying anything I might have saved from the ravages of the war, "unmolested." Fortified by these letters I went to the Provost Marshal in Decatur and told him I would be ready to go to Atlanta to-morrow morning at 8 o'clock, and I wanted to carry some old bed-clothing and other things to my sister, and would be grateful for an ambulance, or an army wagon all to myself, and an Irish driver. He promised that both should be at my service at the time indicated—not, however, without the sarcastic remark that " if the Yankees had been as bad as I had said they were, they would not have left anything for me to carry."

I ran to my mother and imparted to her the glad tidings of success, and in a whispered conversation we soon had definite plans arranged for the consummation of the perilous duty before me. I went to the Federal camp and asked for some crocus sacks such as are used in the transportation of grain, and quite a number were given to me. I shook them thoroughly inside and out, and put them by. A ball of twine and some large needles had found their way into the house. The needles were threaded and placed in convenient proximity to the sacks. Telitha watched every movement with interest and intuitively divined its import. The wardrobe was empty and my very first touch moved it at least one inch in the desired direction, and a helping hand from her soon placed it in favorable position. This much being accomplished, I took a seat by my mother on the front door-steps and engaged in a pleasant conversation with a group of young Federal soldiers, who seemed much attached to us, and with whom I conversed with unreserved candor, and often expressed regret that they were in hostile array towards a people who had been goaded to desperation by infringement upon constitutional rights by those who had pronounced the only ligament that bound the two sections of the country together, "a league with hell, and a covenant with the devil." This I proved to them by documents published at the North, and by many other things of which they were ignorant.

While thus engaged, Captain Woodbury approached and said : "I learn that you are going out into Dixie, Miss Gay."

"Yes, for a few days," I replied.

"I am prepared to furnish a more pleasant conveyance to Atlanta than the one you have secured," said he, and continued, "I have a handsome new buggy and a fine trotter, and it will take only a few minutes to reach there. Will you accept a seat with me ?"

If all the blood within me had overflowed its proper channels, and rushed to the surface, I could not have flushed more. I felt it in the commotion of my hair, and in the nervous twitching of my feet. The indignation and contempt that I felt for the man! That one who was aiding and abetting in the devastation of my country and the spoliation of my home, should ask me to take a seat with him in a buggy which he doubtless had taken, without leave or license, from my countrymen, was presumptuous indeed, and deserved a severe rebuke. But "prudence being the better part of valor," I repressed all that would have been offensive in word and act, and replied with suavity, "Thank you, Captain Woodbury, for the honor you would have conferred upon me, but I cannot accept it." Receiving no reply, I added :

"Let me in candor make a statement to you, and I think you will approve the motive that prompts my decision. I have not sought to conceal the fact that my only brother is in the Confederate army ; he is there from motives purely patriotic, and not as a mercenary hireling. He is fighting for the rights guaranteed by the Constitution of the United States, a constitution so sacred that our people have never violated it in any particular, and of which we have shown our highest appreciation by adopting it *verbatim*, as the guiding star of the Southern Confederacy. You are in an army claiming to be fighting for the Union, and yet the government that sent you out on this glorious mission ignores every principle of fraternal relation between the North and the South, and would subvert every fundamental principle of self-government and establish upon the wreck a centralized despotism. Could I, while you and I are so antagonistic, accept your offer and retain your good opinion ? I think not, and I prefer to go in the conveyance already stipulated."

Silence, without the slightest manifestation of anger, assured me that my argument against taking a buggy drive with him to Atlanta had not been lost on Captain Woodbury, of Ohio, a member of Garrard's Cavalry.

After this episode we bade our callers " good-even-
ing," went into the house and busied ourselves with
the important work before us—a work which probably would not attract attention because of the darkness that would surround the scene of its execution.
The table and chair had been placed, as once before,
by the wardrobe already mentioned, and a little
respite was employed in viewing the situation. The
door connecting our room and this dining-room was
generally kept shut. At length night came on with
its friendly, helpful darkness. The shutters of the
windows had been closed for weeks, and secured by
nails, and the house had been too often searched and
plundered to be suspected of containing valuables.
Therefore, we felt that if no unusual sound attracted
notice we would accomplish our object unsuspected.
But I was anxious and nervous in view of what was
before me, and wanted the perilous work over with.
So when the darkness of night fully enshrouded the
earth, with no other light than that which found its
way from the camp-fires of the enemy through the
latticed shutters, I stepped into the chair and thence
upon the table, and Telitha followed and drew the
chair up after her. Then with her strong dusky
hands she seized the wardrobe as if it had been a toy
in her hands. I steadied the chair by the wardrobe
and stepped into it, and another step landed me on
top of the wardrobe. My fingers penetrated the crev-
ice between the slats which I wanted to pull off, and
to a slight effort they yielded. Lest the noise occasioned by dropping them might attract notice, I
stooped and laid each piece down as I drew it off the

joist. When the aperture thus made was sufficient, I began to draw from their hiding place the precious Confederate overcoats and other winter apparel confided to my keeping (as already related), by soldiers of General Joseph E. Johnston's army, when they were at Dalton. One by one each piece was taken out and dropped down upon the floor. But by a lamentable oversight we afterwards found that one article had been left—a woolen scarf for the neck, knitted for my brother by his loving young wife in Texas.

Carefully I descended, and, with the aid of the girl, placed the chair, the table, and the dear old wardrobe (which deserves to be immortalized in song and story), in less suspicious positions, and then proceeded to pack in the sacks, already mentioned, the precious articles. The thought occurred to me that my mother would like to have a hand in this labor of love, and I opened the door between us. I shall never forget her appearance as she stood as if riveted to the spot, near a window, watching the moving figures without. I approached her and in a cheerful whisper told her that I was now putting the things in the sacks, and I knew she would like to have an interest in the job. She tried to respond, but she was too nervous to do so. Slowly but surely she was yielding to the pressure upon nerve and brain. As each sack was filled, a threaded needle securely closed the mouth. In a short while a number of these sacks stood in a group, as erect as if on parade, and I verily believe that if the host of profane, godless braggarts (with but few exceptions) who surrounded the house could have seen them at that time and known their contents, they would have evacuated Decatur in mortal fear of the ghosts of "Johnnie Rebs."

This important work having been accomplished without discovery or even a shadow of suspicion, I felt vastly relieved, and thanked the Lord with all my heart for the health, strength, and ingenuity which had enabled me to consummate it. My mother and I lay down upon the same bed, and were soon blessed with the invigorating influence of "tired nature's sweet restorer."

The song of the lark had ceased to be heard in this war-stricken locality ; chanticleer had long since furnished a savory meal for camp followers, and the time-pieces had either been spoiled or stolen ; but there was a silent, unerring chronometer within that never deviated, and needed no alarm attachment to arouse me from slumber, and the dawn found me up and preparing for the duties and perhaps the dangers of the day.

Telitha had become quite an attraction to a bevy of men who occupied soldiers' quarters, and wore soldiers' uniforms, and drew pay for doing so, from Uncle Sam's coffers ; and as she had been trained to ideas of virtue and morality she often came in frowning and much ruffled in temper by their deportment towards her. Being almost entirely deaf and dumb, her limited vocabulary was inadequate to supply epithets expressive of the righteous indignation and contempt which she evidently felt—she could only say, "Devil Yank, devil," and these words she used with telling effect both to the amusement and chagrin of the Yankees. This state of affairs convinced me that for her protection she would have to be kept within doors, and I therefore assumed the task of drawing the water, and a few other jobs indispensable even in life's rudest state. On this occasion, when I went to the well for a bucket of water, before preparing our frugal breakfast, I was asked by early marauders why I did not let " that young colored lady draw the water." I candidly answered them, and told them I was going to ask the officers of the encampment to protect her while I was gone, and I also would ask them to report any misdemeanor toward her, that they might witness, at headquarters.

After a good night's rest my mother's nerves seemed all right again, and by 7 o'clock we had finished our breakfast, which consisted of bread and butter and coffee—the latter luxurious beverage being furnished by one whose heart was in touch with humanity. That the aperture in the ceiling of the dining room might not be discovered until I got the contraband goods out of the house, I had brought the sacks containing them into the adjoining room, and it was therefore the work of a very few minutes to convey them to the wagon, when that vehicle, drawn by a span of fine horses, under the guidance of the Irish driver, drove up to the front door. "Put those sacks into the wagon," I said, pointing to them. When the last one of them was stored away safely in that moving repository, one of those feelings of relief and security came over me that had more than once given me courage to brave successfully impending danger— and I donned my hat, and bade my mother and the

faithful girl an almost cheerful "Good-bye," and
took my seat by the driver, *en route* for Dixie. Would
I get there? Ah! that was the question that had
blanched my mother's cheek when I said "Good-bye."
But hope, etc., " eternal in the human breast, " whispered "yes," and thus encouraged, I spoke grateful
words to the Irish driver, and asked him many questions
about the land of the shamrock and sunny blue skies.
He was evidently flattered by my favorable knowledge
of the Emerald Isle, and would have done anything
within his power for me. God bless the Irish forever!

I asked him to drive under my direction to the residence of my estimable friends, Mr. and Mrs. Posey
Maddox, the parents of the accomplished and erudite
Charles K. Maddox, of Atlanta. To my great joy I
saw wagons in the yard, already laden with their
household goods, to be carried to the depot and turned
over to the Federal authorities, who assumed the
transportation of them to Jonesboro and the safe delivery of them to the Confederate authorities, who in
turn assumed the transportation and delivery of them
to the nearest Confederate station. Mr. Maddox had
secured the use of an entire freight car, and gladly
consented to take me and my baggage in with theirs.
Mrs. Maddox was particularly glad to have me go with
them, and to her I confided the character of my baggage, and received in return many words of sympathy
and approbation. Those who have studied mythical
lore, and dwelt in imagination upon the attributes of
mythical characters, especially those of an evil nature,
can perhaps form some idea of the confusion and disquiet

of an entire city yielding its possession to an alien
army, which now, that success had been achieved by
brute force, was bent upon the utter impoverishment
of the people, and their extreme humiliation.   Curses
and imprecations too vile to repeat, and boisterous
laughter, and vulgar jests resounded through the
streets of Atlanta.   Federal wagons followed in the
tracks of Confederate wagons, and after a few light
articles were placed in the latter for Southern destination, the former unblushingly moved up to receive
pianos and other expensive furniture which found its
way into every section of the North.   And this highway robbery was permitted by William Tecumseh
Sherman, the Grand Mogul of the Army of the Republic.   Truly had the city of Atlanta been turned into a
veritable pandemonium.

At length our time came to move in the worse than
death-like processions going southward, and in a
short while we were at Jonesboro, our destination, so
far as Federal aid extended.   As soon as I stepped
from the car I wended my way to the Confederate
officer of the day, whom I recognized by his regalia,
and told him of my success in concealing and bringing
out of Federal lines the winter clothing of our soldiers.
He listened with polite attention and said it was a
wonderfully interesting story, but altogether improb-
able.

" Go with me and I will prove to you the truthfulness of it," I eagerly said.

As it was a bleak equinoctial day, and drizzling
rain, Mr. and Mrs. Maddox had not yet left their car
(by way of parenthesis, I would say that the favors

shown to these excellent people was in consideration of Mr. Maddox being a very prudent minister of the gospel), and, when we reached it, I asked Mr. Maddox to roll one of my sacks to the door. He did so, and I then asked the officer to examine its contents. A blade of a pen-knife severed the twine with which the edges of the mouth had been sewed together, and the loved familiar gray and brass buttons, and other articles, verified the truth of my statement. He looked amazed, and exhausted his vocabulary of flattering encomiums upon me, and, what was more desirable and to the point, he asked what he could do in the matter, and assured me that there was nothing within the range of his jurisdiction that he would not do. I told him that the object of my coming to him was to ask that he send me and my precious charge to General Granbury's headquarters, as, among other overcoats, I had one of his in charge, as well as many other things belonging to his staff officers. He told me the finest span of Confederate horses and the best ambulance on the ground should be at my service as soon as possible.

During the interim, I opened wide my eyes and took in the situation in all its horrible details. The entire Southern population of Atlanta, with but an occasional exception, and that of many miles in its vicinity, were dumped out upon the cold ground without shelter and without any of the comforts of home, and an autumnal mist or drizzle slowly but surely saturating every article of clothing upon them; and pulmonary diseases in all stages admonishing them of the danger of such exposure. Aged grandmothers tottering upon the verge of the grave, and tender

maidens in the first bloom of young womanhood, and
little babes not three days old in the arms of sick
mothers, driven from their homes, were all out upon
the cold charity of the world.

Apropos, I will relate an incident that came under
my observation during my brief stay at this station :
When one of the long trains from Atlanta rolled in
with its living freight and stopped at the terminus, a
queenly girl, tall and lithe in figure and willowy in
motion, emerged from one of the cars, and stood, the
embodiment of feminine grace, for a moment upon the
platform.   In less time than it takes to chronicle the
impression, her Grecian beauty, classic expression and
nobility of manner, had daguerreotyped themselves
upon the tablets of my memory never to be effaced by
mortal alchemy.   The pretty plain debeige dress,
trimmed with Confederate buttons and corresponding
ribbon, all conspired to make her appear, even to a
casual observer, just what she was—a typical Southern
girl who gloried in that honor.   She stood only a
moment, and then, as if moved by some divine inspiration, she stepped from the car, and falling upon
her knees, bent forward and kissed the ground.
This silent demonstration of affection for the land of
Dixie touched a vibrating chord, and a score or more of
beautiful girlish voices blended in sweetest harmony
while they told in song their love for Dixie. I listened
spellbound, and was not the only one thus enchanted.
A United States officer listened and was touched to
tears.   Approaching me, he asked if I would do him
the favor to tell him the name of the young lady who
kissed the ground.

" I do not think she would approve of my telling you her name, and I decline to do so," I said in reply. Not in the least daunted by this rebuff he responded : "I shall learn it ; and if she has not already become the wife or the affianced of another, I shall offer her the devotion of my life."

The Confederate officer of the day, God forever bless him ! came for me. The army wagon was ready and standing by Mr. Posey Maddox's car, waiting to receive its precious freight, and a few minutes sufficed to transfer it from car to wagon, and, after waiting to see the last sack securely placed in the wagon, I, too, got in and took my seat by the driver. A long cold drive was before us, but I was so robust I had no fear of the result.

The driver was a veritable young Jehu, and we got over the ground rapidly ; but, owing to a mistake in following directions, it was a long time before we reached our destination, the course of which must have been due west from Jonesboro, and through a dense forest. And oh, the beauty of that forest ! It will remain a living, vivid memory, as long as life endures. Its rich and heavy foliage had been but lightly tinged by the frosts of autumn, and it was rendered more beautiful by the constant dripping of rain drops from every leaf and blossom. As the evening came on, dense, impenetrable clouds canopied the earth, and shut out every ray of sunlight, and almost every ray of hope. At length night came on, dark and weird, and silent, and we were still in the woods, without compass or star.

Just as my brave heart was about to succumb to

despair, a vision of delight burst upon me—a beacon
light, yea, hundreds of beacon lights, appeared before
me, and filled my soul with joy. The camp-fires of
General Cleburne's brave men beckoned us onward,
and gave us friendly greeting. Every revolution of
the wagon wheels brought us perceptibly nearer the
haven of rest. Sabbath-like quiet reigned throughout
the encampment. No boisterous sounds nor profane
imprecations broke the stillness. But there was a
sound that reached my ear, filling my soul with joy
unspeakable. A human voice it was. I had heard it
before in the slight wail of infancy; in the merry
prattle of childhood; in the melodious songs of youth;
in the tender, well-modulated tones of manhood; and
now—there was no mistaking it—in the solemn, earnest invocation to the Lord of Hosts for the salvation
of the world, for the millenial dawn, and that "peace
on earth, and good will to men," which would never
again be broken by the clarion of war, or earth's rude
alarms. No sweeter voice ever entered the courts of
Heaven.

My obliging young driver stopped the horses at a
favorable distance, and I heard the greater part of
that grand prayer, and wept for joy. When it was
finished, we moved on, and were hailed by a sentinel
who demanded the countersign, I believe it is called.
The driver satisfied him, and calling to a soldier, I
asked him if he knew Lieutenant Stokes. "Like a
book," he answered. "Please tell him his sister Mary
is here," I said. In a moment I was clasped in his
arms with the holy pressure of a brother's love. His
first thought on seeing me was that some calamity

must have occurred, and he said, "Sister, is Ma or Missouri dead?" "No, Thomie, but Toby is."

His brave head bowed low and he wept—sobbed audibly. I told him of Toby's loving mention of him, and of the boy's hope of Heaven. After his natural paroxysm of grief had subsided, he looked up, and with an ineffable smile, said:

"Sister, I know you have a secret to tell—what is it?"

"It is this; I have saved all those precious things that were sent to me from Dalton, and I have brought them to deliver to their rightful owners. Help me to do so as quickly as possible, that I may go back to Jonesboro to-night."

Had a bombshell exploded at his feet, the effect could not have been more electrical. He bounded to General Granbury's tent with the agility of a deer; he told the news to him and the others assembled there; and he came back, and they all came with him; and had I been a magician, I could not have been an object of greater interest. General Granbury protested against my return to Jonesboro through the darkness of the night, and offered his tent for my occupancy, saying he would go in with some of the other officers. Colonel Robert Young, a friend of years' standing, was also earnest in his efforts to keep me from carrying out my purpose to go back, and I gave it up. I knew that I was with friends, and permitted myself to be lifted out of the wagon and conducted to the General's tent. I took a seat upon a camp stool which was placed for me about the

13

center of the tent. The General and his staff officers
sat around, and my dear brother was very near me.
Thus arranged, a conversation was commenced which
continued with slight interruptions into the "wee
sma' hours" of the night. Colonel Young seemed to
have something upon his mind which rendered him
indifferent to society, or some duty to perform which
required his attention outside the tent. At length,
however, he came to the door and asked my brother to
come out awhile. In a short time both of them came
in together, and Colonel Young, after asking us to
excuse the interruption of the conversation, remarked
that there was something outside that he would like
for us to see. My brother took me by the hand and
led me out in front of the tent, and all the officers
stood in a group around. Imagine my surprise when
I perceived a long line of soldiers before us, and an
officer on horseback galloping from one end of the
line to the other. I ventured to ask my brother if
they were going to have a moonlight drill without the
moon? He smiled, and a faint pressure of the hand
indicated that there was something on the tapis that
.would please me, but I must wait until it was revealed
to others as well. In much less time than it has taken
to record this episode a signal was given, and one of
the grandest cheers ever heard by mortal man
resounded through the midnight darkness and the
dense forest, and was echoed over hill and dale.
Another signal and another cheer, and yet another of
each, and I broke down completely and cried heartily.
What had I done that my name should thus be honored

by men enduring all the hardships of warfare and
fighting for my principles; and yet to me it was the
most acceptable compliment ever paid to living woman.
I often fancy I hear those voices now blending in one
grand harmonious shout of praise to the great God of
Heaven and earth, who has doubtless given rest to
many of those weary ones.

Once more in General Granbury's tent, at the
earnest solicitation of all present, I continued the
rehearsal of all the Federal army news that I had
gleaned from close perusal of the United States newspapers and from careless and unsuspicious talkers.
General Granbury was evidently startled when I told
him that I had heard Federal officers say "Hood was
working to their hand precisely in going back to
Tennessee, as Thomas was there with an army that
was invincible, and would whip him so bad that there
would not be a Johnnie Reb left to tell the tale;" and
they criticised severely the "generalship" of giving
an invading army unobstructed route to the goal of
their ambition, which, in this case, was South Carolina. I was asked by one of my auditors to give my
impression of the situation, and I did so. As I
described the magnitude of the Federal army, and its
vindictive spirit as I had seen it, and its implacable
feeling towards the South, I saw a shade of sadness
pass over the noble faces of all present. "Have you
lost hope of the ultimate success of our cause?" was a
question I was compelled to answer, because anxiously
asked. I, however, imitated a Yankee by asking a
question in reply, as to what our resources were, and

if they were deemed adequate to cope with a foe
which had the world to draw from, both for men
and means? "But have you lost hope?" was the
question I was called upon to answer without equivo-
cation.

Silence and tears which would well up were inter-
preted to mean what my tongue refused to speak.
My brother perceiving this, put his hand on mine as
it lay motionless upon my lap, and said, "Cheer up,
sister mine; if you could have seen 'Old Pat's' men
on drill this afternoon, you would think we are some
ourselves."

Colonel Young continued to seem very much engaged outside, and, since the demonstration in my
honor, had given us only an occasional glimpse of
himself. At length he came to the door and said,
"Lieutenant, I should like to speak to you." My
brother responded to the call, and soon returned and
said : "As there is a hard day's march before us for
to-morrow, we must let the General get a little sleep,
and this brave sister of mine must need it, too. Come,
let me conduct you to your room."

Good-byes were spoken that night which, in the
providence of God, were destined never to be repeated,
and Thomie and Colonel Young led the way to a bran
new tent, never used before, and opened the door that
I might enter. Thomie said, "My room is next to
yours, sister. Pleasant dreams, and refreshing slum-
bers," and he kissed me good night. "Good night,
dear brother." "Good night, dear friend," said I, as
he and Colonel Young left the tent. By the dim light

I surveyed the "room" and its furnishings, and wept
to think that dear Confederate soldiers had deprived
themselves of comforts that I might be comfortable.
A handsome buffalo robe lay on the ground; and a
coat nicely folded for a pillow, and a gray blanket
for a cover, invited me to repose. A small pan of
water for morning ablution, and a towel, and a mirror about the size of a silver dollar, and a comb and
brush, furnished every needed convenience. I removed the skirt of my dress that it might not be
wrinkled in the morning, and my mantle for the same
cause, and lay down and slept, oh, how sweetly, under
the protecting care of those noble men, until awakened
by the sweet familiar voice of my brother, saying,
"Get up, sister, or you will not be ready for the roll-
call," was his never-to-be-forgotten morning salutation. "As a short horse is soon curried," it required
only a few moments to make myself presentable, and
just as I was about announcing myself in that condition, Thomie again appeared at the door with a
plate containing my breakfast in one hand, and
a tin cup containing a decoction, which he called
coffee, in the other. "Here is your breakfast, sister;" and he added, "the ambulance is waiting to
carry you to Lovejoy's station. Lieutenant Jewell
and myself have been detailed to accompany you
there."

The army wagons were already falling in line one
after another and moving onward in a northwesterly
direction; and what remained of the infantry and
cavalry of that once magnificent army, which so often

had achieved victory under General Joseph E. Johnston, had made their last grand bivouac on Georgia
soil, and were moving onward in the line of march to
Tennessee, under the command of Hood. They were
leaving many a gallant comrade who had bitten the
dust and drenched the soil of Georgia with their life-
blood, and although they must have feared that the
flag they loved so well was now leading them to defeat, yet not one of those true hearts would have
deserted it for the wealth of India. As they marched
in a different direction from that I was going to take,
and the demand for rapid movement was imperative,
I could not follow them long with my eye, but the
memory of the little I saw will ever be fresh,
and, like an inspiration yet to me, their bayonets
glittered in a perfect halo of glory, for the mists
and clouds of the preceding day had passed away
during the night, and a blue sky and bright sun
gladdened the earth.

The two young lieutenants took seats opposite to
me in the ambulance. Thus arranged, I caught every
movement and look of that dear brother from whom I
was so soon to part. He never looked more handsome, or appeared to greater advantage. I was his
guest, and he entertained me with a "feast of reason
and a flow of soul." At my request he sang some of
the songs of "auld lang syne," but he preferred to
talk of our mother and our sister. He recalled incidents of his childhood, and laughed heartily over
some of them. He spoke of his Mary in Texas and
his love for her, and he took from his vest pocket the

impression of the foot and hand of his only child, a dear little boy whom he had never seen, and kissed them, then folded them carefully and put them back in his pocket and said :

"I must hurry back to Texas."

But back of all this glee and apparent hopefulness I saw, in characters unmistakable, that he was almost bereft of hope, and sustained only by Christian resignation.

We knew, by the immense crowd of people standing and sitting around on improvised seats, that we were approaching the station. The two soldiers got out of the ambulance with the elasticity of youth and health, and Thomie assisted me out. I stood for a moment, as if uncertain where to go, and Lieutenant Jewell grasped my hand and said :

Good-bye, dear Miss Mary !" and stepped back into the wagon and resumed his seat.

Seeing a large, square old house, which appeared to be full of people, Thomie and I advanced toward it a few steps. Suddenly, as if admonished that a soldier's duties should have precedence over everything else, he took me in his arms and kissed me fervently once, twice, thrice. I understood for whom they were intended—that trio of kisses. Not a word did he speak, and when he turned his back on me I saw him brush off the silent tears, and more than one step was uneven before his nerves became steady and he ready to report for duty. I felt intuitively that I should never look upon his face again, and I watched him with riveted eyes until I could no longer see him, and then I gazed upon the vehicle containing him until it, too, disappeared forever from my sight.   Then, and not till then, I gave way to pent-up sorrow, and cried as one without hope—unreservedly.

CHAPTER XIX.

THE RETURN HOME.

From Jonesboro via Augusta—Scenes and Incidents by the way.—The lonely journey from Stone Mountain to Decatur.

Dazed by a full realization that my brother and every male relative and friend were in the octopus arms of war, cruel and relentless, I stood riveted to the spot where my brother had parted from me, until a gentle hand touched my shoulder, and a pleasant voice gave me friendly greeting. Turning I saw Mrs. Anderson, sister of the brave and gallant Robert Alston, whose tragic fate is known to every reader in this country.

"I am glad to see you. I have just seen your brother Robert," I said.

"Where? Where? Do tell me that I may go to him!" cried his devoted sister, laughing and weeping alternately.

Having ascertained that the long train of exiles would not leave the station for several hours, I offered to conduct the tender-hearted woman to the camp-fire of her brother. The route took me over the same ground which only a few moments ago I had traveled with my own dear brother; and along which I had seen so vividly a lean, gaunt, phantom hand pointing

at his retreating from. Even the horses' tracks and
the ruts made by the wheels could be plainly traced
by their freshness and the yet quivering sands ; and as
I gazed upon them, I fancied they were connecting
links between me and him which were binding our
souls together, and which I would never grow weary
in following. These reflections were often disturbed
by questions about " my dear brother Robert," and by
alternate sobs and laughter. The distance seemed
much greater, now that I was walking it, but at
length we attained our destination, the headquarters
of a few of General John Morgan's gallant defenders
of Southern homes and firesides. It would require the
descriptive power of a Sims or a Paul Hayne to give
an adequate idea of the meeting on this occasion of
this demonstrative brother and sister. I will not
undertake to do so. He, too, was ready to move in
that disastrous campaign, which lost to us the *creme
de la creme* of the Army of the Tennessee, and which
aided, as if planned by the most astute Federal tactician, Sherman, in his " march to the sea."

During the interview between Colonel Alston and
his sister, it developed to him that his pretty home
had been abandoned to the tender mercies of the enemy by the family in whose care he had left it, and
that the Yankees had shipped his wife's elegant European piano, mirrors and furniture, as well as his
library, cut glass and Dresden china to the North;
and, besides, in the very malignity of envy and sectional hate, had mutilated and desecrated his house
in a shameful manner. His imprecations were fearful; and his vows to get even with the accursed Yan-

kees were even more so. The lamb of a few moments ago was transformed into a lion, roaring and fierce. He accompanied his sister and myself on our return to the station; and never will I forget that walk.

The station reached, the scene of separation of brother and sister was again enacted, and he, too, went to battle-fields, sanguinary and relentless, she to peaceful retreats undisturbed by cannon's roar.

Here, as at Jonesboro, the face of the earth was literally covered with rude tents and side-tracked cars, which were occupied by exiles from home—defenseless women and children, and an occasional old man tottering on the verge of the grave, awaiting their turn to be transported by over-taxed railroads farther into the constantly diminishing land of their love. During the afternoon I boarded an already well-filled southbound train, and moved about among its occapants as if at home. For were we not one people, the mothers, wives and sisters of Confederates ? The diversity of mind, disposition and temper of this long train of representative women and children of Atlanta, and many miles contiguous, who were carrying minds and hearts brimful of memories never to be obliterated, but rather to harden into asphalt preservation, was illustrated in various ways. Some laughed and talked and jested, and infused the light and warmth of their own sunny natures into others less hopeful ; some were morose and churlish, and saw no hope in the future and were impatient with those who did see the silver lining beyond the dark cloud suspended over us; and some very plainly indicated that if our cause failed, they would lose all faith in a prayer-answering

God; and others saw wisdom and goodness in all His ways and dispensations, and were willing to submit to any chastisement if it only brought them nearer to the Mercy Seat.

After many delays and adventures, not of sufficient importance to relate, I reached Griswoldville. Here I was received with open arms by that good old father and mother in Israel, Rev. Dr. John S. Wilson and his wife, and his excellent family, whom I found residing in an old freight car. But they were living in a palace compared to many of their neighbors and friends, who had scarcely a shelter to protect them from the inclemency of the weather. Every moment of time with these good people was spent in answering questions and receiving blessings. Not long after this pleasant meeting, Stoneman's raiders came into Griswoldville, and the household effects of Dr. Wilson's family were consumed by devouring torches. All their winter clothing, the doctor's library and his manuscript sermons, were burned to ashes. These sermons were the result of the study and experience of forty years. But this grand old soldier of the cross, although on the verge of threescore years and ten, faltered not; for his eye was fixed on the goal of his heavenly inheritance. Wherever he went, he still preached, and died a few years afterwards at his post in Atlanta, having missed but two preaching appointments in all his ministry, one of these on the Sabbath before he died.

By a circuitous route, which I can now scarcely recall, in the course of time I reached Augusta, the beautiful. I wended my way through the crowded

thoroughfares to the residence of friends on Green
street, where my sister had sojourned for several
weeks, far from the distracting confusion of warfare.
After all these long and varied years, I never see that
Elysian street without feeling as if I would like to
kneel and kiss the ground whereon she found surcease
of hostile tread and rancorous foe.

I could scarcely approach the house, in exterior
beautiful in all that makes a home attractive. I
feared that within sorrowful tidings might await me.
No word of the absent sister had come through the
enemy's lines since they were first established, and
now I dreaded to hear. More than once I stood still
and tried to nerve myself for the worst tidings that
could be communicated. And then I ascended the
stone steps and rang the door-bell. When the butler
came, I hurriedly asked if Miss Stokes was in. As if
apprehending my state of feelings, he answered with
a broad African grin : "She is, ma'am."

The pressure of a mountain was removed from my
heart, and with a lighter step than I had taken for
some time I entered that friendly portal, a welcome
guest. A moment sufficed for him to carry the joyous
tidings of my presence to my sister, and, as if by
magic, she was with me. O, the joy and the sadness
of our meeting ! To say that each of us was glad
beyond our ability to express it, would be a tame
statement; and yet neither of us was happy. There
was too much sadness connected with ourselves and
our country to admit of happiness; yet the report of
our mother's fortitude and usually good health, and
the hopeful spirit of our brother, and his numerous

messages of love and playful phraseology, cheered my
sister so much that she rallied and did all she could to
render my brief stay with her as pleasant as possible.
And there was a charm in her sweet voice and pleasant
words that were soothing to me, and did much to
assuage my own grief. Nor were our good friends
wanting in efforts of like character. They, too, had
drank deep of Marah's bitter waters. Two noble
boys, yet in their teens, had been laid upon the sacrificial altar, an oblation to their country. And a fair
young girl had gone down into the tomb, as much a
sacrifice to Southern rights as if slain on the battle-
field. One other girl and her war-stricken parents
survived, and they were devoting their lives to the
encouragement of those similarly bereaved.

Although I knew it would pain her greatly, I
thought it would be wrong to leave without telling
my sister about Toby's death, and, therefore, I told
her. Like our brother, she wept, but not as one without hope. She had been his spiritual instructor, and
thoroughly taught him the great and yet easy plan of
salvation; and I have never doubted that he caught on
to it, and was supported by the arm of Jesus, as he
"passed through the dark valley and the shadow of
death."

The time for leaving this peaceful retreat came,
and was inexorable; nor would I have stayed if I
could. There was a widowed mother, whose head
was whitened, not so much by the frost of winters as
by sorrow and care, grief and bereavement, awaiting
my coming—oh, so anxiously! Waiting to hear from
the soldier son, who, even for her sake, and that of

his gentle young wife and baby boy in Texas, would listen to no plan of escape from the dangers involved by his first presidential vote. Waiting to hear from the fair young daughter, whom she preferred to banish from home rather than have her exposed to the rude chances of war. That she might not be kept in painful suspense, I determined not to linger on the way. I, therefore, took the morning train on the good old reliable Georgia Railroad for Social Circle. The parting from my sister pained me exceedingly; but I knew she had put her trust in the Lord, and He would take care of her. It may be asked why I did not have the same faith regarding the preservation of my brother. He, too, was a Christian. "He that taketh the sword shall perish by the sword," is a divine assertion, and it was constantly repeating itself in my ears; yea, I had heard him repeat it with emphasis.

The trip from Augusta to Social Circle was replete with melancholy interest, and differed very materially from the trip from Atlanta to Jonesboro. Here those who had the courage to do so were returning to their homes, and were on the *qui vive* for every item of news obtainable from within the enemy's lines; but nothing satisfactory encouraged their hope of better treatment. One marked difference appeared in the character of those who were venturing homeward. There was scarcely any young persons—not a single young lady. The good old mother railroad was very deliberate in her movements, and gave her patrons time to get acquainted and chat a little on the way, and this we did without restraint.

We discussed the situation, and narrated our diversified experiences, and this interchange of thought and feeling brought us very near together, and made us wondrous kind to one another. At one of the stations at which the train stopped, and had to wait a long while, I saw several of the young soldiers from Decatur. Among them was Ryland Holmes, and, I think, Mose Brown.

About a dozen ladies were going within the enemy's lines and would there separate for their respective homes. We agreed to hire a wagon team and driver at Social Circle, that we might take it "turn about" in riding to Stone Mountain. As I was the only one going beyond that point, I determined to take my chance from there for getting to Decatur, and go on foot if need be. Our plan was successful, as, after much effort, we obtained an old rickety wagon, which had doubtless done good service in its day, and a yoke of mis-mated oxen, and a negro driver. For this equipage we paid an enormous sum, and, thinking we ought to have the full benefit of it, we all got into the wagon to take a ride. Compassion for the oxen, however, caused first one and then another to descend to the ground, and march in the direction of home, sometimes two abreast and sometimes in single file. Night overtook us at a house only a short distance from the Circle, and in a body we appealed for shelter beneath its roof. The man of the family was at home, under what circumstances I have never heard, and to him we appealed, and from him we received an ungracious "permit" to stay in his house. Seeing no inviting prospects for rest and repose, I established myself in a corner and took out of my reticule some nice German wool that had been given to me by my friends in Augusta, and cast on the stitches for a throat-warmer, or, in the parlance of that day, "a comforter." Mine host watched the process with much interest. When the pattern developed, he admired it, and expressed a wish to have one like it. Glad of the privilege to liquidate my indebtedness for the prospective night's shelter, I told him if he would furnish the material I would knit him one just like it. The material seemed to be in waiting, and was brought forward, soft, pretty lambs' wool thread, and I put it in my already well-filled hand satchel to await future manipulation. The accommodation in the way of bedding was inadequate, and more than one of our party passed a sleepless night; but what mattered it? Were we not Confederate soldiers, or very near akin to them?

As the first sunbeams were darting about among the tree tops, I donned my bonnet and bade adieu to our entertainers, and started on my journey homeward, walking. Being in the very vigor of womanhood, and in perfect health, I never experienced the sensation of fatigue, and I verily believe I could have walked to my desolated home sooner than the most of the resources within our means could have carried me; and I was impatient under the restraint and hindrance of slow teams. Hence my start in advance of the other ladies. And I wanted to be alone. The pent-up tears were constantly oozing out of my eyes and trickling down my face, and I wanted to open the flood-gates and let them flow unrestrainedly.

14

I wanted to cry aloud like a baby. I plunged into
the woods, for the seldom traveled road was scarcely a
barrier to perfect solitude.   I walked rapidly, and
closed my eyes to all the attractions of nature lest
they divert my mind, and appease my hungry heart.
I wanted to cry, and was even then doing so, before I
got ready for it.   At length I came to a rivulet of
crystal water, as pure as the dew drops of Arcadia.   I
sat down beside it and mingled the anguished tears of
my very soul with its sparkling, ever-changing, nec-
tarian waters.   I bathed my hot face and hands in the
pellucid stream, and still the lachrymal fountain
flowed on.   I thought of my lonely mother, surrounded by those who were seeking the subversion of
all that her heart held dear, and I cried.   I thought of
my brother—of his toilsome marches and weary limbs,
and of his consecrated life—and I cried.   I thought of
the fair young sister, still hopeful in early womanhood, and I refused to be comforted, and wept bitterly.
In this disconsolate frame of mind, I was ready to
give up all hope and yield to direful despair.   At this
fearful crisis a still, small voice whispered, "Peace,
be still!" The glamour of love invested sky and
earth with supernal glory. The fountain of tears
ceased to flow, and I looked around upon the handi-
work of the Great Supreme Being in whose creation I
was but an atom, and wondered that He should have
been mindful of me—that He should have given surcease of agony to my sorrowing soul.   All nature
changed as if by magic, and the witchery of the scene
was indescribable. The pretty wildwood flowers, as I
bent my admiring gaze upon them, seemed to say in

beatiful silent language, "Look aloft." The birds, as they trilled their morning roundelay, said in musical numbers, "Look aloft;" and the merry rivulet at my feet affected seriousness, and whispered, "Look aloft." Thus admonished, "in that moment of darkness, with scarce hope in my heart," I looked aloft— looked aloft.

By and by the ladies came in sight, some walking and others riding in the wagon; and I pitied most those who were in the wagon. As soon as they were within speaking distance, one of the ladies said: "You should have stayed for breakfast. It was quite appetizing." Reminded of what I had lost, I was led to compare it with what I had gained, and I would not have exchanged loss and gain for anything in the world. I had to admit, however, that there was a vacuum that needed replenishing; but I was inured to hunger, and, save a passing thought, I banished all desire for food, and thought only of the loved ones, so near and yet so far, and in spite of myself the fountain of tears was again running over.

The long tramp to Stone Mountain was very lonely. Not a living thing overtook or passed us, and we soon crossed over the line and entered a war-stricken section of country where stood chimneys only, where lately were pretty homes and prosperity, now departed. Ah, those chimneys standing amid smoldering ruins! No wonder they were called "Sherman's sentinels," as they seemed to be keeping guard over those scenes of desolation. The very birds of the air and beasts of the field had fled to other sections. By constant and unflagging locomotion we reached Stone

Mountain sometime during the night. We went to the hotel and asked shelter and protection, and received both, but not where to lay our heads, as those who had preceded us had filled every available place. I had friends in the village, but I had no assurance that they had remained at home and weathered the cyclone of war. Therefore, early in the morning, hungry and footsore, I started all alone walking to Decatur. The solitude was terrific, and the feeling of awe was so intense that I was startled by the breaking of a twig, or the gruesome sound of my own footsteps. Constantly reminded by ruined homes, I realized that I was indeed within the arbitrary lines of a cruel, merciless foe, and but for my lonely mother, anxiously awaiting my return, I should have turned and run for dear life until again within the boundaries of Dixie.

I must have walked very rapidly, for, before I was aware of it, I found myself approaching Judge Bryce's once beautiful but now dilapidated home. He and his good wife gave me affectionate greeting and something to inflate a certain vacuum which had become painfully clamorous. And they also gave me that which was even more acceptable—a large yam potato and a piece of sausage to take to my mother.

I begged Judge Bryce to go with me at least part of the way to Decatur, but he was afraid to leave his wife. His experience with the Yankees had not been an exceptional case. They had robbed him of everything of value, silver, gold, etc., and what they could not carry away they had destroyed, and he denied most emphatically that there was a single gentleman in the Federal army. In vain did I tell him that we owed the preservation of our lives to the protection extended us by the few gentlemen who were in it.

After a brief rest, I resumed my way homeward, and oh, with what heart-sickening forebodings I approached that sacred though desolate abode ! Anon the little town appeared in the distance, and upon its very limits I met several of Colonel Garrard's calvary officers. Among them a diversity of temper was displayed. Some of them appeared very glad to see me, and, to anxious inquires regarding my mother, they replied that they had taken good care of her in my absence, and that I ought to have rewarded them for having done so by bringing "my pretty young sister" home with me. Although I did not entertain one iota of respect for the Federal army as a whole, I knew there were a few in its ranks who were incapable of the miserable conduct of the majority, and my heart went out in very tender gratitude to them, especially those who had sought to lessen the anguish of my mother. These men threw the reins into the hands of out-riders, and got off their horses and walked with me to the door of my home. Their headquarters were still in the yard and had been ever since first established there, with the exception of a very few days. My return was truly a memorable occasion. Manifestations assured me that the highest as well as the lowest in that command was glad to see me, and in their hearts welcomed me home. To good Mr. Fred Williams I was indebted, in a large measure, for kindly feeling and uniform respect from that portion of the* Federal army with which I came in contact.

My mother had seen me coming and had retreated into as secluded a place as she could find, to compose herself for the meeting, but the effort was in vain. She trembled like an aspen leaf, her lips quivered and her tongue could not articulate the words she would have spoken. Alas! the tension was more than she could bear. I dwelt upon the fact that Thomie and Missouri were well and had sent her a world of love. I tried to infuse hope and cheerfulness into everything I told her, but she could not see it, and her poor over-taxed heart could bear up no longer, and she cried as Rachel weeping for her children, long and piteously. No purer tears were ever borne by heaven-commissioned Peri into the presence of a compassionate Savior, than those shed by that patriotic though sorrowing mother.

CHAPTER XX.

ON THE VERGE OF STARVATION.

A worn-out army horse is found—Uncle Mack makes a wagon—
I make a unique trip—Starvation is warded off—Dangers and
scenes by the way.

" What is it, Ma ?   Has anything happened ?"

" No, only Maggie Benedict has been here crying
as if her heart would break, and saying that her children are begging for bread, and she has none to give
them.   Give me a little of the meal or hominy that
you have, that we may not starve until we can get
something else to eat, and then take the remainder to
her that she may cook it as quickly as possible for her
suffering children."

We had spent the preceding day in picking out
grains of corn from cracks and crevices in bureau
drawers, and other improvised troughs for Federal
horses, as well as gathering up what was scattered
upon the ground.   In this way by diligent and persevering work, about a half bushel was obtained from
the now deserted camping ground of Garrard's cavalry,
and this corn was thoroughly washed and dried, and
carried by me and Telitha to a poor little mill (which
had escaped conflagration, because too humble to attract attention), and ground into coarse meal.   Returning from this mill, and carrying, myself, a portion of
the meal, I saw in the distance my mother coming to

meet me. Apprehensive of evil, I ran to meet her and asked :

"What is it, Ma ? Has anything happened ?"

With flushed face and tear-toned voice she replied as already stated. My heart was touched and a division was soon made. Before starting on this er- rand, I thought of the probable delay that inexperi- ence and perhaps the want of cooking utensils and fuel might occasion, and suggested that it would hasten the relief to the children to cook some bread and mush and carry it to them already for use. A boiling pot, left on the camping-ground, was soon on the fire ready to receive the well-prepared batter, which was to be converted into nutritious mush or porridge. Nor was the bread forgotten. While the mush was cooking the hoe-cakes were baking in good old plantation style. These were arranged one upon another, and tied up in a snow-white cloth ; and a tin bucket, also a trophy from the company, was filled with hot mush. I took the bread, and Telitha the bucket, and walked rapidly to Doctor Holmes' resi- dence, where Maggie Benedict, whose husband was away in the Confederate army, had rooms for herself and her children. The Rev. Doctor and his wife had refugeed, leaving this young mother and her children alone and unprotected.

The scene which I witnessed will never be oblit- erated from my memory. On the doorsteps sat the young mother, beautiful in desolation, with a baby in her arms, and on either side of her a little one, pite- ously crying for something to eat. " Oh, mama, I want something to eat, so bad." " Oh, mama, I am so hungry—give me something to eat." Thus the children were begging for what the mother had not to give. She could only give them soothing words. But relief was at hand. Have you ever enjoyed the satisfaction of appeasing the hunger of children who had been without food until on the verge of starvation ? If not, one of the keenest enjoyments of life has been denied you. O, the thankfulness of such a privilege ! And oh, the joy, melancholy though it be, of hearing blessings invoked upon you and yours by the mother of those children !

While this needful food was being eaten with a zest known only to the hungry, I was taking in the situation, and devising in my own mind means by which to render more enduring relief. The meal we had on hand would soon be exhausted, and, though more might be procured in the same way, it would be hazardous to depend upon that way only. " God helps those who help themselves," is a good old reliable proverb that cannot be too deeply impressed upon the mind of every child. To leave this young mother in a state of absolute helplessness, and her innocent little ones dependent upon the precarious support which might be gleaned from a devastated country, would be cruel indeed ; but how to obviate this state of affairs was a serious question.

The railroad having been torn up in every direction communicating with Decatur, there seemed to be but one alternative—to walk—and that was not practicable with several small children.

" Maggie, this state of affairs cannot be kept up ; have you no friend to whom you can go ?"

"Yes," she replied. "Mr. Benedict has a sister near Madison, who has wanted me and the children to go and stay with her ever since he has been in the army, but I was too independent to do it."

"Absurd! Well, the time has come that you must go. Get the children ready, and I will call for you soon," and without any positive or defined plan of procedure, I took leave of Maggie and her children. I was working by faith, and the Lord directed my footsteps. On my way home I hunted up "Uncle Mack," a faithful old negro man, who preferred freedom in the midst of privation with his own white people, to following the Federal army around on "Uncle Sam's" pay-roll, and got from him a promise that he would construct a wagon out of odds and ends left upon the streets of Decatur. The next thing to be done was to provide a horse, and not being a magician, nor possessed of Aladdin's lamp, this undertaking must have seemed chimerical to those who had not known how often and how singularly these scarcely formulated plans had developed into success. This day had been one of constant and active service, and was only one of the many that furnished from sixteen to eighteen working hours. No wonder, then, that exhausted nature succumbed to sleep that knew no waking until the dawn of another day.

Next morning, before the sun rose, accompanied by the Morton girls, I was on my way to "the cane-brakes." I had seen many horses, whose places had been taken by others captured from farmers, abandoned and sent out to the cane-brake to recuperate or to die, the latter being the more probable. Without

any definite knowledge of the locality, but guided by
an over-ruling providence, I went direct to the cane-
brake, and there soon made a selection of a horse,
which, from the assortment at hand, could not have
been improved upon. By a dextrous throw of a lasso,
constructed and managed by the young friends already
mentioned, he was soon captured and on his way to
Decatur to enter "rebel" service. His most con-
spicious feature was a pair of as fine eyes as ever
illuminated a horse's head, large, brown and lustrous. There were other conspicuous things about
him, too ; for instance, branded upon each of his sides
were the tell-tale letters, "U. S.," and on his back
was an immense sore which also told tales. By twelve
o'clock, noon, Uncle Mack appeared upon the scene,
pulling something which he had improvised which
baffled description, and which, for the sake of the
faithful service I obtained from it, I will not attempt
to describe, though it might provoke the risibilities of
the readers. Suffice it to say that as it carried living
freight in safety over many a bridge, in honor of this
I will call it a wagon. Uncle Mack soon had the
horse secured to this vehicle by ropes and pieces of
crocus sack, for harness was as scarce a commodity as
wagons and horses. I surveyed the equipage from
center to circumference, with emotions pathetic and
amusing. It was awfully suggestive. And as I viewed
it in all its grotesqueness my imagination pictured
a collapse, and my return home from no very distant
point upon my all-fours, with one of the fours drag-
ging after me in a dilapidated condition. I distinctly
heard the derisive gibberish and laughter of old Mo-

mus, and thought I should explode in the effort to keep from joining in his mirthfulness. As I turned my head to take a sly glance at my mother, our eyes met, and all restraint was removed. With both of us laughter and sobs contended for the mastery, and merriment and tears literally blended. Thus equipped, and with a benediction from my mother, expressed more by looks and acts than by words, I gathered the ropes and started like Bayard Taylor to take "Views Afoot," and at the same time accomplish an errand of mercy which would lead me, as I led the horse, over a portion of country that in dreariness and utter desolation baffles description—enough to know that Sherman's foraging trains had been over it. Leading the horse, which was already christened "Yankee," to Dr. Holmes' door, I called Maggie to come on with her children.

"I can't bring my things out, Miss Mary. Somebody must come to carry them and put them in the wagon."

"I can," I said, and suiting the action to the word, ran into the house where, to my amazement, three large trunks confronted me. What was to be done? If they could be got into the wagon, what guarantee was there that poor Yankee could haul them in that tumblesome vehicle? However, I went for Uncle Mack to put the trunks in the wagon, and in front of them, in close proximity to the horse's heels, was placed a chair in which Maggie seated herself and took her baby in her lap, the other children nestling on rugs at her feet.

Poor Yankee seemed to feel the importance of his

mission, and jogged along at a pretty fair speed, and I, who walked by his side and held the ropes, found myself more than once obliged to strike a trot in order to maintain control of him. Paradoxical as it may seem, I enjoyed this new phase in my service to the Confederacy—none but a patriot could render it, and the whole thing seemed invested with the glamour of romance, the sequel of which would be redemption from all connection with a people who could thus afflict another people of equal rights. While Maggie hummed a sweet little lullaby to her children, I contemplated the devastation and ruin on every side. Not a vestige of anything remained to mark the sites of the pretty homes which had dotted this fair country before the destroyer came, except, perhaps, a standing chimney now and then. And all this struck me as the willing sacrifice of a peerless people for a great principle, and looking through the dark vista I saw light ahead—I saw white-robed peace proclaiming that the end of carnage had come. Even then, as I jogged along at a snail's pace (for be it known Yankee was not uniform in his gait, and as his mistress had relaxed the tension of the ropes, he had relaxed the speed of his steps) up a pretty little hill from whose summit I had often gazed with rapturous admiration upon the beautiful mountain of granite near by, I had so completely materialized the Queen of Peace that I saw her on the mountain's crest, scattering with lavish hand blessings and treasures as a recompense for the destruction so wantonly inflicted. Thus my hopeful temperament furnished consolation to me, even under darkest circumstances.

Maggie and the children became restive in their pent-up limits, and the latter clamored for something to eat, but there was nothing to give them. Night was upon us, and we had come only about eight miles, and not an animate thing had we seen since we left Decatur, not even a bird, and the silence was unbroken save by the sound of the horse's feet as he trod upon the rocks, and the soft, sweet humming of the young mother to her dear little ones. Step by step we seemed to descend into the caverns of darkness, and my brave heart began to falter. The children, awe-struck, had ceased their appeal for bread, and nestled closer to their mother, and that they might all the more feel her protecting presence, she kept up a constant crooning sound, pathetic and sad. Step by step we penetrated the darkness of night—a night without a moon, starless and murky. The unerring instinct of an animal was all we had to guide us in the beaten road, which had ceased to be visible to human ken.

A faint glimmer of light, at apparently no very great distance, gave hope that our day's journey was almost ended. Yankee also caught the inspiration and walked a little faster. Though the time seemed long, the cabin, for such it proved to be, was finally reached, and I dropped the ropes, and, guided by the glimmer of light through the cracks, went to the door and knocked, at the same time announcing my name. The door was quickly opened. Imagine my surprise when recognized and cordially welcomed by a sweet friend, whose most humble plantation cabin was a pretty residence in comparison with the one she now occupied. Maggie, too, as the daughter of a well-known physician, received cordial welcome for herself and children. And thus a kind Providence provided a safe lodging place for the night.

Nature again asserted itself, and the children asked for something to eat. The good lady of the house kissed them, and told them that supper would soon be ready. The larger one of her little sons drew from a bed of ashes, which had been covered by glowing coals, some large yam potatoes which he took to a table and peeled. He then went outside the cabin and drew from a keg an earthen-ware pitcher full of sparkling persimmon beer, which he dispensed to us in cups, and then handed around the potatoes. And how much this repast was enjoyed! Good sweet yams thoroughly cooked, and the zestful persimmon beer! And I thought of the lonely mother at a desolated home, whose only supper had been made of coarse meal, ground from corn which her own hands had helped to pick from crevices and cracks in improvised troughs, where Garrard's cavalry had fed their horses. After awhile the sweet womanly spirit that presided over this little group, got a quilt and a shawl or two, and made a pallet for the children. The boys put more wood upon the fire, and some in the jambs of the fireplace, to be used during the night; and then they went behind us and lay down upon the floor, with seed cotton for pillows, and the roof for covering. Our kind hostess placed additional wraps over the shoulders of Maggie and myself, and we three sat up in our chairs and slept until the dawn.

Accustomed to looking after outdoor interests, I went to see how Yankee was coming on, and found him none the worse for the preceding day's toil. Everything indicated that he had fared as sumptuously as we had—a partly-eaten pumpkin, corn, whole ears yet in the trough, and fodder near by, plainly showed the generosity of the noble little family that took us in and gave us the best they had. After breakfast we bade adieu to the good mother and her children, and went on our way, if not rejoicing, at least feeling better for having seen and been with such good people. There was a strong tie between us all. The husband and father was off in the army, like our loved ones. The generous feeding given to our steed had so braced him up that he began to walk faster, and was keenly appreciative of every kind word ; and I and he formed a friendship for each other that continued to his dying day. The road was very rough and hilly, and more than once he showed signs of fatigue ; but a word of encouragement seemed to renew his strength, and he walked bravely on. Maggie would perhaps have lightened his load by walking now and then, but the jolting of the wagon kept the trunks in perpetual motion, and the lives of the children would thereby have been jeopardized.

Nothing of special interest transpired this second day of our journey. The same fiend of destruction had laid his ruthless hand upon everything within his reach. The woods had been robbed of their beauty and the fields of their products ; not even a bird was left to sing a requiem over the scene of desolation, or an animal to suggest where once had been a habitation. Once, crouching near a standing chimney, there was a solitary dog who kept at bay every at-

tempt to approach—no kind word would conciliate or
put him off his guard. Poor, lonely sentinel! Did
he remember that around the once cheerful hearth-
stone he had been admitted to a place with the family
group ? Was he awaiting his master's return ? Ah,
who can know the emotions, or the dim reasonings of
that faithful brute ?

Night again came on and I discovered that we
were approaching the hospitable mansion of Mr.
Montgomery, an excellent, courtly country gentleman,
who was at home under circumstances not now
remembered. He and his interesting family gladly
welcomed me and my little charge, and entertained us
most hospitably. The raiders had been here and
helped themselves bountifully, but they had spared
the house for another time, and that other time came
soon, and nothing was left on the site of this beautiful home but ubiquitous chimneys.

An early start the next day enabled Yankee to
carry Maggie and her children and the trunks to
Social Circle in time to take the noon train for Madison. So far as Maggie and her children were concerned, I now felt that I had done all that I could, and
that I must hasten back to my lonely mother at Decatur ; but Maggie's tearful entreaties not to be left
among strangers prevailed with me, and I got aboard
the train with her, and never left her until I had
placed her and her children in the care of good Mr.
Thrasher at Madison, to be conveyed by him to the
home of Mrs. Reeves, her husband's sister.

In Madison, I too had dear friends and relatives,
with whom I spent the night, and the morning's train

15

bore me back to Social Circle, then the terminus of the
Georgia Railroad—the war fiend having destroyed
every rail between there and Atlanta. Arriving there,
imagine my surprise and indignation when I learned
that Mr. R——, whom I had paid in advance to care
for Yankee while I was gone to Madison, had sent him
out to his sorghum mill and put him to grinding cane;
and it was with much difficulty and delay that I got
him in time to start on my homeward journey that
afternoon. Instead of his being rested, he was literally broken down, and my pity for him constrained
me to walk every step of the way back to Decatur.
While waiting for the horse, I purchased such articles
of food as I could find. For instance, a sack of flour, for
which I paid a hundred dollars, a bushel of potatoes,
several gallons of sorghum, a few pounds of butter,
and a few pounds of meat. Even this was a heavy
load for the poor jaded horse. Starting so late I could
only get to the hospitable home of Mr. Crew, distant
only about three miles from "The Circle."

Before leaving Mr. Crew's the next morning, I
learned that an immense Yankee raid had come out
from Atlanta, and had burned the bridge which I had
crossed only two days ago. This information caused
me to take another route to Decatur, and my heart
lost much of its hope, and my step its alacrity. Yet
the Lord sustained me in the discharge of duty. I
never wavered when there was a principle to be guarded
or a duty to be performed. Those were praying days
with me, and now I fervently invoked God's aid and
protection in my perilous undertaking, and I believed
that He would grant aid and protection.

That I might give much needed encouragement to Yankee, I walked by his side with my hand upon his shoulder much of the time, an act of endearment which he greatly appreciated, and proved that he did so by the expression of his large brown eyes. One of my idiosyncrasies through life has been that of counting everything, and as I journeyed homeward, I found myself counting my steps from one to a thousand and one. As there is luck in odd numbers, says Rory O'Moore, I always ended with the traditional odd number, and by telling Yankee how much nearer home we were. And I told him many things, among them, *sotto voce*, that I did not believe he was a Yankee, but a captured rebel. If a tuft of grass appeared on the road side, he was permitted to crop it; or if a muscadine vine with its tempting grapes was discovered, he cropped the leaves off the low shrubbery, while I gathered the grapes for my mother at home with nothing to eat save the one article of diet, of which I have told before.

A minute description of this portion of the war-stricken country would fill a volume; but only the leading incidents and events of the journey are admissible in a reminiscence of war times. In the early part of the day, during this solitary drive, I came to a cottage by the wayside that was a perfect gem—an oasis, an everything that could thrill the heart by its loveliness. Flowers of every hue beautified the grounds and sweetened the air, and peace and plenty seemed to hold undisputed sway. The Fiend of Destruction had not yet reached this little Eden. Two gentlemen were in the yard conversing. I

perceived at a glance that they were of the clerical
order, and would fain have spoken to them; but not
wishing to disturb them, or attract attention to myself,
I was passing by as unobtrusively as possible, when I
was espied and recognized by one of them, who proved
to be that saintly man, Rev. Walter Branham. He
introduced me to his friend, Professor Shaw of Oxford.
Their sympathy for me was plainly expressed, and
they gave me much needed instruction regarding the
route, and suggested that I would about get to Rev.
Henry Clark's to put up for the night. With a hearty
shake of the hand, and "God bless you, noble woman,"
I pursued my lonely way and they went theirs. No
other adventure enlivened the day, and poor patient
Yankee did the best he could, and so did I. It was
obvious that he had done about all he could. Grinding
sorghum under a hard taskmaster, with an empty
stomach, had told on him, and he could no longer
quicken his pace at the sound of a friendly voice.

At length we came in sight of "Uncle Henry
Clark's" place. I stood amazed, bewildered. I felt
as if I would sink to the ground, yea, through it. I
was riveted to the spot on which I stood. I could not
move. At length I cried—cried like a woman in
despair. Poor Yankee must have cried too (for water
ran out of his eyes), and in some measure I was quieted,
for misery loves company, and I began to take in the
situation more calmly. Elegant rosewood and mahog-
any furniture, broken into a thousand fragments,
covered the face of the ground as far as I could see;
and china and glass looked as if it had been sown.
And the house, what of that? Alas! it too had been

scattered to the four winds of heaven in the form of
smoke and ashes.   Not even a chimney stood to mark
its site.   Near by stood a row of negro cabins, intact,
showing that while the conflagration was going on
they had been sedulously guarded.   And these cabins
were occupied by the slaves of the plantation.   Men,
women and children stalked about in restless uncertainty, and in surly indifference.   They had been led
to believe that the country would be apportioned to
them, but they had sense enough to know that such a
mighty revolution involved trouble and delay, and
they were supinely waiting developments.   Neither
man, woman nor child approached me.   There was
mutual distrust and mutual avoidance.

It took less time to take in the situation than it
has to describe it.   The sun was almost down, and as
he turned his large red face upon me, I fancied he
fain would have stopped in his course to see me out of
this dilemma.   What was I to do ?   The next nearest
place that I could remember that would perhaps give
protection for the night was Mr. Fowler's, and this
was my only hope.   With one hand upon Yankee's
shoulder, and the ropes in the other, I moved on, and
not until my expiring breath will I forget the plead-
ing look which that poor dumb animal turned upon
me when I started.   Utterly hopeless, and in my
hands, he wondered how I could thus exact more of
him.   I wondered myself.   But what was I to do but
to move on ?   And with continuous supplication for
the Lord to have mercy upon me, I moved on.   More
than once the poor horse turned that look, beseeching
and pathetic, upon me.   It frightened me.   I did not

understand it, and still moved on. At last the hope of making himself understood forsook him, and he deliberately laid himself down in the road. I knelt by his side and told him the true state of affairs, and implored him not to desert me in this terrible crisis. I told him how cruel it would be to do so, and used many arguments of like character; but they availed nothing. He did not move, and his large, lustrous brown eyes seemed to say for him: "I have done all I can, and can do no more." And the sun could bear it no longer, and hid his crimson face behind a great black cloud.

What could I do but rise from my imploring attitude and face my perilous situation? "Lord have mercy upon me," was my oft-repeated invocation. The first thing which greeted my vision when I rose to my feet was a very distant but evidently an advancing object. I watched it with bated breath, and soon had the satisfaction of seeing a man on muleback. I ran to meet him, saying: "O, sir, I know the good Lord has sent you here." And then I recounted my trouble, and received most cordial sympathy from one who had been a Confederate soldier, but who was now at home in consequence of wounds that incapacitated him for further service. When he heard all, he said:

"I would take you home with me, but I have to cross a swimming creek before getting there, and I am afraid to undertake to carry you. Wait here until I see these negroes. They are a good set, and whatever they promise, they will, I think, carry out faithfully."

The time seemed interminable before he came

back, and night, black night, had set in; and yet a quiet resignation sustained me.

When my benefactor returned, two negro men came with him, one of whom brought a lantern, bright and cheery. "I have arranged for you to be cared for here," said he. "Several of the old house servants of Mrs. Clark know you, and they will prove themselves worthy of the trust we repose in them." I accepted the arrangement made by this good man, and entrusted myself to the care of the negroes for the night. This I did with great trepidation, but as soon as I entered the cabin an assurance of safety filled my mind with peace, and reconciled me to my surroundings. The "mammy" that presided over it met me with a cordial welcome, and assured me that no trouble would befall me under her roof. An easy chair was placed for me in one corner in comfortable proximity to a large plantation fire. In a few minntes the men came in bringing my flour, potatoes, syrup, bacon, etc. This sight gave me real satisfaction, as I thought of my poor patient mother at home, and hoped that in some way I should yet be able to convey to her this much needed freight. I soon espied a table on which was piled many books and magazines; "Uncle Henry Clark's" theological books were well represented. I proposed reading to the women, if they would like to hear me, and soon had their undivided attention, as well as that of several of the men, who sat on the doorsteps. In this way several hours passed, and then "mammy" said, "You must be getting sleepy." "Oh, no," I replied, "I frequently sit up all night reading." But this did not satisfy her; she had devised in her own mind something more hospitable for her guest, and she wanted to see it carried out. Calling into requisition the assistance of the men, she had two large cedar chests placed side by side, and out of these chests were taken nice clean quilts, and snow-white counterpanes, and sheets, and pillows—Mrs. Clark's beautiful bed-clothing—and upon those chests was made a pallet upon a which a queen might have reposed with comfort. It was so tempting in its cleanliness that I consented to lie down. The sole occupants of that room that night were myself and my hostess—the aforesaid black "mammy." Rest, not sleep, came to my relief. The tramping of feet, and now and then the muffled sound of human voices, kept me in a listening attitude, and it must be confessed in a state of painful apprehension. Thus the night passed.

With the dawn of day I was up and ready to meet the day's requirements. "Mammy's" first greeting was, "What's your hurry?" "I am accustomed to early rising. May I open the door?" The first thing I saw was Yankee, and he was standing eating; but he was evidently too weak to attempt the task of getting that cumbersome vehicle and its freight to Decatur. So I arranged with one of the men to put a steer to the wagon and carry them home. This he was to do for the sum of one hundred dollars. After an appetizing breakfast, I started homeward, leading Yankee in the rear of this turnout. Be it remembered, I did not leave without making ample compensation for my night's entertainment.

No event of particular interest occurred on the way

to Decatur. Yankee walked surprisingly well, and the little steer acquitted himself nobly. In due time Decatur appeared in sight, and then there ensued a scene which for pathos defies description. Matron and maiden, mother and child, each with a tin can, picked up off the enemy's camping-ground, ran after me and begged for just a little something to eat—just enough to keep them from starving. Not an applicant was refused, and by the time the poor, rickety, cumbersome wagon reached its destination, its contents had been greatly diminished. But there was yet enough left to last for some time the patient, loving mother, the faithful Telitha, and myself.

A summary of the trip developed these facts: To the faithfulness of Uncle Mack was due the holding together of the most grotesque vehicle ever dignified by the name of wagon; over all that road it remained intact, and returned as good as when it started. And but for the sorghum grinding, poor Yankee would have acted his part unfalteringly. As for myself, I labored under the hallucination that I was a Confederate soldier, and deemed no task too great for me to essay, if it but served either directly or indirectly those who were fighting my battles.

CHAPTER XXI.

A SECOND TRIP FOR SUPPLIES.

Gathering "fodder" from a cane-brake as a preliminary—The lonely journey—Changing Yankee's name—I meet the Federal raiders.

At an early hour in the morning of a bright autumnal day, that memorable year 1864—the saddest of them all—Yankee was roped (not bridled, mark you), and crocus sacks, four for him, one for Telitha, and one for myself, thrown over his back, and we three, boon companions in diversified industries, scampered off to a neighboring cane-brake—a favorite resort in those days, but now, alas for human gratitude ! never visited for the sake of " auld lang syne."

Perfect health—thanks to the parents who transmitted no constitutional taint to my veins—unusual strength, and elasticity of motion, soon carried me there, and having secured Yankee to a clump of canes luxuriant with tender twigs and leaves, sweetened by the cool dew of the season, Telitha and I entered upon the work of cutting twigs and pulling fodder.

There being no drainage in those times, I often stepped upon little hillocks, covered with grass or aquatic vegetation, that yielded to my weight, and I sunk into the mud and water ankle deep, at least, and Telitha was going through with similar experiences. I often laughed at her grimaces and other expressions of disgust in the slough of despond, and rejoiced with her when she displayed the trophies of success, consisting of nice brittle twigs, generously clad in tender leaves and full growth ; Yankee, too, was unmindful of small difficulties, and did his "level" best in providing for a rainy day by filling his capacious paunch brimful of the good things so bountifully supplied by Providence in the marshes of old DeKalb. By the time the aforesaid half dozen sacks were filled, the enlargement of that organ of his anatomy suggested that he proposed carrying home about as much inside of him as might be imposed upon his back—of this sagacity he seemed conscious and very proud, and when the sacks of cane were put over his back, pannier fashion, he pursued the path homeward with prouder air and nobler mien than that which marked his course to the cane-brake.

When we three were fully equipped for starting back to the deserted village, Yankee, as already described, and I with a sack of cane thrown over my right shoulder, and reaching nearly to my heels, and Telitha, in apparel and equipment an exact duplicate of myself, I was so overcome by the ludicrous features of the scene that for the time I lost sight of the pathetic and yielded to inordinate laughter. As memory, electrical and veracious, recapitulated the facts and circumstances leading to this state of affairs, I realized that there was but one alternative—to laugh or to cry—but the revolutionary blood coursing through my veins decided in favor of the former, and I laughed until I could no longer stand erect, even though braced by an inflexible bag of cane, and I ignominiously toppled over. As I lay upon the ground I laughed, not merrily, but grimly, as I fancy a hyena would laugh. The more I sought the sympathy of Telitha in this hilarious ebullition, the more uncontrollable it became. Her utter want of appreciation of the fun, and a vague idea that she was in some way implicated, embarrassed her, and, judging from her facial expression, ever varying and often pathetic, wounded her also. In vain did I point to our docile equine, whose tethering line she held. His enlarged proportions and grotesque accoutrements failed to touch a single risible chord, or convey to her utilitarian mind aught that was amusing, and she doubtless wondered what could have so affected me.

In due time we reached Decatur. After passing the Hoyle place, the residence being then deserted, Telitha indicated by signs too intelligible to be misunderstood that she would go home with her sack of stock provender, leading the horse, and then come back for mine, and I could go by a different route and not be known as a participant in the raid upon the cane-brake; but I was too proud of my fidelity to the Southern Confederacy to conceal any evidences of it that the necessities of the times called into action, and I walked through the stricken village with my sack of cane in my arms instead of upon my back; and would have walked as proudly to the sacrificial altar, myself the offering, if by so doing I could have retrieved the fortunes of my people and established for them a government among the nations of earth.

The lowing of our cow reached me as I entered the court-house square, and I hastened my gait and soon displayed before her, in her stall in the cellar, a tempting repast. And my mother, who possessed the

faculty of making something good out of that which
was ordinary, displayed one equally tempting ·to me
and Telitha—milk and mush, supplemented by coffee
made of parched okra seed.

"Tired nature's sweet restorer" faithfully performed its recuperative service that night. When I
opened my eyes upon the glorious light of another
day, I was so free from the usual attendants upon
fatigue that I involuntarily felt for my body—it seemed
to have· passed away during the night, and left no
trace of former existence. I found it, though, perfectly intact, and ready to obey the behests of my will
and serve me through the requirements of another
day. And my mother seemed to be in her usual health
and willing for me to do anything I thought I ought
to do. She could not close her eyes to the fact that
our store of supplies was nearly exhausted, and that
there was only one way to replenish it; and she had
the wisdom and the Christian grace to acquiesce to
the inevitable without a discouraging word. Telitha,
upon whose benighted mind the ridiculous phases of
the previous day's adventures had dawned sometime
in the interim, laughed as soon as she saw me, and in
well-acted pantomime made me fully aware that she
enjoyed at this late hour the ludicrous scene that had
so amused me. And Yankee evidently smiled when
he saw me, and greeted me with a joyous little whicker
that spoke volumes.

A good breakfast for women and beast having
been disposed of, I wended my way in quest of
Uncle Mack. He alone understood the complicated

process of harnessing Yankee in ropes to the primitive vehicle manufactured by his own ingenious hands, and to him I always went when this important task had to be performed. On this occasion, as upon others, it was soon executed. When all was ready and the unbidden tears dashed away, as if out of place, I seized the ropes and started ? Where ? Ah, that was the question. There was only one place that offered hope of remuneration for the perilous undertaking, and forty miles had to be traversed before reaching it. Forty miles through a devastated country. Forty miles amid untold dangers. But in all the walks of life it has been demonstrated that pluck and energy, and a firm reliance upon Providence, are necessary to surmount difficulties, and of all these essentials I had a goodly share, and never doubted but that I would be taken care of, and my wants and those of others supplied. "God helps those who help themselves," is an adage which deserves to be emblazoned upon every tree, and imprinted upon every heart. That vain presumption that folds the hands, and prays for benefits and objects desired, without putting forth any effort to obtain them, ought to be rebuked by all good men and women as a machination of Satan.

These and similar reflections nerved me for the task before me, and I started in earnest. When I got to the " blacksmith shop," I looked back and saw my mother standing just where I left her, following me with her eyes. I looked back no more lest I dissolve in tears. As I passed the few abodes that were tenanted, my mission " out " was apprehended, and I was besought in tearful tones to bring back with me all I could, by those who told me that they and their children were upon the verge of starvation. I took all the sacks which were handed to me and rolled them together, and by the aid of a string secured them to the cart, and amidst blessings and good wishes pursued my devious way; for, be it remembered, many obstructions, such as breast-works and thorny hedge-wood, presented formidable barriers to rapid travel for a considerable distance from Decatur.

While leisurely walking beside Yankee, I was struck with the agility of his motion and his improved figure since we traveled over these grounds a few weeks before. He had taken on a degree of symmetry that I never supposed attainable by the poor, emaciated animal which I captured in the cane-brake. His hair had become soft and silky, and in the sunlight displayed artistic shades of coloring from light to deepest brown ; and his long, black tail, which hung limp and perpendicular, now affected a curve which even Hogarth might have admired, and his luxuriant and glossy mane waved prettily as a maiden's tresses. And his face, perfect in everylineament, and devoid of any indication of acerbity, lighted by large, liquid, brown eyes, would have been a fit model—a thing of beauty—for the pencil of Rosa Bonheur. Rubbing my hand over his silky coat and enlarged muscles, I decided to enjoy the benefit of his increased strength and gently ordered a halt. Stepping from the ground to the hub of the wheel, another step landed me into the cart, vehicle, wagon or landau, which ever you see

proper to denominate it ; I do not propose to confine
myself to any one of these terms.

Yankee understood the movement, and doubtless
felt complimented. As soon as I took my seat in the
chair—a concomitant part of the equipage—he started
off at a brisk gait, which, without a word of command,
he kept up until we came to the base of a long hill,
and then he slackened his speed and leisurely walked
to the summit. I enjoyed going over ground without
muscular effort of my own, and determined to remain
in the cart until he showed some sign of fatigue. I
had only to hold the ropes and speak an encouraging
word, and we traveled on right merrily. Ah, no!
That was a misnomer. Callous indeed would have
been the heart who could have gone merrily over that
devastated and impoverished land. Sherman, with
his destructive host, had been there, and nothing remained within the conquered boundary upon which
"Sheridan's Crow" could have subsisted. Nothing
was left but standing chimneys, and an occasional
house, to which one would have supposed a battering
ram had been applied. I looked up and down, and in
every direction, and saw nothing but destruction, and
the gaunt and malignant figure of General Starvation
striding over our beautiful country, as if he possessed
it. I shook my head defiantly at him and went on,
musing upon these things. I never questioned the
wisdom or goodness of God in permitting them, but I
pondered upon them, and have never yet reached their
unfathomable depths.

At the end of the first day's journey, I found myself twenty miles, or more, from the starting point,

and tenderly cared for by a good family, consisting, in these war times, only of a mother and several precious little children, who were too glad to have company to consider my appeal for a night's entertainment intrusive. This desolate mother and children thought they had seen all the horror of warfare illustrated by the premeditated cruelty of the Yankee raiders, and could not conceive how it could have been worse. But when I got through with my recital of injuries, they were willing that theirs should remain untold. A delicious supper, like manna from Heaven, was enjoyed with a zest unknown to those who have never been hungry.

The light of another day found us all up in that hospitable household, and an appetizing breakfast fortified me for another day's labor in any field in which I might be called to perform it. The little boys, who had taken Yankee out of the rope harness the evening before, remembered its intricacies and had no difficulty in getting him back into that complicated gear. When all was ready, and grateful good-byes had been uttered, I again mounted "the hub," and got into the vehicle. After I had taken my seat, the good lady handed me a package, which proved to be a nice lunch for my dinner. She also had a sack of potatoes and pumpkins stored away in the landau; and being a merciful woman, she thought of the horse, and gave some home-cured hay for his noonday meal.

All day I followed in the track of Sherman's minions, and found the destruction greater than when I had passed in this direction before. Coming to a hill,

16

the long ascent of which would be fatiguing to Yankee, I ordered a halt and got out of the wagon. Taking position by his side, we climbed the hill together, and then we went down it together, and continued to journey side by side, I oblivious to everything but the destruction, either complete or partial, on every side. At length we came to a lovely wee bit stream of water, exulting in its consciousness that no enemy could arrest it in its course to the sea, or mar its beauty as it rippled onward. We halted, and I loosened the ropes so that Yankee might partake of the flowing water before eating his noonday meal. And I am sure epicure never enjoyed luncheon at Delmonico's with more zest than I did the frugal meal prepared for me by the friendly hands of that dear Confederate woman. Much as I enjoyed it, I finished my dinner sometime before Yankee did his, and employed the interim in laving my hands and face in the pure water, and contemplating myself in the perfect mirror formed by its surface. Not as Narcissus did I enjoy this pastime, but as one startled by the revelation. Traces of care, sorrow, apprehension for the future, were indelibly imprinted upon forehead and cheek, and most of all upon that most tell-tale of all features, the mouth. I wept at the change, and by way of diversion turned from the unsatisfactory contemplation of myself to that of Yankee. This horse, instinct with intelligence, appreciated every act of kindness, and often expressed his gratitude in ways so human-like as to startle and almost affright me. I am sure I have seen his face lighted by a smile, and radiant with gratitude. And no human being ever expressed more forcibly by word or act his sorrow at being unable to do all that was desired of him in emergency, than did this dumb brute when he gave me that long, earnest, pathetic look (mentioned in a former sketch) when, from sheer exhaustion, he lay down near the heap of ashes where once stood the beautiful residence of my friend of honored memory, Rev. Henry Clark.

The more I contrasted the treatment which I, in common with my country women and my country, had received at the hands of the Yankees (the then exponents of the sentiment of the United States towards the Southern people), and the gentle, friendly demeanor of the animal upon whom I had unthoughtedly bestowed a name constantly suggestive of an enemy, the more dissatisfied I became with it, and I determined then and there to change it. Suiting the action to the decision, I gathered the ropes and led the noble steed to the brink of that beautiful little brooklet, and paused for a name. What should it be ? "Democrat?" I believed him to be a democrat, true and tried, and yet I did not much like the name. Had not the Northern democrats allowed themselves to be allured into abolition ranks, and made to do the fighting, while the abolitionists, under another name, devastated the country and enriched themselves by the booty. "Copperhead ?" I did not like that much. It had a metallic ring that grated harshly upon my nerves, and I was not then aware of their great service to the South in restraining and keeping subordinate to humanity, as far as in them lay, the hatred and evil passions of the abolitionists. "Johnny Reb ?" Ah,

I had touched the keynote at last, and it awakened a
responsive chord that vibrated throughout my very
being. I had a secret belief, more than once expressed in words, that my noble equine was a captured
rebel "held in durance vile" until bereft of health
and strength, then abandoned to die upon the com-
mons. "Johnny Reb!" I no longer hesitated. The
name was electrical, and the chord with which
it came in contact was charged to its utmost capacity.
With the placid waters of that ever-flowing stream,
in the name of the Southern Confederacy, I christened
one of the best friends I ever had "Johnny Reb," a
name ever dear to me.

This ceremony having been performed to my satisfaction and to his, too—judging by the complacent
glances, and, as I fancied, by the suggestion of an
approving smile which he bestowed upon me—I
mounted the hub, stepped into the cart, seated myself, and with ropes in hand continued my way to "The
Circle," and arrived there before night. Not being
tired, I immediately struck out among the vendors
of home-made products—edibles, wearing apparel,
etc.—for the purpose of purchasing a wagon load to
carry to Decatur, not for the ignoble purpose of
speculation, but to bestow, without money and without price, upon those who, like my mother and myself, preferred hunger and privation rather than give
up our last earthly home to the destroying fiend that
stalked over our land and protected Federal bayonets.

Before the shades of night came on I had accomplished my object. As a matter of history I will

enumerate some of the articles purchased, and annex
the prices paid for them in Confederate money :

One bushel of meal $10 00
Four bushels of corn........................ 40 00
Fifteen pounds of flour...................... 7 50
Four pounds dried apples.................... 5 00
One and half pounds of butter............... 6 00
A bushel of sweet potatoes.................. 6 00
Three gallons of syrup...................... 15 00
Shoeing the horse........................... 25 00
For spending the night at Mrs. Born's, self
     and horse............................. 10 00

Not knowing the capabilities of " Johnny Reb," I
feared to add one hundred and thirty-six pounds
avoirdupois weight to a cart already loaded to
repletion, and the next morning on starting took my
old familiar place by his side. To my slightest touch
or word of encouragement, he gave me an appreciative
look and obeyed to the letter my wishes with regard
to his gaits—slow or fast in adaptation to mine. In
due time we again rested on the banks of the beautiful little stream hallowed by the memory of repudia-
ting a name, rendered by the vandalism of its legitimate owners too obnoxious to be borne by a noble
horse, and by the bestowing upon him of another
more in keeping with his respect for ladies and other
fine traits of character which he possessed. Neither
he nor I had lunch with which to regale ourselves ;
and whilst he moved about at will cropping little
tufts of wild growth and tender leaves, which instinct taught him were good for his species, I abandoned myself to my favorite pursuit—the contempla-

tion of nature. Like Aurora Leigh, I " found books among the hills and vales, and running brooks," and heid communion with their varied forms and invisible influences. To me they ever spoke .of the incomprehensible wisdom and goodness of God. My heart, from my earliest recollection, always went out in adoration to Him who could make alike the grand old Titans of the forest and the humblest blade of grass; and now I beheld them under circumstances peculiarly calculated to evoke admiration. Change had come to everything else. The lofty trees stood in silent grandeur, undisturbed by the enemy's step or the harsh clarion of war—as if defiant of danger—and gave shelter and repose to the humblest of God's creatures who sought their protecting arms. Beguiled by the loveliness of the woodland scenery, I often found myself stopping to daguerreotype it upon the tablets of my memory, and to feast my senses upon the aromatic perfume of wildwood autumn flowers. "Strong words of counseling" I found in them and in " the vocal pines and waters," and out of these books I learned the " ignorance of men."

> " And how God laughs in Heaven when any man
> Says, ' Here I'm learned ; this I understand ;
> In that I am never caught at fault, or in doubt.' "

A word of friendly greeting and renewed thanks to mine hostess of two nights before, and her dear little children, detained me only a very short and unbegrudged space of time ; and during that time I did not forget to refer to the potatoes and the pumpkin so kindly given to me by them on my down trip, and which I could have left in their care until my return, had I thought of it.

Night again came on, and this time found me picking my way as best I could over the rocks shadowed by Stone Mountain. On I plodded through the darkness, guided rather by the unerring step of Johnny Reb than any knowledge I had of the way. At length the poor faithful animal and myself were rewarded for perseverance by seeing glimmering lights of the mountain village. We struck a bee line for the nearest one, and were soon directed to "a boarding house." I was too glad to get into it then, to descant upon its demerits now. I assured the landlady that I needed no supper myself, and would pay her what she would charge for both if she would see that the horse was well fed. I think she did so. My valuable freight could not remain in the cart all night, and there was no one to bring it in. In vain did she assure me that I would find it all right if I left it there. I got into the cart and lifted the sacks and other things out of it myself, and, by the help of the aforesaid person, got everything into the house. I fain would have lain down by these treasvres, for they had increased in value beyond computation since leaving Social Circle, and would have done so but for repeated assurance of their safety.

An early start next morning gave me the privilege of going over the ground familiar to my youth in the loveliest part of the day, and when the sun looked at me over the mountain's crest, I felt as if I was in the presence of a veritable king, and wanted to take my bonnet off and make obeisance to him. His beneficent

rays fell alike upon the just and the unjust, and
lighted the pathway of the destroyer as brightly as
that of the benefactor. Amid destruction, wanton
and complete, and over which angels might weep, I
stepped the distance off between Stone Mountain and
Judge Bryce's; not a living thing upon the face of the
earth, or a sound of any kind greeting me—the desolation of war reigned supreme. I again stopped at
Judge Bryce's, and implored his protection to Decatur,
but, as on the former occasion, he was afraid to leave
his wife to the tender mercy (?) of the enemy. He
told me he feared I would not reach home with my
cart of edibles, as "Yankee raiders had been coming
out from Atlanta every day lately," and that the set
that was now coming was more vindictive than any
that had preceded it. Good, dear Mrs. Bryce, trusting
in the Lord for future supplies, took a little from her
scanty store of provisions and added it to mine for her
friend, my mother.

With many forebodings of evil, I took up the line
of march to Decatur. I looked almost with regret upon
my pretty horse. Had he remained the poor ugly
animal that was lassoed in the cane-brake, I would
have had but little fear of losing him, but under my
fostering care, having become pretty, plump and
sprightly, I had but little hope of keeping him. Being
absorbed by these mournful reflections and not having
the ever-watchful Telitha with me to announce danger from afar, I was brought to a full realization of
its proximity by what appeared to be almost an army
of *blue-coats*, dashing up on spirited horses, and for
the purpose of humiliating me, hurrahing "for Jeffer-

son Davis and the Southern Confederacy." As a flag
of truce, I frantically waved my bonnet, which act
was misapprehended and taken as a signal of approval
of their "hurrah for Jefferson Davis and the Southern
Confederacy," which was resounding without intermission.

Seeing several very quiet, dignified looking gentlemen, who, although apart from the others, seemed to
be exercising a restraining influence, I approached
them and told them how I had gone out from Decatur
unprotected and all alone to get provisions to keep
starvation from among our defenseless women and
children, and that I had to go all the way to Social
Circle before I could get anything, and that I had
walked back in order to save the horse as much as
possible. These men, however, although seemingly
interested, questioned and cross-questioned me until I
had but little hope of their protection. One of them
said, "I see you have one of our horses. How did
you come by him?" And then the story of how I
came by him was recapitulated without exaggeration
or diminution. This narrative elicited renewed hur-
rahs for Jefferson Davis and the Southern Confederacy.
A few minutes private conversation between these
gentlemen ensued, and all of them approached me,
and the spokesman said, "Two of us will escort you
to Decatur, and see that no harm befalls you." It
seemed, then, that no greater boon could have been
offered under the canopy of Heaven, and I am sure no
woman could have experienced more gratitude or been
more profuse in its expression.

The sight of my nervous, gray-haired mother, and her pretty mother ways, touched another tender chord in the hearts of these gentlemen, and if constraint existed it was dispelled, and they became genial and very like friends before they left. They even promised to send us some oats for noble Johnny Reb, who displayed the greatest equanimity all through these trying scenes.

CHAPTER XXII.

NEWS FROM THE ABSENT BROTHER.

He marches into Tennessee with Hood—Extracts from his letters written on the way—Two ears of parched corn—The night burial of a soldier.

After the majority of these sketches were written, I was permitted by my sister to take a few extracts from the cherished letters of our brother, which she numbered and carefully laid away as her most precious treasure. To these we are indebted for all that we know of his history during those trying days and weeks of which I have just been writing. Where was he, and how did he fare? Few and far between were the letters now, in these dark days of the war. The soldiers themselves had but little opportunity to write, and the mail facilities were poor. But I feel sure that to the survivors of the "Lost Cause," these meagre scraps concerning that brave but disastrous march into Tennessee will be read with melancholy interest:

"On the Line of Alabama and Georgia,
Near Alpine, Ga., 8 o'clock at night, Oct. 17, 1874.

"MY DEAR SISTER—As there is a probability of the mail courier leaving here eary in the morning, I hastily scratch you a few lines that you may know that under the blessings of a kind Providence I am yet alive, and, though somewhat wearied, enjoying good health. Yours of 28th of September has been received, but under circumstances of hard marches, etc., there has been but one opportunity of writing to you since leaving Palmetto, and then had just finishèd one to Texas, and was fixing to write to you, when the order came to ' fall in.'

"Well, leaving camps near Palmetto on the 29th of September, we crossed the Chattahoochee below, marched up to Powder Springs, threatened Marietta, and at the same time threw Stewart's corps around above Big Shanty to cut the railroad, which was torn up for about thirteen miles, French's Division attàcking Allatoona, where he sustained some loss, having works to charge. Ector's Texas Brigade, and some Missourians, carried their part of the works, but A——'s Brigade failed to do their part, hence the advantage gained was lost. By this time the enemy were concentrating at Marietta, and General Hood's object being accomplished, he then marched rapidly towards Rome, flanking the place, and making a heavy demonstration as if he intended crossing the river and attacking the place. The enemy then commenced a concentration at Kingston and Rome. We then moved around Rome and marched rapidly up the Oostanaula, and, on the evening of the 11th inst., sent a division of infantry with some cavalry across the river, and captured Calhoun with some stores. Moved on the next morning by a forced march, flanking Resaca, and striking the railroad immediately above, tearing it up to Tilton where there were about three hundred Yankees in a block-house. A surrender was demanded. A reply was returned: 'If you want us come and take us.' Our artillery was soon in position and a few shots soon made them show the 'white rag.' We tore

up the road that night, and the next morning by nine
o'clock, to Tunnel Hill, burning every cross-tie and
twisting the bars. Dalton surrendered without a
fight, with a full garrison of negroes and some white
Yankees. The block-house above, at a bridge, refused
to surrender, and we had to bring the artillery into
requisition again, which made them succumb. They
all seemed to be taken by surprise and were hard to
convince that it was a cavalry raid. They evacuated
Tunnel Hill. Thus after five months of fighting and
running, the Army of Tennessee re-occupied Dalton.
Sherman has been taken by surprise. He never
dreamed of such a move. General Hood's plans all
being carried out, so far as the State road was concerned, we marched across the mountains to LaFay-
ette, in the vicinity of which we camped last night,
and have marched twenty-three miles to-day. To-
morrow we cross the Lookout Mountain, and will, I
suppose, make directly for the Tennessee river, though
of this I'm not certain. Hood has shown himself a
general in strategy, and has secured the confidence of
the troops. Wherever we go, may God's blessing
attend us. Pray for me. In haste.

Your affectionate brother,

Tom Stokes.

"P. S.—Cherokee Co., Ala., Oct. 18, 1864.

" The courier not leaving this morning, I have a
little more time left. We did not travel so far to-day
as I heard we would, having come only ten miles, and
have stopped to rest the balance of the evening. I
find you dislike to have your communications cut off,
so I see you are below Madison. Would to Heaven

that, in one sense of the word my communication
was cut off forever ; yea, that every channel leading
me in contact with *the world*, in any other character
than as a minister of 'the meek and lowly Savior,'
was to me forever blocked up. I am tired of confusion and disorder—tired of living a life of contin-
ual excitement *   *   *. You spoke of passing
through a dark cloud. 'There is nothing true but
Heaven,' and it is to that rest for the weary, alone,
to which we are to look for perfect enjoyment.
We are to walk by faith, and though the clouds
of trouble thicken, yet we should know that if we
do our duty we shall see and feel the genial sunshine of a happier time. Yes, my sister, though we
knew our lives should be lengthened one hundred
years, and every day should be full of trouble ; yet if
we have a hope of Heaven, that hope should buoy up
the soul to be cheerful, even under earth's saddest
calamities.

"I think we will cross the Tennessee river and
make for Tennessee, where it seems to be understood
that we will have large accessions to our army, both
there and from Kentucky *   *   *."

The next letter is enclosed in an envelope which
came through no postoffice, as it was furnished by
my sister, and upon it she wrote : "This letter was
sent to me on the 27th of November, by some one who
picked it up upon the street in Madison. The post-
office had been rifled by the Federals who (under command of Slocum) passed through Madison, November 18th and 19th. Though found without an en-

velope, and much stained, it has reached me, because signed with his full name."

This letter is dated "Near Decatur, Ala., October 28th, 1864." We give a few items :

"We invested this place yesterday, and there has been some skirmishing and artillery firing until an hour ago, when it seems to have measurably ceased. We are in line of battle southwest of Decatur, about one and a quarter miles. I went out reconnoitering this morning and saw the enemy's position. They have a large fort immediately in the town, with the 'stars and stripes' waving above. I hear occasional distant artillery firing which I suppose is Forrest, near Huntsville. * * * We were several days crossing Sand Mountain. Have had delightful weather until a day or two ago it rained, making the roads very muddy, in consequence of which we have been on small rations, the supply trains failing to get up. We had only half rations yesterday, and have had none to-day (now nearly three o'clock), but will get some to-night. We try to be cheerful. * * * No letter from Texas yet. No one of our company has had any intelligence from Johnson county since last May. I can't see what's the matter. I have been absent nearly one year and have received but one letter." (Of course the dear loved ones in Texas wrote to their soldier braves on this side the Mississippi river ; but such are the misfortunes of war that these missives were long delayed in their passage).

"Saturday, October 29th.—The condition of affairs this morning at sunrise remains, so far as I know, unchanged. * * * Yesterday evening we drew two

ears of corn for a day's ration; so parched corn
was all we had yesterday; but we will get plenty
to-day."

And now we come to the last of the letters ever
received. It is probable it was among the last he
ever wrote. It is dated "Tuscumbia, Ala., Nov. 10,
1864.— .   .   . We arrived at this place the 31st
of October, and have been here since, though what
we are waiting for I can't tell. The pontoons are
across the river, and one corps on the other side at
Florence. We have had orders to be ready to move
several times, but were countermanded. We were to
have moved to-day, and even our wagons started off,
but for some cause or other we have not gone. The
river is rising very rapidly, which may endanger the
pontoons.

"November 12th.—I thought to send this off yesterday morning, but, on account of the rain a few
days ago, the mail carrier was delayed until last night,
which brought your dear letter of date October 31st.
It was handed me on my return from the graveyard,
where I had been to perform the funeral ceremony of
a member of the 6th Texas, who was killed yesterday
morning by the fall of a tree. He had been in
every battle in which this brigade was ever engaged;
an interesting young man, only nineteen years of
age.

"The scene at the graveyard was a solemn one,
being some time in the night before we arrived. The
cold, pale moon shone down upon us, and the deep
stillness which pervaded the whole scene, with the

rough, uncouth, though tender-hearted soldiers with uncovered heads, forming a large circle around the grave, made it, indeed, a scene solemnly impressive. The print of my Bible being small, I could not read, but recited from memory a few passages of Scripture suitable to the occasion, the one upon which I dwelt chiefly being a declaration of Paul to the Corinthians, 'For we must all appear before the judgment seat of Christ.' I then spoke of the certainty of that change from life to death; that with the soldier, even, death is not confined to the battlefield; spoke of our comrade, who but in the morning bade as fair for long life as any of us, but within the space of a few short hours was lying in the cold embrace of death; of another of our brigade who was instantly killed a short time since by a stroke of lightning; closed with an exhortation to all to live nearer to God, and be prepared at all times to meet their God in peace. Oh, how sad! Far away from his home to be buried in a land of strangers. How the hearts of his father, mother and sisters must bleed when they receive the sad tidings.

"I expect we will leave here for Middle Tennessee next Monday, as the river will be falling by that time. There is much talk of this brigade being sent home after this campaign. Major Rankin has been exchanged, and is with us. I gave Lieutenant Collins' overcoat to his company to take care of for him.

"Am so glad to hear from ma and sister. We get no letters from Texas; but are continually sending some over, as all the disabled of the last campaign are be-

17

ing retired and sent across. Poor Uncle James! His Joseph is gone. . . . Write to me often.

Affectionately,

YOUR BROTHER."

Ah, could the history of these brave men be written, what a record it would be of endurance, of daring, of heroism, of sacrifice! And the heart-breaking pathos of the last chapters of their experience, ere the furling of the flag they followed! Pat Cleburne and his fallen braves—

> "On fame's eternal camping ground,
>   Their silent tents are spread,
> And glory marks with solemn round
>   The bivouac of the dead."

CHAPTER XXIII.

AN INCIDENT OF THE WAR.

Related to the writer by Hon. Roger Q. Mills, of Texas.

The night was black as Erebus. Not a scintillant of light from moon or star penetrated the dense forest, and no eye save that of God discerned the danger of the situation. Hill and dale, mountain and precipice, creek and surging stream, presented barriers that none but men inured to hardship, and unknown to fear, would have attempted to surmount.

Obedient to the command of the superior officer, the remnant of that magnificent and intrepid army, once guided by the unerring wisdom of Joseph E. Johnston, plodded their way uncomplainingly over these trying difficulties. The Lord must have been amazed at their temerity, and shook the very earth in rebuke, and ever and anon by the lightning's flash revealed glimpses of the peril to which they were exposed; and yet in unbroken lines they groped their way, not knowing whither. At length bewildered, and made aware of impending danger, the general in command ordered a halt. The martial tread ceased, and all was still as death. In the midst of this stillness a voice, sweet as that of a woman, was heard repeating that grand old hymn, which has given comfort to many weary ones treading the wine press :

" How firm a foundation, ye saints of the Lord,
Is laid for your faith in His excellent Word!
What more can He say than to you He hath said,
You who unto Jesus for refuge have fled.

" In every condition, in sickness, in health,
In poverty's vale, or abounding in wealth,
At home and abroad, on the land, on the sea,
As thy days may demand shall thy strength ever be.

" Fear not, I am with thee, O ! be not dismayed,
I, I am thy God, and will still give thee aid ;
I'll strengthen thee, help thee and cause thee to stand,
Upheld by My righteous, omnipotent hand.

" When through the deep waters I call thee to go,
The rivers of woe shall not thee overflow ;
For I will be with thee, thy troubles to bless,
And sanctify to thee thy deepest distress.

" When through fiery trials thy pathway shall lie,
My grace all sufficient shall be thy supply ;
The flame shall not hurt thee ; I only design
Thy dross to consume, and thy gold to refine.

" E'en down to old age, all My people shall prove
My sovereign, eternal, unchangeable love ;
And when hoary hairs shall their temples adorn,
Like lambs they shall still in My bosom be borne.

" The soul that on Jesus hath leaned for repose,
I will not, I will not desert to his foes ;
That soul, though all hell should endeavor to shake,
I'll never, no never, no never, forsake."

General Mills said that during the rendition of this
beautiful hymn, not even the breaking of a twig, or
the changing of a footstep broke the silence of the
midnight tranquillity. The rain drops ceased to

fall; the electricity darted harmlessly through the tree tops; and the muttering of the thunder lulled.

After a most impressive silence of several minutes, the same voice, which had rendered the hymn so effectually, repeated from memory an appropriate passage of Scripture and proceeded to expatiate upon it. He had not uttered a dozen words before another flash of lightning revealed the upturned heads and listening attitudes of the men composing that weird congregation, and each one of them knew as if by instinct that he was going to hear something that would help him on his journey to the Land of Beulah. Strong in the faith, he carried many of the truths and promises of the Holy Word within his mind, and now, as many times before, he opened them by the magic key of memory and unfolded to view their unsearchable riches. He begged his fellow-men and comrades in arms to accept them without money and without price—to accept them that they might wear kingly robes and royal diadems, and be with Jesus in His Father's regal mansions throughout the grand eternities. And as he told the old, old story of divine love, it assumed a contemporaneous interest and seemed a living present reality. Every man who heard it felt the living force and energizing influence of the theme. And thus by earnest, aggressive appeals, he exerted a wonderful power for good over the minds of his hearers; and those men, even now with phantom hands pointing gaunt fingers at them, by their deep interest testified to the warm suffusing purpose which made itself felt in every word that he uttered, as he told of the Fatherhood of God and the ever-present sympathy of a benignant and infinite parent, who delighted not in the death of sinners, but rather that all should come to Him and have eternal life. General Mills added that, as the fine resonant voice of the speaker penetrated the dense forest and found its way to his hearers in distinct enunciation of well-chosen words, the deep-toned thunder emphasized the impressive points, and made it a scene which for grandeur and sublimity has never been surpassed, while the vivid flashes of lighning revealed again and again the earnest face and solemn mien of my brother, Lieutenant Thomas J. Stokes, of the Tenth Texas Infantry of Cleburne's Division.

CHAPTER XXIV.

Picking up minie balls around Atlanta—Exchanging them for bread.

After mingling renewed vows of allegiance to our cause, and expressions of a willing submission to the consequences of defeat—privations and evil dire, if need be—with my morning orison ; yet I could not be oblivious to the fact that I was hungry, very hungry. And there was another, whose footsteps were becoming more and more feeble day by day, and whose voice, when heard at all, was full of the pathos of despair, who needed nourishment that could not be obtained, and consolation, which it seemed a mockery to offer.

In vain did I look round for relief. There was nothing left in the country to eat. Yea, a crow flying over it would have failed to discover a morsel with which to appease its hunger; for a Sheridan by another name had been there with his minions of destruction, and had ruthlessly destroyed every vestige of food and every means of support. Every larder was empty, and those with thousands and tens of thousands of dollars, were as poor as the poorest, and as hungry too. Packing trunks, in every house to which refugees had returned, contained large amounts of Confederate money. We had invested all we possessed except our home, and land and negroes, in Confederate bonds, and these were now inefficient for purchasing purposes. Gold and silver had we none. A more favored few had a little of those desirable mediums of purchase, and sent a great distance for supplies; but they offered no relief to those who had stayed at home and borne the brunt of battle, and saved their property from the destroyers' torch.

What was I to do? Sit down and wait for the inevitable starvation? No; I was not made of such stuff. I had heard that there had been a provision store opened in Atlanta for the purpose of bartering provisions for munitions of war—anything that could be utilized in warfare. Minie balls were particularly desirable. I therefore took Telitha by the apron, and had a little talk with her, and when I was through she understood that something was up that would bring relief to certain organs that had become quite troublesome in their demands, and she was anxious to take part in the performance, whatever that might be. I went also to my mother, and imparted to her my plans of operation, and she took that pathetic little backward step peculiar to herself on occasions which tried her soul, and with quivering lip she assented in approving, though almost inaudible words.

With a basket in either hand, and accompanied by Telitha, who carried one that would hold about a peck, and two old dull case-knives, I started to the battle-fields around Atlanta to pick up the former missiles of death to exchange for food to keep us from starving.

It was a cold day. The wind was very sharp, and over the ground, denuded of forest trees and undergrowth, the wind was blowing a miniature gale. Our wraps were inadequate, and how chilled we became in that rude November blast! Mark you, it was the 30th of November, 1864. But the colder we were, the faster we walked, and in an incredibly short time we were upon the battle-field searching for lead.

I made it a point to keep very near the road in the direction of Atlanta, and soon found myself on the very spot where the Confederate magazine stood, the blowing up of which, by Confederate orders, shook the very earth, and was distinctly heard thirty-five or forty miles distant. An exclamation of glad surprise from Telitha carried me to her. She had found a bonanza, and was rapidly filling her basket with that which was more valuable to us than gold. In a marshy place, encrusted with ice, innumerable bullets, minie balls, and pieces of lead seemed to have been left by the irony of fate to supply sustenance to hungry ones, and employment to the poor, as all the winter those without money to send to more favored and distant points found sure returns from this lead mine. It was so cold ! our feet were almost frozen, and our hands had commenced to bleed, and handling cold, rough lead cramped them so badly that I feared we would have to desist from our work before filling the baskets.

Lead ! Blood ! Tears ! O how suggestive ! Lead, blood and tears, mingled and commingled. In vain did I try to dash the tears away. They would assert themselves and fall upon lead stained with blood. "God of mercy, if this be Thy holy will, give me fortitude to bear it uncomplainingly," was the heart-felt invocation that went up to the throne of grace from over lead, blood and tears, that fearful day. For relief, tears did not suffice. I wanted to cry aloud ; nature would not be satisfied with less, and I cried like a baby, long and loud. Telitha caught the spirit of grief, and cried too. This ebullition of feelings on her part brought me to a realization of my duty to her, as well as to my poor patient mother to whom the day must seem very long, and I tried to stifle my sobs and lamentations. I wondered if she had the forebodings of coming bereavement that were lacerating my own heart. I did not doubt but that she had, and I cried in sympathy for her.

At length our baskets were filled, and we took up our line of march to the desolated city. There were no labyrinths to tread, no streets to follow, and an occasional question secured information that enabled us to find the "commissary" without delay. Telitha was very ambitious that I should appear a lady, and wanted me to deposit my load of lead behind some place of concealment, while we went on to deliver hers, and then let her go back for mine. But I was too much a Confederate soldier for that, and walked bravely in with my heavy, precious load.

A courteous gentleman in a faded grey uniform, evidently discharged because of wounds received in battle, approached and asked what he could do for me. "I have heard that you give provisions for lead," I replied, "and I have brought some to exchange." What seemed an interminable silence en-

sued, and I felt without seeing that I was undergoing
a sympathetic scrutiny, and that I was recognized as
a lady "to the manor born."

"What would you like in exchange," he asked.
"If you have sugar, and coffee, and meal, a little of each
if you please," I timidly said. "I left nothing to eat
at home." The baskets of lead were removed to the
rear and weighed, and in due time returned to me
filled to the brim with sugar, coffee, flour, meal, lard,
and the nicest meat I had seen in a long time.

"O, sir,"I said, "I did not expect so much."

"You have not yet received what is due you," this
good man replied, and handed me a certificate which
he assured me would secure as much more on presentation.

Joy had gone out of my life, and I felt no thrill of
that kind ; but I can never describe the satisfaction
I experienced as I lifted two of those baskets, and
saw Telitha grasp the other one, and turned my face
homeward.

CHAPTER XXV.

The Decatur women's struggle for bread—Sweet singing in
hard places—Pleasant visitors—I make a trip to Alabama—
The news of my brother's death.

The tug of war was upon us from the mountains
to the sea-board, and ingenious was the woman who
devised means to keep the wolf, hungry and ravenous,
from the door. The depreciation of our currency, and
its constant diminution in value, had rendered it an
unreliable purchasing commodity,, and we had nothing to give in exchange for food. I, therefore, felt
that I had literally rubbed against Aladdin's lamp
when I saw much needed food, good and palatable,
given in exchange for minie balls, and for any kind
of metal convertible into destructive missiles, and I
was anxious that others should share the benefit
accruing from the lead mines mentioned in a former
sketch. In pursuance of this humane desire, I proclaimed its discovery and results from house to house;
for, mark you, we had no "Daily Courier," nor mes-
senger boy to convey the glad tidings to the half-
famished women and children in and around Decatur.
And if my words could have been changed into diamonds by the magic wand of a fairy, not one of those
starving people would have accepted the change of
diamonds for bread.

It required only a short time to raise a large company of women, girls and little boys, who were ready

to do service for themselves and their country by digging lead with case-knives from mines providentially
furnished them. And was it not serving the cause of
the Confederacy? I thought so; and never walked
with more independent step than when acting as gen-
eralissimo of that band of devoted, patriotic women,
en route to the "lead mines" around Atlanta. Telitha,
too, evidently felt that she was an important adjunct
in the mining enterprise, and a conspicuous personage
in the scenes being enacted, and emphasized her
opinion by strong and suggestive gesticulation. On
this occasion she playfully wrenched from my hand
the small vessel with which I had supplied myself
and which I carried on the former trip, and substituted
a larger one, while for herself she got at least a half-
bushel measure.

All who remember the month of December, 1864,
know that it abounded in clouds and rain and sleet,
and was intensely cold in the Confederate States of
America; and in the latitude embracing Atlanta, such
severity of weather had never been known to the
oldest inhabitant. But what mattered it? Each one
in that little band of women was connected by a bright
link to the illustrious armies that were enduring
greater privation and hardship than those to which
she was exposed, and counted it a willing oblation
upon his country's altar, and why should she not prove
faithful to the end, and suffer the pangs of hunger
and privation too?

The work of picking up minie balls began as soon
as we reached the battle-field, and, consequently, we
carried several pounds some distance unnecessarily.

The "mine" proper, I doubt not, could have filled
several wagons. As "a little fun now and then is
relished by the wisest men," I found a grim smile as-
serting itself at the quaint and ready wit of those estimable girls, the Misses Morton, whose Christian
names I have forgotten and who, alas! have long
since joined the silent majority.   One of them assumed the character of a Confederate soldier and the
other that of a Federal, and the conversation carried
on between them, as they "exchanged coffee and tobacco," was rich, rare and racy.   The exchange having
been effected, the signal of combat was given. "Look
out, Billy Yank!"   "Look out, Johnnie Reb!" were
simultaneous warnings from opposing forces, and
minie balls whizzed through the air, much to the merriment of the little boys who wished themselves men,
that they might be with their fathers, whizzing minie
balls from musket mouths.

The sham battle over, the work of digging lead
was resumed, and in an amazingly short time our
vessels were filled to overflowing.   I watched Telitha
with interest.   She was eager to fill her basket, and
more than once she said, "Me full!" and added a little gutteral laugh that always indicated pleasure.
Her attempt to raise the basket from the ground,
and her utter failure to do so surprised her amazingly,
and her disappointment was pathetic.   With great
reluctance she saw her treasure reduced to her capacity of handling.   Each member of the party experienced similar disappointment on attempting to raise
her burden, and we left more exhumed lead and other
valuables than we carried away.

We took up our line of march, and as there were no obstructions in the way (for, be it remembered, Sherman had been there, and with torch and explosive removed all obstructions save the standing chimneys and carcasses of horses and cattle shot by his order to prevent the possibility of use to the rebels), we struck a bee-line to the commissary. As the first to take advantage of this industry, I took the lead, and the vigor of young womanhood, and "a heart for every fate," gave elasticity to my steps, and I soon outdistanced even the girls. In due time we reached the commissary, and in a short while a most satisfactory exchange was made, thanks to one whose great heart beat in unison with ours, and in lieu of the heavy burden which we laid down, we picked up food for the nourishment of our tired bodies and those of our loved ones at home. Oh, how light, comparatively, it seemed ! I verily believe if it had weighed the same number of pounds, it would have seemed lighter, and the change would have seemed restful. "Good-bye, noble ladies and sisters in a righteous cause," was the parting salutation of our no less noble benefactor.

With our respective packages of food we again turned our faces homeward, solemn as a funeral march, for, strive against them as we would, we all had forebodings of ill, and the swaying of our bodies and our footsteps kept time with the pulsations of our sad hearts. I fancied as I approached standing chimneys and other evidences of destroyed homes, that the spirit of Sherman, in the guise of an evil spirit, was laughing over the destruction his diabolism had wrought. In the midst of these reflections a

song, which for sweetness and tranquilizing melody
I have seldom heard equalled and never surpassed,
broke the stillness of the scene and added to the melancholy interest of the occasion.   It was the well
known ballad, then familiar to every child in the Confederacy, "When this Cruel War is Over," and sung
by those gifted sisters mentioned as a part of the
lead digging company.   The pure, sweet soprano
voice of one of the girls put to flight the spirit of
Sherman, and when it was joined by the flute-like
alto of the others, every evil spirit within and without
was exorcised, and the spirit of submission took its
place.   And yet as the words rang out and found an
echo in my own heart, I had to walk very straight,
and turn my head neither to the right nor to the left,
lest I betray the copious tears trickling down my
cheeks.   At length pent-up feelings burst the fetters,
and an audible sob removed restraint, and we cried as
women burdened with great sorrow.   Precious tears!
Nature's kind alleviator in time of trouble.

> "The day was cold and dark and dreary,
> And it rained and the winds were never weary,"

and yet I was nerved for its duties and toil by the
consciousness of having met, uncomplainingly, the
work which the preservation of my own principles
made me willing to endure.   Several days subsequent to this trip to Atlanta, the Morton girls came
running in and told me that we had some delightful
friends at the "Swanton place," who requested to see
us.   My mother was too much exhausted by anxiety
and waiting for that which never came, to go, but

approved my doing so. I, therefore, donned my sun-
bonnet and went ; and whom should I meet but Mrs.
Trenholm and her sweet young daughters, Essie and
Lila ? I was delighted to see them, and invited them
to go home with me. Ma received them in a spirit of
cordial hospitality, and they were invited to remain
at her house. Without hesitation, Mrs. Trenholm
accepted the proffered kindness, and returned to her
wayside rendezvous only to send her trunks, bedding
and other household 'goods. And truly the coming
of that saintly woman and those lovely girls was a
rare benediction, especially at that time. Day by day
ma looked in vain for tidings from " the front "—
wherever that might be—and day by day her health
and strength was perceptibly weakened by disappointment. Mrs. Trenholm's sympathy with her in
her suspense regarding the operations of Hood's
army, and the fate of her beloved son, was both
touching and consoling. Seeing that my mother and
myself were hoping almost against hope, she endeavored to bring us to a realization of that fact, and a
complete submission to the will of God, even though
that will deprived us of our loved one. All of her
Christian arguments and consolations had been pondered over and over by mother and daughter, but
they never seemed so sweet and potent as when coming in the chaste and simple language of a precious
saintly woman.

With the tact peculiar to the refined of every
clime and locality, Mrs. Trenholm assumed management of the culinary department, and her dinner-
pot hung upon our crane several weeks, and

18

daily sent forth appetizing odors of bacon and peas. How we enjoyed those peas and that bacon, and the soup seasoned with the only condiments at our command—salt and red pepper—and the good hoe cakes! Mrs. Trenholm had a large sack of cow peas, and a sack of dried fruit, and other articles of food which she had provided for herself and her family before she left Southwest Georgia *en route* to her home in Marietta, which she left in obedience to the order of William Tecumseh Sherman, and which she learned, before reaching Decatur, had shared the fate of nearly all other homes which had to be thus abandoned. Although magnanimously proffered, we were averse to sharing Mrs. Trenholm's well-prepared and ofttimes tempting *cuisine*, unless our proportion of food equaled hers; and fearing even the appearance of scanty supplies, I set about to gather up "the miners," so that we might appoint a day to again go lead digging, if that which we left in as many little heaps as there were members of the company had been, in the interim, gathered up by others.

On former occasions I had led my company to victory over that malignant general left by Sherman to complete his work, and styled by him "General Starvation," and they were willing to go wherever I led. Now, I had two recruits of whom I was very proud. Telitha, too, had gathered from observation that the sweet young Trenholm girls were going with us, and she set about to provide very small baskets for their use, which, with gestures amusing and appropriate, she made us understand were large enough to contain all the lead that girls so pretty and so ladylike ought to carry. To their credit, however, they repudiated that idea, and carried larger vessels. By appointment the "lead diggers" were to meet at the tanyard, those arriving first to wait until the entire number came. "Man proposes and God disposes." Just as my last glove was drawn on, Telitha, ever on the alert, said "Morton, Morton," and I looked and saw the girls coming. "We needn't go—the commissary has folded its tents, and silently stolen away," was the voluntary announcement. Imagine my consternation and disappointment—the last hope of supply cut off! Ma saw the effect upon me, and said in a more hopeful voice than was her wont, "The Lord is my shepherd, I shall not want." And good Mrs. Trenholm said her sack of peas was like the cruse of oil that never seemed to diminish in quantity, however much was taken out of it. An examination, too, of our own resources was quite gratifying; but I knew I ought to be "providing for a rainy day."

I pass now over an interval which brings me to the latter part of January, 1865. My sister returned home from Madison and spent several weeks with us, but had accepted an offer to teach at Grantville, on the LaGrange and West Point Railroad. I had a precious aunt, my mother's sister, Mrs. Annie Watson, whom I loved dearly, and of whom I had not heard a word since the interruption of the mail communication by the siege of Atlanta, and my mother's frequent mention of her determined me to go and see if this beloved aunt was living, and, if so, in what condition. I knew she was one of the favored ones of earth, viewed from a worldly standpoint, but I knew not what changes had come over her or her worldly possessions. Rumor conveyed startling accounts of the atrocious deeds of Wilson's raiders, and I knew that they were operating in that rich cotton belt of Alabama which embraced my aunt's plantation and beautiful home. I could scarcely hope that that home and its valuable appointments had escaped the cupidity of an organized band of robbers protected by the United States Government.

When I think of my mother's fond affection for her children, and her tender solicitude for their welfare, I am constrained to think that she thought I was endowed with a sort of charmed existence not subject to the perils which beset the pathway of ordinary mortals, and hence her ready acquiescence to my proposition to undertake a journey of many miles, under circumstances of imminent danger, inspired with confidence amounting to certainty that I would be preserved by an All-wise Providence for future usefulness. I had very little preparation to make for the contemplated trip. A pretty, small-checked dress, which had done service through many a changing scene, and was good for as many more, and a hat—well, I beg to be excused from describing it—and gloves upon which I had expended skill in darning until it was difficult to perceive where the darning ceased and the glove began, completed my toilet, and I bade to all appearance a cheerful good-bye to my mother and kind friends, and went by private conveyance to Fairburn. There I took the train for Cowles' Station, Alabama.

Nothing of particular interest transpired on the way. My country was prostrate and bleeding from many lacerations, and my tears flowed so freely that by the time I reached my railroad destination I had a very sick headache. That "there is a providence that shapes our ends" was again illustrated. Some of my aunt's neighbors, who knew me at least by name, were at the station, and kindly offered to carry me to her residence, a distance of ten miles. I found my aunt in feeble health, and all alone save her usual dusky attendant. Her only child, Mrs. Mary E. Seaman, had gone to Tuskeegee to see her little daughter, who was there going to school in care of a friend and relative, Col. Smith Graham. My closest scrutiny failed to detect any change in my aunt's mode of living. The same retinue of servants came into the house to see and shake hands with mistress' niece, and after many questions about "our white folks in Georgia," retired from my presence with the same courtesy that had marked their demeanor towards me in ante-bellum days.

My aunt manifested her joy at seeing me in many ways, and wept and smiled alternately, as I related my adventures with the Yankees. "And my sister, what was their treatment of her?" My evasive answer, "It could have been worse," heightened her desire to learn particulars, and I told them to her. She was grateful for all leniency shown by them, and affected to tears by unkindness. As the day waned, and the middle of the afternoon came on, my aunt proposed walking "to meet Mary." I supported her fragile form, and guided her footsteps in the best

part of the road. How like her beloved sister in
Georgia she seemed! Accustomed to this little diversion, for she always went to meet Mary, she had
reckoned accurately regarding the time of her daughter's coming, and we had not gone far when we saw
the carriage descending a declivity in the distance.
Nelson, the coachman, had also recognized "Mistress
and Miss Mary," and announced his discovery to my
cousin. Increased speed in the gait of the horses
soon brought us together, and she opened the door
and stepped to the ground. After kissing her dear
mother, she encircled me in her arms, and kissed me
time and again, and then assisted me into the carriage, and she and her mother followed. I greeted
the coachman in a cordial manner, because of past
service and present fidelity to " mistress and my white
folks " generally.

With my rapidity in conversation, I could scarcely
keep up with my cousin's questions. Happy woman!
She had never seen any " Blue-coats," or, in the parlance of the times, " Yankees," and she enjoyed my
description of them, especially when in answer to the
question, " Do they look like our men ?" I attempted
to define the difference. It was amusing to me to hear
her describe the preparations she made for the coming of Wilson and his raiders.

After reaching home, she left her mother and myself only a few minutes. I scarcely perceived her absence, and yet when she returned the disparity in our
dress was not so apparent. The elegant traveling suit
had been exchanged for her plainest home attire, and
every article of jewelry had disappeared. The brief

period spent with these dear relatives was spent in mutual efforts to entertain and amuse each other. My aunt's conversation was like sweet music in which minor chords abounded. Her love for her sister, and apprehension of evil, gave a pathetic turn to every conversation she attempted, and it was evident to me that she had given up all hope of my brother's safety, and her resignation under similar circumstances was a great support to me.

Much as I enjoyed this luxurious home, and its refined appointments, there was a controlling motive—a nearer tie—that made me willing to again take up the hardships and perils of warfare, and battle for life with that relentless enemy left by Sherman to complete his cruel work, the aforesaid General Starvation.

After many farewell words were spoken, I left my aunt, accompanied by her daughter, who went with me to the station for the purpose of seeing me on the train bound for Fairburn, then the terminus of the railroad. It was past noon when the train left the station, and in those days of slow railroad locomotion, it was all the afternoon reaching West Point. I learned before reaching there that I would have to remain over until the next morning, and, therefore, as soon as I stepped from the cars, started to hunt a place at which to spend the night. Wending my way, solitary and alone, through the twilight, I saw Mr. John Pate, the depot agent at Decatur, coming towards me.

"Oh, Mr. Pate, have you heard anything from ma in the last week?"

"Yes; it went very hard with her, but she was some better this morning."

I did not have to ask another question. I knew it all, and was dumb with grief. The thought that I would never see my darling brother again paralyzed me. I saw him in the mirror of my soul, in all the periods of his existence. The beautiful little baby boy, looking at me the first time out of his heavenly blue eyes, and his second look, as if not satisfied with the first, followed by the suggestion of a smile. Ah, that smile! It had never failed me through successive years and varying scenes. The boyhood and youth— honest, truthful and generous to a fault—and the noble, genial boyhood, had all developed within my recollection, and I loved him with an intensity bordering on idolatry. These scenes and many others rushed through my mind with kaleidoscopic rapidity and made me so dizzy that I had no knowledge of how I reached the "hotel." My heart cried and refused to be comforted. From the consolation of religion and patriotism it recoiled and cried all the more. A great tie of nature had been sundered, and the heart, bruised and crushed and bleeding, pulsated still with vitality that would have flickered out but for the hope of giving comfort to the poor bereaved mother and sister in our great sorrow. Good ladies bathed my throbbing temples and kissed my cheeks and spoke comforting words, for they were all drinking the bitter waters of Marah, and knew how to reach the heart and speak of the balm of Gilead.

"Killed on the battle-field, thirty steps from the breastworks at Franklin, Tennessee, November 30th,

1864," was the definite information regarding my brother's death, left for me by Mr. Pate.

Interminable as the darkness of night appeared, it at length gave way to the light of day, and I was ready with its dawn to take the train. But, oh, the weight of this grief that was crushing me! Had the serpents which attacked Laocoon, and crushed him to death by their dreadful strength, reached out and embraced me in their complicated folds, I could not have writhed in greater agony. I did not believe it was God's will that my brother should die, and I could not say to that Holy Being, "Thy will be done." In some way I felt a complicity in his death— a sort of personal responsibility. When my brother wrote to me from his adopted home in Texas that, having voted for secession, he believed it to be his duty to face the danger involved by that step, and fight for the principles of self-government vouchsafed by the Constitution of the United States, I said nothing in reply to discourage him, but rather I indicated that if I were eligible I should enter the the contest. These, and such as these were the harrowing reflections which accused me of personal responsibility for the demon of war entering our household and carrying off the hope and prop of a widowed mother.

I found my poor stricken mother almost prostrate. The tidings of her son's tragic death did the work apprehended by all who knew her nervous temperament. Outwardly calm and resigned, yet almost paralyzed by the blow, she was being tenderly cared for by our saintly neighbor, Mrs. Ammi Williams and her family, who will always be held in grateful remembrance by her daughters.

CHAPTER XXVI.

MY MOTHER'S DEATH.

Rev. Dr. John S. Wilson performs the funeral service

In sympathy with a disappointed people who had staked all and lost all in the vain effort to defend the inherited rights of freemen, and had not yet rallied from the depression occasioned by defeat, the spring of 1866 had withheld her charms, and, instead of donning a mantle of green, decorated with pansies, violets and primroses, hyacinths, bluebells and daffodils, verbenas, phlox and geraniums, and bloom of vine and briar in endless variety, the first day of April found her wounded, bleeding bosom wrapped in the habiliments of sorrow and despondency. A few brave old apple trees, as if to encourage the more timid, had budded and blossomed and sent forth sweet fragrance as of yore, and a few daring sprigs of grass suggested spring-time and sunny skies. Loneliness, oppressive and melancholy, and a spirit of unrest, prompted me to go to the depot in quest of something that never came, and my sister had stepped over to our neighbor, Mrs. Williams'.

Our mother loved the spring-time. It had always been her favorite season of the year. Fifty-nine vernal suns had brought inspiration and hope to her sensitive, tender heart, and given impulse to a checkered life ; but now no day-star of hope shed its effulgence for her. As I mentioned in a former sketch, her

only son had fallen mortally wounded upon the sanguinary battle-field of Franklin, and she had never
recovered from the shock.

After a few months of patient endurance, an attack of paralysis had occurred, and during many days
life and death contended for the victory. But the skill
of good physicians, among them Dr. Joseph P. Logan, and faithful, efficient nursing, aided in giving
her a comfortable state of health lasting through several months. But the fiat had gone forth, and now
after a pathetic survey of earth, mingled with thankfulness even then to the God of the spring-time, she
succumbed to the inevitable.

Returning from the depot, I espied in the distance
the approaching figure of Telitha. As she came up to
me she was the very picture of despair. With one
hand clasped to her head, she fell on the ground and
lay as if dead for a moment. My worst apprehen-
sions were more than realized. I found my mother
speechless, and never more heard her voice—never
more heard any sound emanating from her lips except
labored, heavy breathing. It was all so sudden and
strange and sad, I cannot describe it. Neighbors and
friends came in by the score, and did all they could
to mitigate our great sorrow. "Johnnie" Hardeman
stayed until all was over, and mother never received
from loving son kinder care or more unremitting attention. Paul Winn also remained and manifested
deep sympathy, and so did other neighbors. Oh, the
sorrow, the poignant sorrow, to see a mother in the
embrace of death, and to have no power over the
monster! About thirty hours of unconsciousness,

and without a struggle, "life's fitful dream was over," about 9 o'clock p. m., April 1st, 1866. The silent hush that ensued was sacred, and scarcely broken by the sobs of those most deeply afflicted.

Loving hands fashioned a shroud, and a beautiful casket was obtained from Atlanta. When all was done, and our mother arrayed for the tomb, she looked like the bride of Heaven. I gazed long and earnestly upon her face and figure, and went away and came back, and gazed again admiringly. For every lineament was formed into a mold that compelled admiration.

During the two days that she lay there, I often lingered by her side ; and I recalled the many scenes, ofttimes perilous and sad, and ofttimes joyous and gay, through which we had gone together. Although a wee bit girl, scarcely turned in my fifth year at the time of my mother's second marriage, I remembered her as a bride. I remembered our journey by gig and wagon to Cassville, then, paradoxical as it may sound now, situated in the heart of a wilderness of beauty and savagery. The war-whoop of an uncivilized race of Indians, justly angry and resentful, reverberated though the impenetrable forest that belted the little settlement of white people that had the hardihood and bravery to make their homes among them. I remembered how she soon became a favorite, and was beloved by every one in that sparsely-settled locality, and won even the hearts of the Indians, by kindness towards them. She taught them how to make frocks and shirts, and clothes for their children, for the Cherokees were an ambitious people, and aspired to assimilation with the white race; and, to please them, she learned to bead moccasins, and other articles, ornamental and useful, just as they did. She also learned their alaphabet, and became able to instruct them in their own language.

I remembered how she had always worked for the poor; not so much in societies (where the good that is accomplished in one way is often more than counterbalanced by the harm that is done in others), as in the quiet of her home, and in the humble habitations of God's poor. I remembered, with a melancholy thrill, how she had worked for our soldiers, and had not withheld good deeds from an invading alien army. Reverently I took in mine her little, symmetrical hand as it lay peacefully over the heart that had ever beat in unison with all that was good. It was weather-beaten, and I could feel the rough places on the palm through the pretty white silk glove in which it was encased. Cold and stark in death, it gave no responsive pressure to my own. I thought of its past service to me in which it never tired. It had trained my own from the rudimentary "straight lines" and "pot hooks," through all the intricacies of skilled penmanship, and from the picturesque letters on a sampler to the complete stitches of advanced embroidery. The little motionless hand that I now held in my own had picked corn from cracks and crevices in bureau drawers, which served as troughs for Garrard's cavalry horses, to make bread with which to

appease her hunger and mine. I gazed upon the pallid
face and finely-chiseled features. The nose never
seemed so perfect, or the brow so fair, or the snow-
white hair so beautiful. The daintiest of mull caps
heightened the effect of the perfect combination of
feature, placidity and intellectual expression.   I
fancied I had never seen her look so beautiful, and
felt that it was meet that we should lay her away in
a tomb where she could rest undisturbed until the
resurrection morn, not doubting that the verdict of a
great and good God would assign her a place among
His chosen ones.

Soothing to our bruised hearts was the sweet
singing of those who watched at night beside her
lifeless form. With gratitude we remember them
still: Laura and Mary Williams, Emma and John
Kirkpatrick, Josiah Willard and John McKoy. One
of the hymns they sang was "Jerusalem, My Happy
Home."

The hour for the funeral service came. Friends
and neighbors and fellow-citizens had been assem-
bling for several hours, and now the house was full,
and the yard was thronged. Where did this concourse of people come from—old men, war-stricken
veterans, and a few young men who had survived
the bloody conflict that had decimated the youth of
the South, and boys and women and girls! All alike
came to pay respect to the deceased friend, and to
show sympathy for the bereaved and lonely sisters.
That sainted man and friend of ours, Rev. John S.
Wilson, took his stand near the casket, and we sat

near him, and those who loved us best got very near
to us. Ah, well do I remember them! I could call
each by name now, and the order in which they came.
An impressive silence ensued, broken by the man of
God uttering in hopeful intonation and animated
manner, "She is not dead, but sleepeth," and a sermon
followed upon the resurrection of God's people, never
surpassed in interest and pathos. All felt the power
of his theme, and the eloquence of his words. He also
spoke of the humble modesty of his friend, who had
counted herself least in the congregation of the righteous, and dispensed favors to others in an unobtrusive
manner, and who practically illustrated the divine
command: "Do unto others as ye would that others
should do unto you." This beautiful funeral tribute
was succeeded by the hymn—

"Rock of ages, cleft for me,"

which was sung with an unction which none but
Christians can feel.

The last earthly look, solemn and earnest, was
taken of our long-suffering, patient, loving mother,
and everybody in the house followed our example
and gazed reverently upon the pretty face, cold in
death. And then the pall-bearers, "Johnnie" Kirkpatrick, "Johnnie" Hardeman, Virgil Wilson and
Mr. G. W. Houston, bore her to the grave.

With uncovered head and grey locks fluttering in
the vernal breeze, Dr. Wilson repeated the beautiful
burial service of the Presbyterian Church. I can
never describe the utter desolation of feeling I experienced as I stood clasped in the arms of my sis-

ter, and heard the first spadeful of earth fall over the remains of our loved one.

But we had heard above all the glorious words, "This mortal shall put on immortality," and "O, death, where is thy sting? O, grave, where is thy victory?"

CHAPTER XXVII.

A REMINISCENCE.

"Sister, you are not paying any attention whatever to my reading, and you are losing the most beautiful thoughts in this delightful book."

"Yes, and I am sorry to do so; but I think I see one of Rachel's children—Madaline or Frances."

My sister closed her book, and, looking in the direction indicated, agreed with me that the negro woman, clothed in the habiliments of widowhood, who was coming up the avenue with a little boy by her side and one in her arms, was one of Rachel's children; and, although she was scarcely in her teens when she went away, she was a mother now, and traces of care were visible in every lineament of her face. I recognized her, however, as Rachel's youngest daughter, Frances, and went to meet her.

"Is that you, Frances?" I asked.

"Yes, Miss Mary, this is me; your same nigger Frances, and these are my children."

"I am glad to see you and your children;" and I extended my hand in genuine cordiality to her who had once been a slave in my mother's family, and I bade her welcome to her old home. Frances was too demonstrative to be satisfied with simply hand-clasping, and putting her boy on the ground, she threw her arms

19

around me and literally overwhelmed me with kisses. My hands, neck and face were covered with them, and she picked me up and carried me in her arms to the house, her children following in amazed astonishment. She now turned her attention to them, and, after deliberately shaking the wrinkles out of their clothes, she as deliberately introduced them to me. The older of the two she introduced as "King by name," and the younger as " Lewis by name."

" You see, Miss Mary, I named my children King and Lewis 'cause my white folks named my brothers King and Lewis.

The ceremony of introducing her sons to *her* old *white folks* being performed to her satisfaction, she again turned her attention to me, and again literally overwhelmed me with caresses.

Entering the house, I asked Frances and her children to come in too.

"Miss Mary, whar's Miss Polly ?"

" Have you not heard, Frances, that ma is dead ?"

"Seem to me I has heard somethin' about it, but some how I didn't believe it. And my poor Miss Polly is dead ! Well, she ain't dead, but she's gone to heaven."

And Frances became quite hysterical in demonstrations of grief.

"And Marse Thomie, what about him, Miss Mary?"

" He was killed by the enemy at Franklin, Tenn., the 30th of Novenber, 1864."

"Miss Mary, did them old Yankees kill him?"

"Yes, he was killed in battle."

And again, whether sincere or affected, Frances became hysterical in demonstrations of grief.

" Miss Mary, whar's Miss Missouri ? Is she dead too ?"

" No ; that was she who was sitting in the portico with me as you were coming up the avenue. She always has to go off and compose herself before meeting any of you—ma was that way, too—I suppose you remind her of happier days, and the contrast is so sad that she is overcome by grief and has to get relief in tears.

"Yes'm, I have to cry, too, and it does me a monstous heap of good. I know it's mighty childish, but I jest can't help it. Jest to think all my white folks is done dead but Miss Mary and Miss Missouri !"

"Our brother left a dear little boy in Texas, and I am going after him next winter. He and his mother are going to live with us, and then we will not be so lonely."

" That's so, Miss Mary."

Frances and her children having partaken of a bountiful supper, she resumed, with renewed vigor, her erratic conversation, which consisted, chiefly, of innumerable questions, interspersed with much miraculous information regarding herself since she left her white folks and became a wife, a mother, and a widow.

"Miss Mary, whar's my children going to sleep tonight?"

"With your help I will provide a comfortable place for them, and, also, for you."

And taking a lantern and leading the way to the kitchen, I entered and pointed to a light bedstead, and told her to carry a portion of it at a time to my room, and we would put it up in there.

"Same old room, jest like it was when me and my mammy used to sleep in it.

"Well, things do look mighty nateral if it has been a long time since I seed it.

"And Miss Mary is agoing to let me and my children sleep in her room. Well!"

The bedstead having been placed in position, a mattress and bed clothing were furnished. And soon the little negro children were soundly sleeping under the protecting roof of their mother's former young mistresses.

"Whar's your teakettle, Miss Mary?" Having been told where to find it, Frances took it to the well and filled it with water, and, by adding a little more fuel to the fire, soon had it boiling.

"Whar's your bath-tub, Miss Mary?"

That, too, was soon produced and supplied with hot water, reduced to proper temperature. Memories of the past left no doubt in my mind as to the use to which the water was to be applied, and I determined to gratify every fancy that would give pleasure to our former handmaid, and, therefore, I made no resistance when garters were unbuckled, shoes and stockings removed, and feet tenderly lifted into the tub. She knew just how long to keep them there, and how to manipulate them so as to give the most satisfaction and enjoyment; and how to dry them—a very important process. And then the shoes and stockings were again put on, and giving me an affectionate pat on the head she told me to sit still until she told me to move.

" Now, whar's your comb and brush ?"

The force of habit must have impelled her to ask this question, as, without awaiting an answer, she went to the bureau and got the articles about which she had asked, and in a few moments she had my long, luxuriant black hair uncoiled and flowing over my shoulders. She was delighted ; she combed and braided it, and unbraided and combed it again and again, and finally, as if reluctant to do so, arranged it for the night.

"Now, whar's your gown ?"

" You will find it hanging in the wardrobe."

Having undressed me, Frances insisted upon putting the gown on me, and then wanted to carry and put me in bed ; this service, however, I declined with thanks. All these gentle manipulations had a soporific effect upon me, and I fain would have slept, but no such pleasure was in store for me. Frances had an axe to grind, and I had to turn the grindstone, or incur her displeasure. Mark her proposition :

" Miss Mary, I come to give you my children."

" Your what ?"

" My children, these smart little boys. I'll go with you to the court-house in the mornin' and you can have the papers drawn up and I'll sign 'em, and these little niggers will belong to you 'til they's of age to do for theyselves ; and all I'll ever ask you to do for me for 'em is to raise them like my Miss Polly raised me."

"That you should be willing to give your children away, Frances, surprises me exceedingly. If you are without a home, and would like to come here and live, I will do all I can for you and your children. The kitchen is not occupied, only as a lumber or baggage room, and you can have that without paying rent; and you can take care of the cow and have all you can make off of her milk and butter, except just enough for the table use of two; and you can have a garden without paying rent, and many other favors—indeed, I will favor you in every possible way."

"Well, I tell you how it is, Miss Mary. You see, mammy wants to open up a laundry, and she wants me to help her. She's done 'gaged several womens to help her, and she wants me to go in with her sorter as a partner, you see. And I wants to get my children a good home, for you knows if I had to take care of 'em I couldn't do much in a laundry."

"And you want me to take care of them?"

"Yes'm; just like you used to take care of your own little niggers before freedom, and after I sign the papers they'll belong to you, *don't you know.*"

"I am sorry to disappoint you, Frances, but I cannot accept your offer. If slavery were restored and every negro on the American continent were offered to me, I should spurn the offer, and prefer poverty rather than assume the cares and perplexities of the ownership of a people who have shown very little gratitude for what has been done for them." Without seeming to notice the last sentence, Frances exclaimed:

"Well, it's mighty strange. White folks used to love little niggers, and now they won't have them as a gracious gift."

Under the cover of night she had made her proposition and received her disappointment, after which she lay down by her children and was soon sleeping at the rate of 2:40 per hour, if computed by the snoring she kept up. In due time morning, cheerful, sunlighted morning, came, and with it many benign influences and good resolutions for the day.

Frances asked where everything was, and having ascertained, went to work and soon had a nice, appetizing breakfast for us, as well as for herself and children. After that important meal had been enjoyed, she inquired about the trains on the Georgia Railroad, and asked what time she could go into Atlanta. I told her she could go at nine o'clock, but I preferred that she should stay until twelve o'clock, m.

"Miss Mary, what was in that trunk I saw in the kitchen last night?"

"I scarcely know; odds and ends put there for safe-keeping, I suppose.

"May I have the trunk and the odds and ends in it? They can't be much, or they wouldn't be put off there."

"We will go and see." Again I took the kitchen key, and the trunk key as well, and having unlocked both receptacles, I told Frances to turn the contents of the trunks out ubon the floor. When she saw them I noticed her disappointment, and I told her to remain there until I called her. I went in the house and got a pair of sheets, a pair of blankets, a quilt, several dresses and underclothing, and many things that she could make useful for her children, and put them together, and then called her and told her to take them and put them in the trunk.

"Look here, Miss Mary, you ain't going to give me all them things, is you?"

"Yes," put them in the trunk and lock it."

A large sack of apples, a gift also, was soon gathered and a boy engaged to carry it and the trunk over to the depot in a wheelbarrow. Promptly at half-past eleven o'clock the trunk and apples, and Frances and her little boys, were on the way to the depot, *en route* to Atlanta, their future home, and even a synopsis of the subsequent achievements of that woman and her unlettered mother would be suggestive of Munchausen.

CHAPTER XXVIII.

HOW THE DECATUR WOMEN KEPT UP THE SABBATH SCHOOL.

A Brief Sketch of the Old Churches and the Union Sunday School—The Resumption of Church Services.

Before the war there were in Decatur but two churches, the Methodist and the Presbyterian ; although Baptist and Episcopal services were occasionally held. The churches first mentioned had been organized• about 1825. The Presbyterians first worshipped in a log church, and afterwards in a frame building, but in 1846 had erected a substantial brick church. In this building was also taught the Decatur Union Sabbath School, organized in 1831, and for twenty-five years preceding the summer of 1864 it had been superintended by that godly man, Mr. Levi Willard.

The Federals had now come in. The church had been rifled of all its contents, including the pews. The faithful Sunday School superintendent with his lovely family soon after went away. Being nearer to our house, I remember more about the dismantling and refurnishing of the Presbyterian church than of the Methodist. So far as can be ascertained, the last sermon at the Presbyterian church had been preached by Rev. James C. Patterson, who was then living at Griffin, but was the stated supply of the pulpit here at that time. He will be remembered as a most godly man, and as a sweet singer of sacred songs.

The Sabbath before the entrance of the Federals, no service was held in the dear old church. The last prayer service had been held on Wednesday afternoon, led by Mr. Levi Willard, who was an efficient elder.

In July, 1864, but few families remained in Decatur; but there was still a goodly number of children and young people whose training must not be neglected. On the southwest corner of the Courthouse stood, and still stands, a long, narrow, two-story house. The lower story was occupied as a residence—the upper story, for many years preceding and succeeding these times, was the quarters of the Masonic Lodge. In the ante-room of this lodge, Miss Lizzie Mortin taught a day school. The first story of the building was now occupied by the family of Mr. John M. Hawkins. Mr. Hawkins had enlisted in the army early in the war, but for some reason had returned home and been elected clerk of the court, which position he held until forced to leave before the advancing foe.

Mrs. Hawkins, whose maiden name was Valeria A. Perkins, the eldest daughter of Reuben Perkins of Franklin county, gladly opened her house on Sunday·mornings that the children might be taught in the Sacred Scriptures. And thus a Sunday School was begun, and Mrs. Hawkins was made the superintendent.

Among the organizers and teachers may be mentioned Miss Cynthia Brown, Mrs. H. H. Chivers, Mrs. Eddleman, Miss Lizzie Morton, and Miss Lizzie McCrary. Mr. and Mrs. Buchanan, Mrs. Ammi

Williams, and Mr. Fred Williams acted as a sort of
advisory board. Rev. Dr. Holmes and Rev. P. F.
Hughes, two elderly Baptist ministers, sometimes
came ; and Mr. R. J. Cooper, a godly layman, came a
few times.

The names of some of these Sabbath school pupils
can yet be re-called :—Charley, Guss and Lizzie Hawkins ; their Cousins John, Sam, Ellen and Lizzie
Hawkins, the children of Mr. Sam Hawkins, who is
still living in Summerville, Georgia ; the children of
Mr. R. J. Cooper, and of Mrs. Eddleman, Mrs.
Chivers, and of Mr. Ed Morton. There were others
whose names I cannot recall.

The number of pupils increased to forty, and the
school, having out-grown its quarters, was moved to
the Court House ; but when the Federals chose to
occupy the Court House, the Sunday school was moved
back to Mrs. Hawkins's home. The Bible was the
text book ; for there were no Sunday-school papers or
song books.

Imagine the scene, if you can. Says one of the
participants, who was then a young girl : "We were
a peculiarly dressed lot. I had a stand-by suit, the
skirt made of a blanket shawl; with this I wore one of
my brother's white shirts and a red flannel jacket. I
had grown so fast that I was taller than my mother,
and there was literally nothing large enough in our
house or circle of friends to make me a whole suit.
One of the ladies wore a gray plaid silk, a pair of
brown jeans shoes, and a woven straw bonnet. She
had nothing else to wear. Many of the children were
rigged out in clothes made from thrown-away uni-

forms, picked up, washed, and cut down by the mothers."

Mrs. Hawkins is still living near Decatur. She remembers that on several occasions the soldiers came in while the school was in session, much to the demoralizing of good order and comfort of mind. On one occasion the raiders piled barrels one on top of another, near the house, and set them afire, frightening the children very much.

When the war was over, the refugees began to return. Among the first were the families of Mr. J. W. Kirkpatrick, Mr. Ezekiel Mason, Captain Milton A. Candler, Dr. W. W. Durham, Dr. P. F. Hoyle, Mrs. Jane Morgan, Mrs. Cynthia Stone, Mr. James Winn, Mr. Benjamin Swanton, Mr. Jonathan Wilson, and Mr. J. N. Pate. But, alas! our faithful old Sunday-school superintendent and his family returned not, but remained in Springfield, Ohio, with the exception of Mr. Josiah J. Willard, who afterwards married Miss Jessie Candler, a sister of Captain Candler.

These returning refugees were devoted to the Sunday-school. Mr. John C. Kirkpatrick, just from the war, and scarce twenty-one, undertook the task of re-seating the Presbyterian church. He went out to a saw-mill and had puncheons sawed and carried to Mr. Kirkpatrick's cabinet shop, where they were fashioned into temporary seats. These were placed in the church, and it was once more opened for the exercises of the union Sunday-school, and also for divine worship. Who conducted those exercises, I can find no one who now remembers. My mother had been stricken in July, 1865, with paralysis, which confined her to her bed for many weeks. It was not to be supposed that her daughters could leave her; so that neither one of them can recollect these sessions of the resumed Sabbath-school.

There lies before me "the Sunday-school register and minute-book of 1866," kindly furnished for inspection by Mr. Hiram J. Williams, who had from early youth been constantly identified with the Sunday-school and church. The Superintendent was Mr. Ben T. Hunter; the librarian, Mr. John C. Kirkpatrick; the treasurer, Mr. John J. McKoy. Mr. Kirkpatrick removed to Atlanta in the August of that year, and Mr. Josiah Willard was elected to fill his place, but resigned in December to go on to Ohio, from whence he soon returned, and died a few years ago in Atlanta.

But I must not forget that I am not writing a history of the Sabbath-school, yet I cannot leave the theme without mentioning the fact that all the faithful ones who had taught in the stormy days of war still came in time of peace, and many others whose hearts had not grown cold by their enforced absence. Let me mention the teachers: Mr. J. W. Kirkpatrick, Dr. P. F. Hoyle, Rev. A. T. Holmes, Mr. W. W. Brimm, Captain Milton A. Candler, Mr. G. A. Ramspeck*, Dr. John L. Hardman, Mr. H. H. Puckett, Mr. W. A. Moore (afterwards a Superintendent), Miss Cynthia Brown, Mrs. H. H. Chivers, Mrs. Eddleman, Mrs. Catharine Winn, Mrs. Jane Morgan, Miss Lizzie Swanton, Mrs. E. A. Mason, Mrs. Valeria A. Hawkins, Mrs. J. J. McKoy and Miss Lee Moore. Miss

---

*This gentleman. who married sweet Maggie Morgan, (the sister of Dewitt and Billy), has now been Sunday school treasurer for twenty-seven years.

M. H. Stokes had been appointed one of the teachers, but her mother's feeble health, and the great shock consequent upon her death, prevented this teacher from attending that year with any regularity.

Among the names of "visitors" we notice those of Mr. Bryce, Rev. P. F. Hughes, Mr. Cooper, and Mr. L. J. Winn.

The re-opening of the Sabbath school at the old church was doubtless a great blessing to many. To one young man the joining of that school, and the acceptance of a teacher's place, meant the first public step to a profession of faith in Christ. Captain Milton A. Candler was the child of pious parents, but so far as he knew, was at this time an unconverted man. He reluctantly and with great diffidence accepted a teacher's place. Said he quite recently: "I attribute my subsequent union with the church to the study of the Bible which I made while teaching a class of little boys, Sabbath after Sabbath, in the old church with its puncheon seats. I taught my pupils, a class of little boys, to read from 'the blue-back speller,' and, when that lesson was over, read to them from the Bible, explaining it to them as best I could in all humility." In a few years he made a public profession of his faith in Christ, and was elected to the Superintendency of the Sabbath-school, (which office he still holds), and has labored for its interests with a love and an unflagging zeal rarely ever equalled.

How sweet were the voices of many of the teachers and pupils! John C. Kirkpatrick sang a fine tenor; and clear and soft and true were the tones of Josiah Willard, sweet as the lovely character of this sainted one. All who knew Rev. J. D. Burkhead remember his singing, and he often led the music. A little later came Mrs. Mary Jane Wood with her magnificent voice, and the grand bass of Joseph Morgan, the son of one of the pioneer teachers, Mrs. Martha Morgan. From this Sunday-school, and from its ex-Confederate soldiers, there went into the ministry W. W. Brimm, Paul P. Winn and Sam K. Winn. Promoted to the Glory Land long ago was Mrs. Jane Morgan; and, more recently, Mrs. Catherine Winn.

In the summer of 1866, a Sabbath-school was organized at the Methodist church, which, while a step in the right direction, was the sundering, in one sense, of ties that were very dear.

I cannot ascertain when the first sermon was preached in the church after the war, but think it must have been in August, as there is this entry in the journal of my sister, Miss Stokes, already quoted from in a former part of this volume : "Sunday, August 27th, 1865.—Dr. Holmes preached in the Presbyterian church, which has been re-opened for divine service, being furnished with puncheon seats without backs. There are a few benches with backs. Next Sabbath, Dr. Wilson will administer the communion of the Lord's supper." This was done at the time appointed—the first communion held in the church after the war. (The Dr. Wilson referred to was the venerable Rev. John S. Wilson, D. D., who had organized the church forty years before.)

So far as is known, the only part of the former church furnishings that ever re-appeared was the melodeon (or "seraphine"), which Rosella Stone, a negro woman, had preserved. She must have done this for the sake of Miss Marian Stone, who had formerly played it in church, and who, if I remember aright, played it again after the resumption of church services.

In the winter of 1865 and 1866, there was preaching for a short while by the Rev. Theodore Smith. Then followed Rev. J. D. Burkhead, and under his preaching, in the early spring, there occurred a protracted meeting, at which many persons were added to the church.

Gladly would I recall, if I could, the preachers who supplied the Methodist church at that time, but my memory fails me as to the exact details. I believe, however, that the Rev. William Henry Clarke, referred to in a preceding sketch, was the first Methodist minister who preached there after the war; and that Rev. Mr. Morgan and Rev. William A. Dodge were the first ministers in charge appointed by Conference.

In ante-bellum times, on many of the large plantations, special services were held for the negroes—some planters paying a regular salary for this purpose. In pious families, members of the household often taught the slaves, especially the house servants, the Bible and Catechism. So far as I can recollect, certain seats were assigned to them in all churches at all services, besides the special services usually held for them on Sabbath afternoons.

After the war, the negroes of Decatur and surrounding country were organized into a Sabbath-school at the Presbyterian Church. They came in large numbers, and were faithfully taught by the people of Decatur. To the kind courtesy of Mr. George A. Ramspeck I am indebted for the loan of the Minute-book of this school, which seems to have been organized in 1867. The pastor was the Superintendent. The Vice-Superintendent was Mr. Samuel K. Winn, the Treasurer, Mr. George A. Ramspeck, and the Librarian, Mr. Moses S. Brown. But after several months the negroes went off to themselves, and eventually founded the African Methodist Episcopal Church. They have also a Baptist Church. In these undertakings they were assisted by the people of the village.

20

CHAPTER XXIX.

POSTAL AFFAIRS.

The Postmaster, Hiram J. Williams—A life that was a reality,
but reads like a romance.

The north side of the court-house square at Decatur is intersected by a public road leading to North
Decatur, Silver Lake, the Chattahoochee River, and
points beyond. On the eastern corner of this inter-
section stands the well-known Bradbury House. The
house itself is an unsightly object, being almost un-
tenable through age and neglect, but occupying a
most desirable location. From its site lovely views of
the surrounding country may be obtained, as the eye
sweeps the circle of the horizon which is bounded on
the north by distant hills, and on the northwest by
the blue peaks of the Kennesaw. In the west is a
near-by plateau, crowned with oaks and pines, beautiful in the morning when covered with a filmy mantle
of faint purple mist—gorgeous at evening, when over-
hung by sunset clouds.

In 1860 the lower part of the Bradbury House was
occupied as a store and postoffice, the proprietor and
postmaster being Mr. William Bradbury. His assistant was Hiram J. Williams, then a lad of fourteen
years. When Mr. Bradbury enlisted in the DeKalb
Light Infantry in 1861, Hiram became in reality the
postmaster. At that early age he manifested the
same traits which have characterized him to this day

—unwearied attention to the business before him, unvarying courtesy, beautiful modesty, calm unbroken serenity of manner, and an unswerving honesty.

During the four years of the war, the mail received and sent out from Decatur was enormous in its quantity, and all the while it was handled by this youth; for when, in 1862, Mr. Bradbury resigned and Mr. John N. Pate was appointed postmaster in his place, Hiram Williams was retained in the office, Mr. Pate simply bringing over the mail from the depot. So great was the quantity of mail matter that sometimes Hiram had to call to his assistance his young friend, John Bowie.

During those war years, there were but few post-offices in DeKalb County, and the people for miles around had their mail sent to Decatur. The soldiers, unless writing to young ladies, rarely ever paid postage on their letters, but left it to be done by their home folks. This unpaid postage had to be collected and kept account of. Often a poor wife or mother, after trudging weary miles to the postoffice, would receive a letter from husband or son and, unwilling to return without answering it, would request Hiram to answer it for her, which he always did. With every package of letters sent out, a way-bill had to go, showing the number of letters, how many were prepaid, how many unpaid, etc, etc. Imagine the work this entailed! Imagine the great responsibility! Imagine the youth who bore this labor and responsibility for four years! Small of stature, quiet in manner, but with an undaunted spirit looking out from his steady but softly bright brown eyes. How brave he must have been, and how his good widowed mother and only sister must have doted on him.

In July, 1864, when the booming of the Federal guns is heard from the banks of the Chattahoochee, the postoffice is closed and for several month thereafter letters, if sent for at all, are sent by hand.

Our brave little postmaster now hies him away to Augusta, and there acts as mailing clerk for " The Constitutionalist," and, after the surrender, for " The Evening Transcript." In 1866 he returns to Decatur and engages in mercantile business with Willard and McKoy, but soon after opens a store of his own.

Early in 1867, Mr. Williams, now arrived at the age of twenty-one, is appointed postmaster at Decatur by Samuel W. Randall, postmaster general of the United States Government. In 1869 Mr. Williams was elected clerk of the Superior Court of DeKalb County, still retaining the office of postmaster, but having an assistant in each position.

In 1871, he was re-elected clerk of the court, and again in 1873. All this time he continued to be postmaster, and was re-commissioned by Postmaster General Jewell in 1875, holding the office up to 1880.

Mr. Williams continued to be Clerk of the Superior Court until 1884, when Mr. Robert Russell, a Confederate veteran, was elected. Mr. Williams then returned for a while to mercantile pursuits. But while pursuing the even tenor of his way, was called to a responsible position in Atlanta (which he still holds) with the G. W. Scott Manufacturing Company, now known as the Southern Fertilizer Company.

From 1870 to 1886, Mr. Williams was a special

correspondent of "The Atlanta Constitution," thus preserving the history of Decatur and of DeKalb county during that period.

So much for a business career of remarkable success. But is this all? What of the higher and nobler life? This has not been neglected. In 1866 Mr. Williams united with the Decatur Presbyterian church. In 1868 he was appointed Librarian of the Sabbath school, an office he still holds. In 1894 he was elected to the office of Deacon, and also appointed church Treasurer. When the Agnes Scott Institute, for girls, was founded in 1891, he was made Secretary and Treasurer.

Mr. Williams has been twice married—in his early manhood to Miss Jennie Hughes, who lived but a short while. His present wife was Miss Belle Steward, who has been a true help-meet. They have a lovely and hospitable home on Sycamore street, where her sweet face, ever beaming with cheerfulness and loving kindness and sympathy for all, must be to him as a guiding star to lead and bless him with its light, as he returns at evening from the city and its business cares and toils, to the rest and peace of home.

If any one should say that this is not strictly a war sketch, I would reply, "no, but who could resist following up at least the salient points of such a life —a life that exemplifies the main elements of success." Dear young readers, have you not seen what they are: —perseverance, fidelity to trusts reposed, punctuality, courtesy, honesty and conscientiousness—in other words, adherence to right principles and to Christian duty.

CHAPTER XXX.

THE TRAGIC DEATH OF SALLIE DURHAM.

The closing days of the war.—A sketch of the Durham family
—The death of Sallie.

On the 9th of April, 1865, at Appomattox Court House, Lee had surrendered his army of twenty-five thousand men to Grant with his four-fold forces. One after another of the Confederate Generals had been forced to yield to superior numbers, and by the last of May the war was over.

"The North had at the beginning of the strife a population of twenty-two millions; the South had ten millions, four millions of whom were slaves. The North had enlisted during the war two million six hundred thousand troops—the South a little more than six hundred thousand. Now the North had a million men to send home—the South but one hundred and fifty thousand."

Jefferson Davis had been captured, and imprisoned in Fortress Monroe. Our worn and ragged soldiers had returned to a devastated country. Our entire people were to begin life over again in the midst of poverty, uncertainty, and under the watchful eye of the conqueror. The war was over, but military rule was not.

It was in these transition days, between the fall of "the Lost Cause" and the more stirring events of

"Reconstruction," that there occurred in our little village a most appalling tragedy. To understand it fully, my readers should know something of the young lady's family. Let us pause here and take a backward glance.

About a hundred years ago Lindsey Durham, a Georgia boy of English descent, graduated from a Philadelphia Medical College and located in Clarke county, in his native State. Drugs were expensive, as they could not be obtained nearer than Savannah, Charleston or New York. Being surrounded by frontiersmen and Indians, he could but notice the efficacy of the native barks and roots used by them as medicines. He was thus led to adopt to a large extent the theories of the Botanic School. He began to cultivate his own medicinal plants, and to prosecute with much zeal his botanical studies and researches. He even went to Europe and procured seeds and plants of medicinal value, until finally his garden of medicinal herbs and plants contained thirteen acres. So great was his fame that patients began to come to him from adjoining States, and he had to build cottages on his plantation in order to entertain them. His marvellous success brought to him ample compensation. He became a millionaire, and lived in all the old-time splendor. Once, by a loan of money, he rescued the Athens bank from utter failure.

Dr. Lindsey Durham left several sons, all of whom were physicians. The eldest of these, and the most eminent, was Dr. William W. Durham, who was born on his father's plantation in Clarke county, in 1823. After a collegiate course at Mercer University, he

graduated from the Jefferson Medical College of Philadelphia, taking high honors, spending five years in
the hospital there, and perfecting himself in surgery.
This talented gentleman married Miss Sarah Lowe, of
Clarke county, and, four years after her death, he
married Mrs. Georgia A. Allen, whose maiden name
was Wood, and who was a native of Franklin, Georgia.

With the children of his first marriage and their
fair young step-mother, Dr. Durham came to Decatur
in 1859. Well do I remember the children; two handsome sons, John and William—two pretty brown-eyed
girls, Sarah and Catherine. It is needless to say that
a large practice awaited the skillful physician, whose
eclectic methods were then comparatively new.

William, the eldest son, went into the Confederate
service at the age of sixteen, remaining the entire four
years, suffering severely at the siege of Vicksburg,
fighting valiantly at the Battle of Atlanta, and coming
out of the war the shadow of his former self, with
nothing but an old army mule and one silver dollar.

Sarah Durham, called Sallie by her family and
friends, was a lovely girl of seventeen. She was tall
and graceful; bright, and full of enthusiasm; kind,
loving and generous. She had just returned from her
grandmother's plantation, for her father had not
sooner dared to have his daughters return, such was
the insolence of the straggling Federals.

On the morning of September 1st, 1865, this dear girl
arose early and noiselessly with a scheme in her kind
heart. The former servants were all gone; her mother
was not well, and she would surprise the household

by preparing for them a nice breakfast. In fancy we see her, as she treads lightly, and chats softly with her tiny half-sister Jennie, and with a little negro girl who in some way had remained with the family.

The Durham residence, which was on Sycamore street, then stood just eastward of where Col. G. W. Scott now lives. The rear of the house faced the site where the depot had been before it was burned by the Federals, the distance being about 350 yards. Hearing an incoming train, Sallie went to the dining room window to look at the cars, as she had learned in some way that they contained Federal troops. While standing at the window resting against the sash, she was struck by a bullet fired from the train. (It was afterwards learned that the cars were filled with negro troops on their way to Savannah, who were firing off their guns in a random, reckless manner.) The ball entered the left breast of this dear young girl, ranging obliquely downward, coming out just below the waist, and lodging in the door of a safe, or cupboard, which stood on the opposite side of the room. (This old safe, with the mark of the ball, is still in the village.)

The wounded girl fell, striking her head against the dining table, but arose, and walking up a long hall she threw open the door of her father's room, calling to him in a voice of distress. Springing from bed, he said:

"What is it, my child?"

"Oh, father," she exclaimed, "the Yankees have killed me!"

Laying her upon a small bed in the room, her father cut away from her chest her homespun dress and made a hasty examination of the wound. Her horror-stricken mother remembers to this day that awful scene in all its details. But we will draw a veil over the grief of the smitten family, as they stood half paralyzed at this sudden calamity, and looked upon the loved one whom they were helpless to save. Mrs. Durham recalls the fact that the first person who came in was Rev. Dr. Holmes, and that throughout this great trial he and his family were very sympathetic and helpful.

Every physician in the village and city, and her father's three brothers were summoned, but nothing could be done except to alleviate her sufferings. She could lie only on her right side, with her left arm in a sling suspended from the ceiling. Every attention was given by relatives and friends. Her grandmother Durham came and brought with her the old family trained nurse. Sallie's schoolmates and friends were untiring in their attentions. Some names that have appeared in previous sketches, will now appear again, for they watched with anxious, loving hearts by the couch where the young sufferer lay. Tenderly let us mention their names, as we tread softly in memory's sacred halls. Among the constant attendants at her bedside were Mrs. Martha Morgan, Mrs. Hughes, Mrs. Morton, Miss Laura Williams (Mrs. J. J. McKoy), Lizzie and Anna Morton, Mrs. H. H. Chivers, Dr. Jim Brown and John Hardeman. During the week that her life slowly ebbed away, there was another who ever lingered near her, a sleepless and tireless watcher, a young man of a well-known family, to whom this sweet young girl was engaged to be married.

Writes Mrs. P. W. Corr, of Hampton, Florida, (formerly Miss Lizzie Morton): "Never can I forget the dreary night when Willie Durham, Kitty Durham and Warren Morton left Decatur with Sallie's body, which was to be buried in the old family cemetery in Clarke county. Mrs. Durham, who was in delicate health, was utterly prostrated and the doctor could not leave her." So Dr. Charles Durham managed the funeral arrangements, chartering the car, and Sallie was buried from the old church her grandfather Lowe had built on his own plantation in Clarke county, and laid to rest in the Durham cemetery near by.

Sallie was shot on Friday at 7:30 A. M., and died the following Friday at 3:30 A. M. While she had suffered untold agony, she was conscious to the last. Throughout her illness she manifested a thoughtful consideration for the comfort of others. Especially did she show tender solicitude for her step-mother, insisting that she should not fatigue herself. While anxious to live, she said she was not afraid to die. In her closing hours she told her friends that she saw her own mother, her grandfather Durham, and her uncle Henry Durham (who had died in the Confederate service), all of whom she expected to meet in the bright beyond.

General Stephenson was in command of the Federal Post at Atlanta. He was notified of this tragedy, and sent an officer to investigate. This officer refused to take anybody's word that Sallie had been shot by a United States soldier from the train; but, dressed in full uniform, with spur and sabre rattling upon the bare floor, he advanced to the bed where the dying girl lay, and threw back the covering "to see if she had really been shot." This intrusion almost threw her into a spasm. This officer and the others at Atlanta promised to do all in their power to bring the guilty party to justice, but nothing ever came of the promise, so far as we know.

As a singular coincidence, as well as an illustration of the lovely character of Sallie, I will relate a brief incident given by the gifted pen already quoted from : "One of the most vivid pictures of the past in my memory is that of Sallie Durham emptying her pail of blackberries into the hands of Federal prisoners on a train that had just stopped for a moment at Decatur, in 1863. We had all been gathering berries at Moss's Hill, and stopped on our way home for the train to pass."

Dr. W. W. Durham lived for nearly twenty years after Sallie's death. During the war he had enlisted as a soldier, but was commissioned by Dr. George S. Blackie, a Medical Director in the Western Division of the Confederate Army, to the position of Inspector of Medicines for the Fifth Depot. This position was given him because of his remarkable botanical knowledge and power of identifying medicines. After the war he was prominent in the reorganization of the Georgia Medical Eclectic College, but refused to take a professorship on account of an almost overwhelming practice. He was a quiet, earnest, thoughtful man ; and highly sympathetic and benevolent in his disposition. His widow, Mrs. Georgia A. Durham, and their daughter, Mrs. Jennie Findley, still reside in Decatur.

Dr. W. M. Durham is a successful physician in Atlanta. He holds a professorship in the Georgia Eclectic Medical College, and edits the Georgia Eclectic Medical Journal. Kitty is Mrs. W. P. Smith, of Maxey's ; and John L. Durham is a physician with a large practice, and a large family, living at Woodville, Georgia.

The Durham residence still stands in Decatur, though not upon the same spot. For years a great stain of blood remained upon the floor, as a grim and silent reminder of this most awful tragedy which so closely followed the horrible and cruel war.

CHAPTER XXXI.

THE DEATH OF MELVILLE CLARK.

The lamented death of Miss Durham was not the only one in our community to be traced to the results of the war.

The period of reconstruction, forcing upon the Southern states the obnoxious Fourteenth Amendment, so humiliating and so unjust, especially at that time, had intensified the prejudices of the negroes against the white people—prejudices already sufficiently aroused by previous abolition teachings and the results of the war.

Several times in this little volume mention has been made of Rev. William Henry Clarke, the staunch patriot and well known Methodist preacher. At this period he had become a resident of Decatur. His son, Melville Clarke, a noble, promising boy, while attempting to rescue a small white child from the abuse of an overgrown negro youth, received wounds from which he died. Memory recalls many other instances of like character, perpetrated at this period, the most disgraceful in the annals of American history.

The subjoined resolutions, passed by the Methodist Sabbath school of which Melville was a beloved scholar, attest the many good traits of his character, and the affection accorded him in the community :

" The committee appointed to draft resolutions on

the death of Melville Clarke, one of our scholars, beg
leave to submit the following:

"In the wise dispensation of Him that doeth all
things well, we are called to pay the last tribute to
departed worth. Melville Clark is no more. The vacant seat says he is no more. The hushed voice says
he is no more. Yes, the impressive, solemn silence of
this moment whispers that another light which shone
brightly the brief space allotted it here has flickered
out. The body which encased the spirit of the noble
Christian boy has been laid away in the silence of the
grave, and his spirit, as we trust, escorted by a con-
voy of angels, has gone to that bright and better
world above.

"*Therefore, Resolved,* That as we gather around the
new-made grave and drop a sympathetic tear (which
speaks more eloquently than any words mortal lips
can utter), we deeply feel the loss of one so full of
promise and usefulness—that noble spirit just burst-
ing into manhood, with a mind that would grasp in a
moment things that men have passed through life and
never comprehended—and a heart lit up with the love
of God, and drawn out by the tenderest cords of affection to do little acts of kindness. Language fails us
to give utterance to the anguish we feel at sustaining
so great a loss. But he has gone. No more shall we
hang upon the eloquence of his gentle, kind words, or
see that face which was so often lit up with an expressive sweetness that we could but recognize as the
reflex of the lamb-like Christian spirit that reigned
within. He has gone, and as we turn from the sad,
solemn scene in that faith which 'hopeth all things,

believeth all things, endureth all things,' we can but exclaim : 'The Lord gave—the Lord hath taken away—blessed be the name of the Lord !'

"*Resolved*, That in the death of one of our members, so young, we recognize an admonition that the young, as well as the old, are swiftly passing away, and that we should pause and reflect seriously upon this important subject.

"*Resolved*, That as a school, our warmest sympathy and condolence be tendered to the family of our dear deceased friend in this, their great bereavement, and that a copy of these resolutions be furnished them."

DR. AVERY,
JOHN N. PATE,
CAPTAIN RANDALL, } Committee
J. R. HAMPTON,

August 30th, 1868.

CHAPTER XXXII.

THE MORTON FAMILY.

Incidents thrilling and affecting.

In several previous sketches references have been made to the Misses Morton. Not only they, but the whole family, bore an interesting and heroic part in the scenes of the war. Mr. Edward L. Morton hoisted the first Confederate flag that ever floated on the breeze in DeKalb county. This he did as soon as he heard that Georgia had passed the ordinance of secession. A few miles from Decatur there was a large mill known as Williams's Mill, situated on Peachtree Creek. At the terminus of the bridge that spanned the creek, near the little hamlet, there grew a tall, graceful Lombardy poplar tree. The flag had been made by Mrs. Morton, Mrs. James Hunter, and other ladies who lived in the neighborhood, and was hoisted by Mr. Morton from the top of the lofty poplar. When the Federals came in they cut down the tree, but another has grown from its roots.

Mr. Morton enlisted with the first company that went from DeKalb, but returned and organized one of his own—Company F, 36th Georgia. From this command he was sent home on account of lung trouble, and placed on special duty. When Hood fell back to Atlanta, Captain Morton joined White's Scouts, a picked band of men. He was also at one time Morgan's guide.

21

After Mr. J. W. Kirkpatrick refugeed, his home on Atlanta street was occupied by Captain Morton's family. Here some stirring incidents occurred. Says one of his daughters: "Pa tried to avoid coming within the Yankee lines, but did several times get caught at home, owing to his extreme weakness. Finally, after the 23d Army Corps was sent back to Tennessee, a raiding party of Federals went out toward Stone Mountain, were fired on a few miles from Decatur, and several killed. They were furious when they got to our house (on their return). Here they found one of 'White's Men' (Pa) ill in bed. They held a court-martial and sentenced him to be hanged as soon as they finished eating dinner. Meanwhile they left a guard in his bed-room. Ma asked the guard to sit in the parlor and leave them alone the short time he had to live. The guard was a kind-hearted man, the house surrounded, the whole detachment eating and feeding their horses on all sides, and Pa was very feeble; so the guard sat in the parlor." Captain Morton then disguised himself, armed himself, and, passing out a side door, went unchallenged through the crowd of soldiers, by Woodall's tan-yard and out into the woods. Continues his daughter: "But when the guard thought he had better see the prisoner, it was discovered that he was gone. They talked of burning the house and made many other threats. For a long time we did not know whether he had escaped or died in the woods. * * * No man that served in the Confederate army more truly laid down his life for the cause than did my father. He never recovered from the lung trouble brought on and aggravated by the exposure and hardships he endured between '61 and '65.''

Warren Morton went into the army at the tender age of fifteen, as a private in his father's company. He was in the siege of Vicksburg—was paroled, and re-entered the army in Cumming's Brigade—and was shot at Kennesaw, near Marietta, while acting as Sergeant-Major on Hood's retreat. The ball struck the bone of the outer angle of the left eye, cutting away the temple plate, and came out just over the ear, cutting off the upper half of the ear. The torn nerves and arteries have always caused him pain. The bullet, while it did not touch his eye-ball, paralyzed the optic nerve on that side. The hardships endured when a growing boy, the long marches in Kentucky, the starvation rations in Vicksburg, and the horrible wound, ruined his constitution. Yet he has been an energetic man, and is living now on a farm near Newnan.

The young ladies—girls they all were at the time of which I write—were Lizzie, Anna, Kelly, Fannie and Eddie.

On the day that Wheeler's Cavalry routed the Federal wagon train at Decatur, Lieutenant Farrar of the 63d Ohio Regiment was killed on a meadow near Mrs. Swanton's residence, just opposite Mrs. Morton's. There was also another Federal, a mere lad, who was mortally wounded. In some way I discovered the dying boy, and, after carrying him some water, I left him to the care of the nearer neighbors. Mrs. James Hunter, Mrs. Morton and her daughters cared for him as best they could, and sat by him until he died.

Miss Lizzie Morton cut from his head a lock of hair and wrote some verses, which Mrs. Swanton kindly sent to his people in Dayton, Ohio. In some way this became known to the Federal officers, and future developments showed that this tender act was much appreciated by them.

On the morning of the 22nd of July, 1864, Mrs. Morton sat on the front steps watching for an officer to whom she might appeal for protection. "Very early General McPherson and his staff rode by. Mrs. Morton ran out and called. General McPherson alighted from his horse, heard her story, bare-headed, with his hat in hand, wrote an order and dispatched it, and then mounting, rode away to his death." That order was to station a guard at the house, and it was never disregarded as long as the Federal line was near. This the family have always attributed to their caring for the dead, and to the kind order of General McPherson.

On the night of the 21st, Mrs. Morton had been badly frightened by some Federal soldiers coming to her house with the accusation that her young daughter "had given information that had led to the capture of their wagon train." Threats of burning the residence were made by the Federals on several occasions. The family feel persuaded that Bill Pittman, a faithful negro, a sawyer who had lived many years at Williams's Mill, prevented these threats from being put into execution.

Soon after the close of the war Captain Morton and his family went to Mississippi. Here he died, and one after another four of the girls, Anna, Kelly,

Fanny, and Eddie. Most touchingly Lizzie (Mrs. P. W. Corr) writes : "When my sister and I were little girls in Decatur, we were very fond of private literary entertainments. Anna's favorite declamation (which always brought down the house) was:

> 'They grew in beauty side by side
> Around one parent knee ;
> Their graves are scattered far and wide
> O'er mountain, plain, and sea.'

"Anna sleeps alone near an old church in Scott county, Mississippi ; Kelly, alone at Pickens ; Pa, Fanny and Eddie side by side at Shiloh, in Holmes county." Anna married Mr. Kearney ; Kelly, Mr. W. S. Cole. Mrs. Morton is still living in the home of her daughter Lizzie, who married Rev. P. W. Corr, of Hampton, Florida. Mrs. Corr is very happily married, being fond and proud of her husband, and her children filling her heart with comfort and pleasure. To crown her earthly blessings, her mother has been spared to her in all life's changing scenes.

Here in her happy Florida home we leave our erstwhile lassie of the war times—now an earnest wife and mother, busy ever with home duties, and also a true helpmeet to her husband in his ministerial and editorial labors.

This sketch, with its incidents, both heroic and pathetic, cannot be more appropriately concluded than by the touching words of Mrs. Corr in a recent letter : "What you say of the 'empty places' is full of suggestiveness. I think I never could have borne my losses and still have moved about among the 'empty

places.' But going always among strangers after
every loss, being removed at once from the scene of
death and not passing that way again, my sisters live
in memory as part of the past, always merry, happy
girls, never to grow heart-weary, never to fade. We,
wandering among strangers in strange and unfamiliar
scenes, have kept the memory of our old Decatur
home and friends intact. There are no empty places
there for us.

"It seems sweet to me to think that in that home
to which we are all traveling, we shall find that those
dear ones who have preceded us have carried with
them that same bright and precious picture, which,
however, is not there a picture of memory, but a reality of which the earthly circle was only a shadow or
prophecy ; and the only empty places there are those
which shall be filled when we get home. Something
there is in the friendships, even, of other days, that
has never died—something that will live again—a
root planted here that there blossoms and fruits eter-
nally. How much more true is this—it must be so—
of those who were heart of our hearts, our own loved
ones. I doubt not that for one sad longing thought
of 'brother, mother, nephew,' all that you have loved
and lost, they have had many sweet and loving
thoughts of you, and joyful anticipations of your coming home 'Some Sweet Day.'"

CHAPTER XXXIII.

HON. JOSEPH E. BROWN'S PIKES AND GUNS.

(This chapter, and the succeeding one, were not placed in the chronological order of events, because they would have broken the continuity of personal experiences).

After an appeal to physical force, as the only means of redressing our wrongs, was fully determined upon, we made many important discoveries, chief of which was that we were not prepared for war. This fact had often been impressively and earnestly set forth by our greatest statesmen, Alexander Hamilton Stephens and Benjamin Harvey Hill, who, though reared in different schools of politics, were fully agreed upon this point, and who urged, with all the eloquence of patriotism and profound understanding of existing facts, the importance of delaying the act of seceding from the United States until we were better prepared for the mighty consequences—either beneficial or disastrous. In no way was the wisdom of this advice made more apparent than by our utter want of the appliances of warfare on land and on sea.

The ordinance of secession having been enacted, Georgia found itself confronted by the scarcity of guns and other munitions of warfare. Hon. Joseph E. Brown, our war Governor, finding it impossible to secure even shot-guns to equip the many regiments eager for the fray, conceived the idea of arming them with pikes; and, undaunted by the Herculean undertaking, put a large force of the best blacksmiths at the W. & A. R. R. shops to making these primitive weapons. To whose fertile brain belongs the honor of evolving the plan or diagram by which they were to be made, has never been revealed to the writer. The blade of the pike was to be about 16 inches long and 2 inches wide, with a spur of about 3 inches on either side, all of which was to be ground to a sharp edge. The shank was to be about 12 inches long, and arranged to rivet in a staff 6 feet long.

In the memorable year, 1861, J. C. Peck owned a planing mill and general wood-working shop on Decatur street, Atlanta, Ga., on the grounds now occupied by the Southern (old Richmond and Danville) R. R. freight depot. There being no machinery at the railroad shops suitable for turning the handles nor grinding the pikes, Mr. Peck contracted to grind and supply with handles the entire number—he thinks ten thousand. Before he finished this work, Governor Brown called a meeting of the mechanics of Atlanta for the purpose of ascertaining if some arrangement could be made for the manufacture of guns for the army. This meeting was adjourned two or three times, and no one seemed willing to undertake the job. At the last meeting a letter was received from the Ordnance Department of the Confederate States, containing a "drawing" of a short heavy rifle to be supplied with a Tripod rest, and an urgent request that the Governor would encourage the making of twenty-five guns after this pattern, as soon as possible. A liberal premium for the sample was offered by the Confederate Ordnance Department. The barrels were to be thirty inches long with one inch bore, and rifled with three grooves, so as to make one complete revolution in the thirty inches. As no one else would undertake this complicated job, Mr. Peck asked for the "drawing," and announced his willingness to do so. He discovered that it would require iron ¾ by 4½ or 5 inches to make the barrels, and for this purpose he procured enough Swede iron at a hardware store on Whitehall street to make thirty barrels. He also discovered that the common Smith bellows would not yield a blast sufficient to secure welding heat on so large a piece, and it was suggested that it could be done at W. & A. R. R. shops; he therefore secured an order from Governor Brown authorizing this important work to be done there under his instruction. An old German smith, whom Mr. Peck found at the shops, rendered him valuable aid in the accomplishment of this portion of the work. As rapidly as the welding was done he had them carried to his shop, and a wood-turner, Mr. W. L. Smith, bored them on a wood turning lath. This was a difficult job, as the boring bits caught in the irregular hole and broke ; finally he devised a sort of rose bit which steadied itself, and he had no further trouble. After successfully accomplishing this portion of the work, Mr. Peck found himself confronted by another difficulty. He had no way of turning iron, but his indomitable will shrank not from the task, and he threw out a search-light which enabled him to discern a Savage, who had been superintendent of Pitts & Cook's gin factory, and he

engaged him to turn it. Mr. Peck then employed an
ingenious blacksmith, who did to his satisfaction all
the smith work he wanted. He made his own taps
and dies for fitting the breech pieces, putting in the
nipples, etc., and forged the hammers, triggers, ram-
rods, etc. The brass mountings were cast by Gullatte
Brothers, who at that time were running a brass
foundry. The locks were purchased by Mr. Peck in
Macon, but, as already intimated, had to be supplied
with new hammers and triggers. As the plan called
for the barrels to be rifled with three grooves, and to
make one complete revolution in the length of the
barrel, there was none in the employ of Mr. Peck who
had any idea how it was to be done. Much perplexed
he went to Mr. Charles Heinz, the gunsmith on
Whitehall street, who explained the process of rifling
done by hand. On this idea Mr. Peck constructed
a machine which he attached to a Daniels planer.
This was a wood machine, with a bed which traveled
backward and forward, similar to the bed of an iron
planer—in such a manner that the backward and forward motion of the bed gave, also, a rotary motion to
the cutters. By this process each barrel was rifled
precisely alike. Mr. Peck had thirty barrels forged,
but some of them were defective and would not bore
through without breaking, and some were burnt in
testing. Only twenty-five of them were finished. He
had an abundance of walnut lumber and did not have
to contend with any obstacle in making the stocks, but
some in clamping them to the barrels. The plan also
showed the usual screw in the extension of the breech
pin, and two bands similar to those on the old style

musket. Mr. Peck forged iron bands, but with his best effort at finishing them they appeared clumsy. Opportunely he chanced to see a wagon on Pryor street containing a lot of hardware and other things, among which was a large brass kettle. Thinking he could make bands out of this vessel, he purchased it and cut it up into those indispensable parts of his famous job, but another obstacle to success presented itself to his patient vision. He could find no one to braze the joints. By reference to his "Mechanic's Companion" he learned the art, and brazed the bands in a skillful style. This being done, he gave his finishing touches to the rifles.

The balls were like minie-balls, one inch in diameter, and two and one-fourth inches long, and weighed four ounces. Mr. Peck made only one set of bullet moulds, which run two bullets at the same time, and he thinks he made only six of the tripod rests. They were—every lock, stock and barrel—tested by several persons expert in the handling of muskets, rifles, shotguns, etc., among whom was Mr. Charles Heinz, still living in Atlanta, and who will vouch for the accuracy of this important item of Confederate history, and the utility of the shot emanating from these wonderful guns. To put it mildly, the effect was almost equal to that of a six-pounder. And the recoil! Well! Wonderful to relate! They must have had infused into their mechanism supernatural or national prescience, and peering through the dim vista of the future saw the beacon light of a re-united country, and disdained partiality in the Fratricidal Contest, for every time one of them was shot at a " Yankee," it kicked a " Rebel " down.

P.S.—Mr. Peck has the original "drawing" sent on from the Ordnance Department at Richmond, and also the receipt for the payment for the barrels. He also has a letter from the Chief of Ordnance at Washington, D. C., informing him that the identical guns described in the above sketch had been found in his department, and that two of them would be exhibited in the Government Building of the Piedmont Exposition, Atlanta, Georgia, in 1895.

CHAPTER XXXIV.

THE PURSUIT AND CAPTURE OF THE ANDREWS RAIDERS.

Captain William A. Fuller and his comrades of the pursuit.—
The race of the engines, "The General" and "The Texas."

In the early part of 1862 the army of the Cumberland and also that of the Tennessee had grown to gigantic proportions. The history of that memorable era establishes the fact that in the month of February of that year the army of the Cumberland, commanded by General Buell, had captured Fort Donaldson and several other strong strategic points on the Tennessee and Mississippi Rivers. Numerically the Federal Army was so much stronger than the Confederate that large detachments could easily be made for incursions into the interior and unprotected sections of middle and West Tennessee, while the main army steadily advanced down the Mississippi Valley. By the first of April, General Mitchell had occupied Shelbyville and other cities, including Nashville ; and the larger towns and railroad stations in the neighborhood South and East of Nashville had been occupied by the Federals.

Recognizing the importance of saving to the Confederate cause everything necessary to sustain life both of man and beast, all that could be brought out of Kentucky and Tennessee had been sent South—to

Atlanta and other important points—so that those States were literally stripped of all surplus food.

The army of the Tennessee, under the command of General Albert Sidney Johnston, sought to meet General Buell and dispute his further advance. Corinth, Mississippi, was selected by General Johnston as a point beyond which the army of the Cumberland should not go. This position commanded the Memphis and Charleston Railroad, as well as others running south of that point. By the fifth of April General Buell's army had massed at Pittsburg Landing, and along a line reaching south and parallel to that of General Johnston. Relatively the armies stood about five to eight, the Confederate of course being the smaller. They met in battle on the 6th day of April at Shiloh, so-called by the Federals, but Southern historians call it the battle of Corinth. The fight was a long and disastrous one—disastrous to both armies—but the Federals, having an unbounded supply of everything needed in war, and being immediately strengthened by large reinforcements which literally poured in, were enabled to rapidly recuperate. The Confederates lost heavily in killed and wounded, and suffered irreparably by the death of General Albert Sidney Johnston. The loss of this noble man was deeply felt and regretted by the entire South. The week following this horrible carnage was mainly taken up by both armies in burying the dead, caring for the wounded, fortifying, receiving reinforcements and maneuvering for advantageous positions.

General Mitchell, as already stated, had occupied Shelbyville, and had a considerable force. Some

cavalry had penetrated as far south-east as Chattanooga, and had several times dropped a few shell into
that town.

After the death of General Johnston the Confederate
Army at Corinth was put under the command of
General Beauregard. There were small detachments
of Confederate troops distributed along the Memphis
and Charleston Railroad to Stephenson, and from
there to Chattanooga ; also from Chattanooga to
Bristol, on the East Tennessee and Georgia Railroad,
and on the Virginia and Tennessee. These were
to guard the railroad bridges, depots, and government
stores, etc. General Ledbetter was stationed at Chattanooga with about three thousand men. There was
a tolerably strong guard at London bridge, where the
East Tennessee railroad crosses the Tennessee river ;
and General E. Kirby Smith occupied Knoxville, with
a sufficient force to protect that important point as
against General Morgan in his immediate front with
a strong force. East Tennessee was very nearly
evenly divided between Federals and Confederate
sympathizers. Neither side was safe from betrayal.
Those who were true to the Southern cause distinguished themselves as officials and soldiers, and those
who were recreant to it were a source of great annoyance and disaster ; and this applies to Kentucky and
West Virginia as well. During the month of April,
1862, Brownlow, and those of his opinion, were
arrested, and imprisoned in Knoxville.

The strict rules of the passport system had not yet
been adopted by southern army commanders, and it was
no difficult matter for friend or foe to pass the lines.

Thus matters stood at that time. The reader, therefore, may be prepared to appreciate one of the most exciting, thrilling and interesting stories of the Civil Contest.

The Western and Atlantic Railroad (often called the State Road) at the time discussed in the preceding pages, was the only line of communication between the southern centre of the Confederate States and the Army of Tennessee. It was worthy of notice that this road was not paralleled by any of the roads now in existence. The Memphis and Charleston Railroad came into the Nashville and Chattanooga at Stevenson as now, and the latter road reached from Nashville to Chattanooga. The East Tennessee and Georgia Road also came into Chattanooga then as now, and also into Dalton. These three railroad lines were "the feeders" for the Western and Atlantic Railroad at Chattanooga and Dalton. At the south or Atlanta end of that line we had the old Macon & Western (now the Georgia Central), the Atlanta and West Point, and the Georgia Railroad, as feeders for the Western and Atlantic, which reached from Atlanta via Dalton to Chattanooga. As has been stated, the Army of Tennessee, under General Beauregard at Corinth, the army under General E. Kirby Smith at Knoxville, the army under General Ledbetter at Chattanooga, and all detailed men on duty along the whole front of the Confederates from Corinth to Bristol, depended upon this single line (the old reliable Western and Atlantic Railroad) for army supplies. There was no other road in the whole distance of eight hundred miles, reaching from Mobile, Alabama, to Rich-

mond, Virginia, that ran north and south. These facts
were well known to northern commanders, and it has
always seemed strange that the road should have been
so unprotected. The many bridges on the Western
and Atlantic were guarded at the time under consideration, April 1862, by a single watchman at each
bridge, and he was employed by the railroad authorities. The bridges were of the Howe Tress pattern, weatherboarded with common wooden boards,
and covered with shingles. They were exceedingly
inflammable and could easily have been set on fire.

One of the rules for the running of the trains was
that "if any two trains failed to make the meeting
point they would be considered irregular trains, and
the conductor of each train should be required to send
a flagman ahead, and thus proceed until the two flag-
men met." This cumbersome rule frequently occasioned great disorder, and sometimes many trains of
all grades were massed together at one station.
Railroad men will understand this condition of affairs.
These things were known and understood not only by
the Confederates, but by the Federals through their
spies. J. J. Andrews especially understood them, as
the sequel will prove.

It is beyond the scope of this article to discuss the
plans adopted by Captain J. J. Andrews and his
twenty-two auxiliaries, to descend into the heart of
the South; suffice it to say, their plans were successful, and they passed the Confederate lines and entered
the pretty town of Marietta, twenty miles north of
Atlanta, unmolested and unsuspected. The solving
of the mystery will appear at the proper time. For

22

present purposes it is enough to state that they not only entered the town mentioned, but boarded the north-bound train on the morning of April 12th, 1862. The well-known and intrepid Captain William A. Fuller was the conductor in charge of that train—the now celebrated "General" was his engine—and Jeff Cain his engineer. There was nothing suspicious in the environments of the occasion. In those days it was not unusual, even in a country town, for a large number of men to board a train, and they were coming in from all over the country to join the Confederate army.

There was a Camp of Instruction at Big Shanty, seven miles north of Marietta, and this fact, as well as many others more important, was known to Andrews, who from the beginning of the war had been "a commercial traveller," "in full sympathy with the South," and had ridden over this line many times. The conductor, therefore, took up the tickets as usual, some to one point and some to another, but the most of them to Big Shanty. The raiders were dressed in various styles and appeared like a good class of countrymen. They claimed to be "refugees from beyond the Lincoln lines."

Big Shanty was a mere station, having only one or two business houses, and noted by the traveling public as having a most excellent "eating-house" for the accommodation of the passenger trains. When Captain Fuller's train arrived at Big Shanty, the passengers and train hands went into the hotel for breakfast. The absence from the table of the large crowd that got on the train at Marietta was noticed by the con-

ductor, and just as he took his seat, which commanded
a view of his train, the gong on the old " General "
rang. It should be stated here that the train was as
follows : "The general," three freight cars, one second and two first-class coaches, a baggage car and
express car. Andrews had detached the entire passenger train, put his surplus men into the three
freight cars, and on " The General " he had with himself his own engineer and fireman.

The very moment the gong rang Captain Fuller
sprang from the table, and with a swift run reached
the main track and pursued the flying train, which
was now fast disappearing around a curve in the road.
As he ran out of the hotel Captain Fuller called to his
engineer, Jeff Cain : "Some one who has no right to
do so has taken our train !" Cain and Mr. Anthony
Murphy joined in the race, but were soon distanced
by the fleet-footed Fuller. The limestone soil between
the tracks was wet and clung to his feet so that fast
running was very fatiguing to Captain Fuller, but he
ran with a determination that overcame all obsta-
cles. Moon's Station, a little more than two miles
from Big Shanty, was reached by him in an incredibly short time. Here he found that the Andrews
raiders had stopped and had taken all of the tools from
the railroad section hands. They had climbed the
telegraph poles, cut the wire, and carried a hundred
feet of it along with them to prevent the repair of the
line in time to thwart their plans. The track hands
were amazed at their conduct, and hurriedly told Captain Fuller what had been done. Up to this time he
had been in doubt as to the true character of the

raiders. He had thought that possibly some of the
Confederates at Camp McDonald, (the Camp of
Instruction at Big Shanty), tired of strict discipline
and confinement, might have taken the train in order
to enable them to pass the environment of their camp.
But from this moment there was no room for doubt.
As quickly as possible Captain Fuller and two track
hands placed upon the rails an old timber car used for
hauling crossties, iron, and other heavy material.
This was an unwieldy and cumbersome medium of
locomotion, but it rendered good service, nevertheless.
Captain Fuller knew that every moment of time was
most valuable, as the raiders were speeding along up
the road and his chances for overtaking and capturing them were very doubtful. While putting on the
hand-car he debated with himself these questions :
" Should he proceed immediately in the pursuit, or
would it be best to push back and get his engineer ?"
He decided to push back for Cain, and when he had
gone nearly a mile he met Cain and Mr. Anthony
Murphy. They were taken on the hand-car and the
pursuit of the raiders, now far ahead, was begun
again. Captain Fuller says that if he had not gone
back, as above stated, he would have captured the
raiders at Kingston, as more than twenty minutes
were lost, and he was quite that close to them at
Kingston. He says, however, he is now glad he did
not do so, as the run from that point furnished the
most thrilling event of his life.

Murphy, Cain, the two track hands, and Fuller,
pushed and ran, and ran and pushed, alternately, and
each and every man on the old hand-car did his full

duty. Soon after passing Moon's Station, where
Captain Fuller got the hand-car, the pursuers came
upon a pile of cross-ties, but they were soon removed
from the track and the race resumed.

The intelligent reader will not for a moment suppose that Captain Fuller and his comrades entertained
any hope of overtaking the raiders on foot, or even by
the hand-car. Captain Fuller's thoughts ran ahead
of his surroundings, and he disclosed his plans to his
comrades in these words : "If we can get to Etowah
by 9:40, we will catch the old Yonah. This we can
do by very hard work, unless hindered by obstructions." This suggestion doubled the energy of every
man, and they abandoned themselves to the task before them. It is difficult to write, with deliberation,
a story so full of push and haste. This run of twenty
miles with an old clumsy hand-car, under so many
difficulties, is replete with interest. At length, after
Captain Fuller and his comrades were thoroughly exhausted, standing on the turn-table at Etowah more
than a mile away, "the old Yonah " was espied. A
yell and cry of great joy went up from these gallant
men ; but, alas, their vision had extended beyond
their immediate danger ! The raiders had removed
an outside rail in a short curve, and unexpectedly the
whole party was thrown into a ditch full of water.
This, however, was a small matter to men of resolute
will and iron nerve. The car was soon carried across
the break in the track and put upon the run again.
One of the track hands was left to watch this break,
to prevent danger to following trains—the other was
left with the hand-car at Etowah. Although the old

Yonah was standing on the turn-table at Etowah,
her tender was on another track.   Willing and eager
hands soon had the engine and tender coupled together, and the Yonah was "pressed into service."
An empty coal car was taken on, and a few Confederate soldiers, who were at the station waiting for a
south-bound train, volunteered to join in the chase.
The engineer of the Yonah, Mr. Marion Hilly, and
his own hands, ran the Yonah from Etowah to Kingston, and Captain Fuller gives them great credit for
their loyalty and faithful service.

A more dangerous run was never made. The track
was in a bad condition, and the line quite crooked; and
the pursuers could not tell at what moment they
might be thrown into a ditch by a removal of rails, or
obstructions placed upon the track; but they were absolutely blind to all personal danger or considerations.
The Yonah had only two drivers and they were six
feet, and she had a very short strike. She was built for
fast running with a small passenger train on an easy
grade.   Under all the difficulties by which he was surrounded, Hilly ran the Yonah from Etowah to Kingston, thirteen miles in fourteen minutes, and came to a
full stop at Cartersvile, and also at Kingston. Several
crossties had been put upon the track, but the pursuers
said "they were literally blown away as the Yonah
split the wind."

At Kingston, Captain Fuller learned that he was
only twenty minutes behind the raiders. At this point,
Andrews had represented himself as a Confederate officer.   He told the railroad agent that he "passed
Fuller's train at Atlanta, and that the cars which he

had contained fixed ammunition for General Beauregard at Corinth." He carried a red flag on "The General," and said that "Fuller's train was behind with the regular passenger train."

This plausible story induced the agent to give him his keys to unlock the switch at the north end of the Kingston railroad yard. Several heavy freight trains were at Kingston, bound southward. Those furthest behind reached a mile or so north of the switch on the main line. Owing to Andrews's "fixed ammunition" story, the agent, being a patriotic man, ordered all trains to pull by, so as to let Andrews out at the north end of the yard. This was done as quickly as possible, though it was difficult to make the railroad men understand why the great haste, and why Andrews should be let pass at so much trouble when Fuller's train would soon be along, and both could be passed at the same time. But Andrews's business was so urgent, and so vitally important, as a renewal of the fight between Beauregard and Buell was expected at any hour, the freightmen were induced to pull by and let him out. This delay gave Captain Fuller an inestimable advantage, and but for the delay at Moon's Station, Andrews and his raiders would have been captured at Kingston.

When Fuller arrived at Kingston on the Yonah, he was stopped by a flagman more than a mile south of the depot, on account of the trains that had pulled by to let Andrews out. He saw at once that he would have to abandon the Yonah, as he could not get her by without much delay. So taking to his feet again, he ran around those freight trains to the depot and held a short conversation with the agent from whom he learned the particulars of Andrews's movements and representations, etc. He then ran to the north prong of the Rome railroad " Y," where that road intersected with the Western and Atlantic mainline. There he found "The Alfred Shorter," the Rome railroad engine, fired up and ready to move. He hurriedly told Wyley Harbin the engineer of " The Alfred Shorter," about the raiders, and he and his fireman, noble fellows, at once put themselves and their engine at his service. The pursuers were gone in thirty seconds. Captain Fuller says that Jeff Cain got into the train, but that Mr. Murphy who was in another part of the car yard, considering some other plan, came near being left ; but Fuller saw him and held Harbin up until he ran up and got on.

Captain Fuller rode on the cowcatcher of the " Shorter," that he might remove crossties and other obstructions that would probably be put on the track. Further down the road, when Andrews was running more at leisure, he loaded the three box cars with ties and other timber, and when he feared pursuit he punched out the rear end of his hindermost car and dropped obstructions in the way of his pursuers. The Alfred Shorter had drivers only four feet—6—, and could make only ordinary time; but Captain Fuller did not consider that of any great disadvantage, as she ran as fast as it was safe to do on account of the many obstruction dropped by raiders upon that part of the road.

Six miles north of Kingston, Captain Fuller found it necessary to abandon the " Shorter," because at that point several rails of the track had been taken up and carried away by the raiders. Knowing the schedule as he did, and seeing he could not get by in less time than thirty minutes, Captain Fuller decided that the best thing to be done was to go to Adairs-ville, four miles north, where he hoped to find a south-bound train, "tied up" because of the delay of his train. Possibly he might meet this train before reaching Adairsville. Leaving the "Shorter," he called upon all who wished to join in one more effort to follow him, and started in a run on foot for another four miles. There were none to follow—all preferred to remain in the Rome passenger coach. (It is not amiss here to state that, at Kingston, Fuller took on one coach belonging to the Rome Railroad, and that some thirty or forty persons had volunteered and boarded the Rome car ; but, when invited to join in a four-mile foot race, they preferred to remain in the coach.)

When Fuller had run about two miles he looked back and saw Murphy just rounding a curve about three hundred yards behind. When he had run about a mile further, to his great delight he met the expected south-bound freight train. Fuller gave the signal, and, having a gun in his hand, was recognized by the conductor, who stopped as quickly as possible. Fortunately Peter I. Brachen was the engineer of the freight, and had "The Texas," a Danforth & Cook, 5 feet 10 driver, as his engine. Captain Fuller knew that Brachen was a cool, level-headed man, and one of the best runners that ever pulled a throttle. As soon as the train stopped, Fuller mounted and was

about to back it, when, seeing Murphy coming, he held
Brachen a few seconds until his comrade got on " The
Texas." Then the long train was pushed back to
Adairsville, where Fuller changed the switch, un-
coupled the train from the engine, and pushed in upon
the side track. In the further pursuit of the raiders,
Captain Fuller never changed his engine or his crew
again.

From hence " The Texas " is after " The General "
—both are new, both 5 feet 10 driver, with the same
stroke—" The General " a Rogers, " The Texas " a
Danforth & Cook. But " The General " was forward, while " The Texas " had to back.

Captain Fuller rode on the back end of the tender,
which was in front, and swung from corner to corner,
so that he could see round the curves and signal to
Brachen. His only chance to hold on was by two
hooks, one at each corner of the tender, such as were
formerly used to secure " spark catchers." Many
times he bounced two feet high when the tender ran
over obstructions not seen in time to stop the engine.
The ten miles from Adairsville to Calhoun was made
in twelve minutes, including the time consumed in removing obstructions. (Here it may be in order to
state that when Andrews had met Brachen at Adairsville, on his south-bound trip before being met by
Fuller, that he told him to hurry to Kingston, as
Fuller would wait there for him. This Brachen was
doing, when Captain Fuller met him a mile south of
Adairsville. But if Fuller had not met and stopped
him, he would not have gone on to Kingston, but
would have plunged into the break in the railroad

where the raiders had taken up the rails at the point where the " Shorter" was abandoned. This was one of Andrews' best moves. He hoped to occasion a disastrous wreck, and block the road.)

As Captain Fuller with "The Texas" and her crew figure exclusively in the remainder of this wonderful chase, he thinks it eminently due them that the names of those actually engaged on the engine should be given. Federal reports of the affair have put under the command of Fuller a regiment or more of armed soldiers. Some illustrations show long trains of cars packed to overflowing with armed men.

From the time he stopped Brachen, a mile south of Adairsville, to the point where Andrews abandoned "The General," three miles north of Ringgold, he had with him only Peter J. Brachen as engineer, Henry Haney, fireman of the engine (who, at the suggestion of Brachen, stood at the brakes of the tender, and had for additional leverage a piece of timber run through the spokes of the brake-wheel), Flem Cox, an engineer on the road, who happened to be along, and fired the "Texas," and Alonzo Martin, train hand of the freight train left at Adairsville, who passed wood to Cox. Thus it is seen that Captain Fuller, Peter J. Brachen, Flem Cox, and Alonzo Martin were the members of the pursuing party in toto, during the last fifty-five miles of the chase.

As has been stated, Mr. Anthony Murphy, of Atlanta, rode on "The Texas" with Brachen from Adairsville to the point at which the Andrews raiders were caught, and there is no doubt he would have aided in their capture at the forfeit of his life had he been called upon to do so.

As the pursuers ran past Calhoun, an enthusiastic old gentleman, Mr. Richard Peters, himself a Northern man, and who died an honored citizen of Atlanta, offered a reward of a hundred dollars each for all the raiders captured. Had this promise been fulfilled Captain Fuller would have received $2,300, which no doubt he would have divided with his comrades in the pursuit.

At Calhoun Captain Fuller met the south-bound "day passenger train," delayed by his unexpected movements. He had his engine run slowly by the depot, and exchanged a few words with the excited crowd of people, who were amazed at the sudden appearance and disappearance of the runaway train which had passed there a few moments before. Here he also saw Ed Henderson, the telegraph operator at Dalton. Discovering that the line was down below Dalton, Henderson had gone down on the passenger train to try to repair the break in the wire. Seeing him, Fuller reached out his hand as he was running by and took the operator into the tender, and as they ran at the rate of a mile a minute he wrote the following dispatch :

" *To General Ledbetter, Chattanoga :*

My train was captured this morning at Big Shanty, evidently by Federal soldiers in disguise. They are making rapidly for Chattanooga, and will no doubt burn the Chickamauga bridges in their rear, if I should fail to capture them. Please see that they do not pass Chattanooga. Signed, W. A. Fuller."

He handed this dispatch to the operator, and instructed him to put it through at all hazards when he should arrive at Dalton.

Just at that moment the pursuers came in sight of the raiders for the first time. They had halted two miles north of Calhoun and were removing a rail from the track. As the pursuers hove in sight, the raiders detached their third car and left it before Captain Fuller could reach them. Coupling this abandoned car to "The Texas," Captain Fuller got on top of it and began the race again. The rails had only been loosened and the intrepid conductor took the chances of running over them. From this point the raiders ran at a fearful rate, and the pursuers followed after them as fast as "The Texas" could go.

One mile and a half further up, the raiders detached another car in the front of the pursuers. This was witnessed by Fuller, who was standing on the rear end of the car he had coupled to when the raiders were first seen. He gave Brachen the signal, and he advanced slowly to the abandoned car and coupled it to the first one obtained in this way. Then getting on top of the newly captured one he was off again in the race with scarcely the loss of a moment's time.

Just in front of the raiders, and not more than a mile away, was an important railroad bridge over the Oostanaula river at Resaca. The pursuers had greatly feared that the raiders would gain time to burn this bridge, after passing over it. But they were pressed so hotly and so closely that they passed over the bridge as rapidly as the "General" could carry

them.   The pursuers were, therefore, greatly rejoiced
on their arrival at Resaca to see that the bridge was
standing, and that it had not been set on fire.   The
two cars picked up as described were switched off at
Resaca, and the pursuers again had "The Texas" un-
trammeled.   The race from Resaca to Dalton has
seldom been paralelled. It is impossible to describe it.

At Dalton the telegraph operator was dropped,
with instructions to put the dispatch to General Ledbetter through to the exclusion of all other matter.
All was excitement at this point.   The unusual
spectacle of a wild engine flying through the town
with only one car attached was bewildering indeed ;
and when Captain Fuller arrived and ran through,
slacking his speed just enough to put the operator
off the train, the excitement became intense.   The
operator was besieged on every side for an explanation, but he knew nothing save that contained in the
dispatch.

Two miles north of Dalton, Andrews stopped.
Some of his men climbed telegraph poles and cut the
wire, while others were engaged in an effort to take
up the track behind them.   The operator at
Dalton had sent the dispatch through to Ledbetter at
Chattanooga ; but just as he had finished and was
holding his finger on the key, waiting for the usual
" O. K.," click went the key, and all was dead.   He
did not know until the next day that Captain Fuller's
dispatch had reached its destination.   Had the raiders
been thirty seconds earlier in cutting the wire, the
dispatch would not have gone through.   As it was
Ledbetter received it, and not being able to hear any-

thing further by telegraph or otherwise he had a regiment placed in ambush (some of the soldiers on either side of the track), and had a considerable part of the track taken up. This was about a mile from Chattanooga, so that by the intervention of the telegram Fuller had Andrews both front and rear.

Andrews was run away from the point where the wires were cut before any material damage was done to the track. The rails had been partially removed, but not so much as to prevent the safe passage over them of "The Texas" and her crew.

Now the last long race begins. The pursued and the pursuers are in sight of one another. In every straight line of the road, Andrews was in plain view. This tended to increase the interest and excitement, if, indeed, the thrilling scenes and incidents of the seconds as they flitted by could have been heightened. I say seconds, because minutes in this case would be too large to use for a unit of time. The experience, practice, and knowledge of machinery possessed by the engineers was brought into full play. "The Texas" was kept at a rate of one hundred and sixty-five pounds of steam, with the valve wide open. Brachen would appear a little pale sometimes, but he was encouraged by Fuller standing the full length of the tender before him, and watching around the curves. At every straight line in the road Andrews was sighted, and a yell went up from the throats of the pursuers, but they did not lose their wits. Their aim was forward, onward, at all hazards. They were now convinced that Andrews had exhausted his supply of obstructive material, and were not so uneasy on that account. But as prudence is the better part of valor, and as they had so few men on board, they dared not approach too close, lest their little band should be fired upon ; or what appeared to be a greater danger, Andrews might suddenly stop and give fight. Captain Fuller had only five person on "The Texas" besides himself, and all accounts heard by them at points below had placed Andrews's party as high as twenty or twenty-five. Fuller knew that the fire-arms he had gathered up early in the race, such as " squirrel guns," and most of them unloaded, would have but little showing in a hand-to-hand contest; so these things had to be considered as they sped along so swiftly. Another danger was to be feared—Andrews might stop, abandon " The General," let her drive back, and thus force a collision with the pursuers.

In approaching the tunnel, seven miles north of Dalton, our brave conductor slackened speed until he could see dimly through the smoke of " The General," which had only passed out of the further end by a few seconds, and was in sight beyond. For the next seven miles from Tunnel Hill to Ringgold, nothing occurred except a race between engines such as has never been excelled. When Ringgold was reached, both engines literally flew through the town, the "Texas" only about one-fourth of a mile behind. When the pursuers were passing through the north end of the town, Captain Fuller noticed a company of militia drilling. Their horses were hitched to the small shade trees near the muster grounds, and this fact fastened itself upon his mind.

In a few minutes the pursuers swung around the

second short curve north of Ringgold, just in time to see Andrews slack his speed, and himself and his men jump off the " General " to seek concealment in the dense woods. The foliage of the trees and undergrowth was about half grown, and it would have been an easy matter to hide in the forest. When the raiders were first seen north of Ringgold, it was obvious that the heroic old " General " was almost exhausted. Her smoke was nearly white, and ran up at an angle of 45 degrees, while before that it lay flat, and appeared to the eyes of the pursuers as if fresh from the stack. When Andrews abandoned the "General," his engineer threw the lever back and gave the engine all the steam it had, but in his haste the brake was left on, so the engine was unable to drive back and collide with the "Texas," as Andrews had hoped it would.

The pursuers ran up to the " General " to which was attached one box car—the one historians and statesmen have so often said was fired and left to burn in a bridge below Ringgold. This car had been fired, but was easily extinguished. It had never been uncoupled from the "General" since Fuller left Atlanta with it that morning. Brachen hastily coupled the "Texas" to this car and the " General." Captain Fuller reminded Brachen of the militia company they had seen drilling at Ringgold a few minutes before, and encouraged him to go back there as soon as possible and tell of the capture of the "General," and to beseech the soldiers to mount their horses and come to his aid, as he, Flem Cox, and Alonzo Martin were already chasing through the woods after Andrews and his men. Mr. Murphy and Henry Haney went back to Ringgold with Brachen after the militia.

It was probably three minutes after the "General" was overtaken before Captain Fuller and his two comrades were ready to take to the woods, as they assisted in getting the car and two engines started back to Ringgold. The raiders, therefore, had the advantage and were deep in the forest before the woodland chase began. Besides, the reader will see at once that the raiders were fresh—that they had done no really hard work, except the fireman and engineer. They had not already run on foot more than twenty miles, as Fuller had done. After the pursuing party had gone about two miles through the woods, they came to a fifty-acre wheat field just in time to see the raiders cross the fence at the further side. It had been raining nearly all day, and the ground was wet. It was limestone soil, and almost as sticky as tar. The boots of the pursuers would clog up, and the mud on them would sometimes weigh doubtless two or three pounds. Another source of annoyance was the growing wheat, which was half leg high and very difficult to tread. Captain Fuller has said that it appeared to be up-hill every way that he ran.

Finally the woods beyond were reached, and, by accident, Captain Fuller and his two comrades got separated. In the afternoon four of the raiders were captured. About 8 P. M. Captain Fuller became completely exhausted. Some old farmers put him on a mule and carried him back to Ringgold, distant seven miles direct route, but by the one he was carried three times that distance. He lay down on the mule's back, and a man on either side held him on.

Soon after they arrived at Ringgold the down night passenger train came, and Captain Fuller was put on board and carried to Atlanta. At Tunnel Hill, seven miles south, a train of soldiers passed them on the way to the scene of interest. The Andrews Raiders had already been captured, and the "General" was safe on the side track at Ringgold, eight hours before. And this train of soldiers just spoken of is "the second pursuing train" that Pittenger so often speaks of in his "Capturing a Locomotive," and "Daring and Suffering."

We have followed Captain Fuller and his wise and intrepid men, in the pursuit of spies no less wise and intrepid, from the first step in an act which, under the usages of war in all countries, meant death to them if captured ; and over that lamentable scene we drop the curtain. We have the testimony of reliable men that they were humanely treated while in prison. After a trial, conducted on the highest principles of military law and honor, eight of these spies were condemned and executed.

The following list gives the names of the Andrews raiders, all of whom were captured in the manner described :

J. J. Andrews,	John Scott,
Wilson Brown,	Perry G. Shadrack,
Marion Ross,	George D. Wilson,
W. H. Campbell,	Samuel Slavens,

These were tried and executed.

S. Robinson,	W. Bensinger,
Ed. Mason,	A. Wilson,
Wm. Knight,	W. Reddie,
Robert Bruffum,	D. A. Dorsey,
William Pittenger,	I. R. Porter,
M. J. Hawkins,	M. Wood,
I. Parroth,	W. W. Brown.

The last named fourteen were never tried.

CONFEDERATE LOVE SONG.

Over the mountains of Winter,
  And the cold, cold plains of snow,
Down in the valleys of Summer,
  Calling my love I go.

And strong in my woe and passion,
  I climb up the hills of Spring,
To listen if I hear his voice
  In songs he used to sing.

I wait in the fields of Autumn,
  And gather a feast of fruit,
And call my love to the banquet;
  His lips are cold and mute.

I say to the wild bird flying:
  " My darling sang sweet as you;
Fly o'er the earth in search of him,
  And to the skies of blue."

I say to the wild-wood flowers:
  " My love was a friend to you;
Send one of your fragrant spirits
  To the cool Isles of Dew,"

" Gold-girt by a belt of moonbeams,
  And seek on their gleaming shore
A breath of the vanished sweetness
  For me his red lips bore."

I stand at the gates of Morning,
  When the radiant angel, Light,
Draws back the great bolt of darkness,
  And by the gates of Night,

When the hands of bright stars tremble
  While clasping their lanterns bright;
And I hope to see him passing,
  And touch his garments white.

O, love ! if you hear me calling,
　Flee not from the wailing cry;
Come from the grottoes of Silence
　And hear me, or I die !

Stand out on the hills of Echo;
　The sensitive, pulsing air
Will thrill at your softest whisper—
　Speak to me, love, from there !

O, love, if I hear you calling,
　Though far on the heavenly side,
My voice will float on the billow :
　" Come to your spirit bride."
　　　　　　　　—MARY A. H. GAY.

TO THE READER,

Who has kindly perused these sketches, I would say, as they have already attained length and breadth not anticipated from the beginning, I will withhold the sequels to many of them for, perhaps, another volume of reminiscences.

Were I possessed of the Sam Weller genius and versatility, and the happy faculty of making the reader wish I had written more, I would throw open the doors of the store-house of my war memories, a structure as capacious as the "Southern Confederacy" and canopied by the firmament, and invite the public to enter and share with me the treasures hidden there. The coruscations of wit and the profound displays of wisdom by many who donned Confederate grey and went forth in manhood's prime to battle for the principles of their country, would employ the minds and feast the intellect of the most erudite. There are living, glowing pictures hanging upon the walls which delineate the mysteries of humanity in all its varied forms, and, by example, demonstrate that we often spurn with holy horror that which is better far than that which we embrace with all the fervor of affection. I would resurrect the loftest patriotism from the most humble graves in the Southern land, and prove by heroic deeds and noble acts that valor on

the battle-field was as often illustrated by the humble
soldier whose name has not been preserved in "storied
urn," as by the gallant son of chivalrous ancestors who
commanded the applause of an admiring multitude. I
would place by the side of those greatest of chieftains,
Robert E. Lee, and our impregnable "Stonewall"
Jackson and Albert Sidney Johnston, many of our soldiers "unknown to fame," in faded grey jackets and
war-worn pants, and challenge the world for the difference. I would dwell with loving interest upon the
innumerable sad, sweet faces of the mighty throng of
bereaved mothers, sisters and aunts, out of whose lives
all light had gone, and who, though hopeless, uttered
no words of complaint against our cause or its leader,
but toiled on with unswerving faith and souls that
borrowed the lustre of heaven. All these sad things
in my gallery I would clothe in living form and glowing color. And, saddest of all, I would live over
with them that melancholy period when the very few,
comparatively, that were left of the noble defenders of
our principles, came back, not with buoyant step and
victor crown, but with blighted hopes and despondent
mien to desolated homes and decimated families. Under the new regime I would tell of despair and suicide,
of hope, energy and success ; I would tell how I have
lived in this gallery—its silent occupants my companions and friends, my inspiration to useful deeds.
There is not a day that I do not arouse by muffled
tread the slumbering echoes of this past, and look
upon the cherished souvenirs of the patriotic friends
now roaming the beautiful gardens of Paradise, or
sleeping the mystic waiting of the resurrection. I

ponder upon their lives, their ambitions, their disappointments, and it requires no effort of the imagination to animate those dead forms and invest them with living attributes. And daily, in imagination I weave for them a laurel crown that shall grow greener and greener as the cycles of Time speed on to Eternity.

APPENDIX.

The author has selected the article, "Gleanings from General Sherman's Despatches," as an appendix for these sketches, not because of a desire to keep up the issues of the war between the States (for she would gladly bury them so deep they could never be resurrected until the great Judge of all issues calls them up to receive sentence by his unerring judgment), but rather, because of the persistent insistence of Northern Republicans to make it appear to the world that the Southern people are a semi-barbarous people, solely responsible for the war and altogether unworthy fraternal consideration in the compact called the Union.

The article mentioned, "Gleanings from General Sherman's Despatches," is to be found, word for word, in The Southern Magazine, May, 1873, Vol. XII. Baltimore : Turnbull Brothers.

GLEANINGS FROM GENERAL SHERMAN'S DESPATCHES.

Those thick, loosely-bound octavos printed on soft and rather dingy paper, which Congress publishes and distributes under the name of Public Documents, are not generally considered very entertaining reading. But there are exceptions ; and one of these is the report of the joint committee of Congress on the conduct of the war. Indeed, compared with such mild pastorals as "Some Accounts of the Cheese Manufacture in Central New York," or "Remarks on the Cultivation of Alfalfa in Western Tennessee," it is quite luridly sensational, and in parts reminds us of those striking reports of the Duke of Alva to his royal master, which have been disinterred in the dusty archives of Simancas. As a study of congressional nature, military nature, and human nature generally, in its least attractive aspects, these eight stout volumes are richly worth perusal. Here the reader is allowed to peep behind the scenes of that portentous drama; here he may see the threads of the intrigues that centered in Washington; may hear a petty newspaper correspondent demonstrating, with an animation that we can scarcely ascribe to fervid patriotism, the incapacity, the ignorance and even the doubtful "loyalty" of the commander-in-chief; may see private malignity and vindictiveness putting on grand Roman airs, and whispering debaters draping themselves in the toga of Brutus.

However, it is not with these aspects of the reports that we at present have to do, but with the despatches of General Sherman on his march through Georgia and South Carolina. A great deal of fiction and some verse,* we believe, have been written about this famous march or grand foray; but here we have the plain matter-of-fact statement of things as they were, and they form a luminous illustration of the advance

---

* One of these poems, "Marching Through Georgia," we learn by the evidence, was a favorite canticle of Murray, the kidnapper and butcher of Captain Polynesius.

of civilization in the nineteenth century as exempli-
fied in the conduct of invasions, showing how modern
philanthropy and humanitarianism, while acknowledging that for the present war is a necessary evil, still
strive to mitigate its horrors and spare all avoidable
suffering to non-combatants. For this purpose we have
thought it worth while to reproduce a few of the most
striking extracts illustrating the man, his spirit, and
his work.

A kind of keynote is sounded in the dispatches to
General Stoneman, of May 14, which, after ordering
him to "press down the valley strong," ends with the
words, "Pick up whatever provisions and plunder you
can."

On June 3, the question of torpedoes is discussed,
and General Stedman receives the following instructions : " If torpedoes are found in the possession of
an enemy to our rear, you may cause them to be put
on the ground and tested by wagon loads of prisoners,
or, if need be, by citizens implicated in their use. In
like manner, if a torpedo is suspected on any part of
the railroad, order the point to be tested by a carload
of prisoners or citizens implicated, drawn by a long
rope." " Implicated," we suppose here meant "residing or captured in the neighborhood."

On July 7, we have an interesting dispatch to
General Garrard on the subject of the destruction of
the factories at Roswell. " Their utter destruction is
right, and meets my entire approval; and to make the
matter complete, you will arrest the owners and employees and send them under guard charged with
treason, to Marietta, and I will see as to any man in

America hoisting the French flag and then devoting his labor and capital to supplying armies in open hostility to our government, and claiming the benefit of his neutral flag. Should you, under the impulse of anger, natural at contemplating such perfidy, hang the wretch, I approve the act beforehand · · · · I repeat my orders that you arrest all people, male and female, connected with those factories, no matter what the clamor, and let them foot it, under guard, to Marietta, whence I will send them by cars to the North. Destroy and make the same disposition of all mills, save small flouring mills, manifestly for local use ; but all saw mills and factories dispose of effectually ; and useful laborers, excused by reason of their skill as manufacturers, from conscription, are as much prisoners as if armed." On the same day he further enlarges on this subject in a despatch to General Halleck :

"General Garrard reports to me that he is in possession of Roswell, where were several very valuable cotton and wool factories in full operation, also paper mills, all of which, by my order, he destroyed by fire. They had been for years engaged exclusively at work for the Confederate government ; and the owner of the woolen factory displayed the French flag, but, as he failed to show the United States flag also, General Garrard burned it also. The main cotton factory was valued at a million of United States dollars. The cloth on hand is reserved for the use of the United States hospitals ; and I have ordered General Garrard to arrest for treason all owners and employees, foreign and native, and send them to Marietta, whence I will send them North. Being exempt from conscription, they are as much governed by the rules of war as if in the ranks. The women can find employment in Indiana. This whole region was devoted to manufactories, but I will destroy every one of them." There are two points specially worth notice in this despatch. The first, that *since* these men and women, by reason of sex, or otherwise, are exempt from conscription, they are, therefore, as much subject to the rules of war as if in the ranks. Why not do less violence to logic and state frankly that factory hands were in demand in Indiana ? The next point is that the Roswell factories, whether French property or not, were destroyed because they were making cloth for the Confederate government, followed presently by the declaration that every manufactory in that region shall be destroyed, evidently without reference to its products or their destination. How much franker it would have been to have added to this last sentence, "and thus get rid of so many competitors to the factories of the North." The South must learn that while she may bear the burden of protective tariffs, she must not presume to share their benefits. Another despatch to General Halleck, of July 9, again refers to these factories. After referring to the English and French ownership, comes this remark : " I take it a neutral is no better than one of our citizens, and we would not respect the property of one of our own citizens engaged in supplying a hostile army." This is the kind of logic proverbially used by the masters of legions. A despatch to General Halleck, of July 13, gives General Sherman's opinion of two great and philanthropic institutions. Speaking of "fellows hanging about" the army, he says: "The Sanitary and Christian Commission are enough to eradicate all traces of Christianity from our minds."

July 14, to General J. E. Smith, at Allatoona : "If you entertain a bare suspicion against any family, send it North. Any loafer or suspicious person seen at any time should be imprisoned and sent off. If guerrillas trouble the road or wires they should be shot without mercy."

September 8, to General Webster after the capture of Atlanta : "Don't let any citizens come to Atlanta ; not one. I won't allow trade or manufactures of any kind, but you will remove all the present population, and make Atlanta a pure military town." To General Halleck he writes : "I am not willing to have Atlanta encumbered by the families of our enemies." Of this wholesale depopulation, General Hood complained, by flag of truce, as cruel and contrary to the usages of civilized nations and customs of war, receiving this courteous and gentlemanly reply (September 12): "I think I understand the laws of civilized nations and the 'customs of war ;' but, if at a loss at any time, I know where to seek for information to refresh my memory." General Hood made the correspondence, or part of it, public, on which fact, General Sherman remarks to General Halleck : "Of course, he is welcome, for the more he arouses the indignation of the Southern masses, the bigger will be the pill of bitterness they will have to swallow."

About the middle of September, General Sherman, being still in Atlanta, endeavored to open private communication with Governor Brown and Vice-President Stephens, whom he knew to be at variance with the administration at Richmond on certain points of public policy. Mr. Stephens refused to reply to a verbal message, but wrote to Mr. King, the intermediary, that if the general would say that there was any prospect of their agreeing upon " terms to be submitted to the action of their respective governments," he would, as requested, visit him at Atlanta. The motives urged by Mr. King were General Sherman's extreme desire for peace, and to hit upon " some plan of terminating this fratricidal war without the further effusion of blood." But in General Sherman's despatch of September 14, to Mr. Lincoln, referring to these attempted negotiations, the humanitarian point of view is scarcely so prominent. He says: " It would be a magnificent stroke of policy if I could, without surrendering a foot of ground or principle, arouse the latent enmity to Davis."

On October 20, he writes to General Thomas from Summerville, giving an idea of his plan of operations : " Out of the forces now here and at Atlanta, I propose to organize an efficient army of 60,000 to 65,000 men, with which I propose to destroy Macon, Augusta, and it may be, Savannah and Charleston. By this I propose to demonstrate the vulnerability of the South, and make its inhabitants feel that war and individual ruin are synonymous terms."

Despatch of October 22, to General Grant " I am now perfecting arrangements to put into Tennessee a force able to hold the line of the Tennessee, while I break up the railroad in front of Dalton, including the city of Atlanta, and push into Georgia and break up all its railroads and depots, capture its horses and negroes, make desolation everywhere; destroy the factories at Macon, Milledgeville and Augusta, and bring up with 60,000 men on the seashore about Savannah and Charleston."

To General Thomas, from Kingston, November 2: "Last night we burned Rome, and in two more days will burn Atlanta" (which he was then occupying).

December 5: "Blair can burn the bridges and culverts and burn enough barns to mark the progress of his head of columns."

December 18, to General Grant, from near Savannah: "With Savannah in our possession, at some future time, if not now, we can punish South Carolina as she deserves, and as thousands of people in Georgia hope we will do. I do sincerely believe that the whole United States, north and south, would rejoice to have this army turned loose on South Carolina, to devastate that State in the manner we have done in Georgia."

A little before this he announces to Secretary Stanton that he knows what the people of the South are fighting for. What do our readers suppose? To ravage the North with sword and fire, and crush them under their heel? Surely it must be some such delusion that inspires this ferocity of hatred, unmitigated by even a word of compassion. He may speak for himself: "Jefferson Davis has succeeded perfectly in inspiring his people with the truth that liberty and government are worth fighting for." This was their unpardonable crime.

24

December 22, to General Grant: "If you can hold Lee, I could go on and smash South Carolina all to pieces."

On the 18th General Halleck writes: "Should you capture Charleston, I hope that by some accident the place may be destroyed; and if a little salt should be sown upon its site, it may prevent the growth of future crops of nullification and secession." To this General Sherman replies, December 24: "This war differs from European wars in this particular—we are not only fighting hostile armies, but hostile people; and must make old and young, rich and poor, feel the hard hand of war, as well as their organized armies. I will bear in mind your hint as to Charleston, and don't think *salt* will be necessary. When I move, the Fifteenth corps will be on the right of the right wing, and their position will naturally throw them into Charleston first; and, if you have studied the history of that corps, you will have remarked that they generally do their work up pretty well. The truth is, the whole army is burning with insatiable desire to wreak vengeance upon South Carolina. I almost tremble for her fate, but she deserves all that seems in store for her.

"I look upon Columbia as quite as bad as Charleston, and I doubt if we shall spare the public buildings there as we did at Milledgeville."

And now we look with interest for the despatches that would settle the vexed question as to whether Sherman or his officers, acting under his orders, burned Columbia on the 17th of February. Unfortunately, a paternal government, not thinking it good that the truth should be known, has suppressed all the despatches between the 16th and the 21st, and every other allusion to the transaction.

On the 23d, he writes to General Kilpatrick: "Let the whole people know the war is now against them, because their armies flee before us and do not defend their country or frontier as they should. It is pretty nonsense for Wheeler and Beauregard and such vain heroes to talk of our warring against women and children and prevent us reaching their homes."

If, therefore, an army defending their country can prevent invaders from reaching their homes and families, the latter have a right to that protection; but if the invaders can break through and reach these homes, these are justified in destroying women and children. Certainly this is a great advance on the doctrine and practice of the dark ages. Another extraordinary moral consequence flows from this insufficiency of defence: "If the enemy fails to defend his country, we may rightfully appropriate what we want." Here, now, is a nice question of martial law or casuistry, solved with the simplicity of an ancient Roman. In other words, when in the enemy's country, the army shall be strictly careful not to seize, capture or appropriate to military or private uses, any property—that it cannot get.

"They (the Southern people) have lost all title to property, and can lose nothing not already forfeited."

What, nothing? Not merely the houses we had built, the lands we had tilled, the churches we worshipped in—had we forfeited the right to drink of the streams, to behold the sun, to breathe the free air of

heaven? What unheard of, what inconceivable crime
had we committed that thus closed every gate of mercy
and compassion against us, and provoked an utterance
which has but one parallel—the death warrant signed
by Philip II. against all Netherlanders? General
Sherman has himself told us what it was: We had
dared to act on the "truth that liberty and government are worth fighting for."

On March 15, he writes to General Gillmore,
advising him to draw forces from Charleston and
Savannah (both then in Federal hands) to destroy a
railroad, etc. "As to the garrisons of those places I
don't feel disposed to be over-generous, and should
not hesitate to burn Savannah, Charleston and Wil-
mington, or either of them, if the garrisons were
needed."

Such are some of the results of our gleanings in
this field. Is it any wonder that after reading them
we fervently echo General Sherman's devout aspira-
tion: "I do wish the fine race of men that people the
United States should rule and determine the future
destiny of America."

SHERMAN'S MARCH TO THE SEA.

It is a proud thing for Americans to feel that there is little to bring the blush of shame to their cheeks in the contemplation of their country's history. It is a glorious thing for our young manhood to know that the annals of their race tell of the earnest and upward progress of a people, Christian from the first, toward an ever higher civilization. It is well to reflect that when the ruthless hand of war has turned American citizenship from the paths of peace it could do little more than array strong man against sturdy foeman in an honest battle for principle, and that outrage and pillage in our broad domain have been the almost undisputed heritage of the Aborigines.

Enduring with patient fortitude the raids of savage foes upon our early frontiers, meeting the armed invasion of foreign hosts with a resistance vigorous but manly, pressing our own victorious arms to the very citadel of our Mexican neighbors without spoliation or rapine, it is sad to realize that it remained for an internecine conflict, where brother stood against brother, for an invasion by an army void of pretext of reprisal or revenge, to write upon American warfare the stigma of vandalism, rapacity and theft.

The movement from Atlanta to Savannah, which figured in history as "The March to the Sea," was, from the standpoint of the tactician, no great achievement; it involved no more than the passage of an invincible army across some three hundred miles of country, where it could gather supplies upon its way, to effect a junction with its naval allies at a practically defenceless city. It was peculiarly lacking in the daring which is customarily ascribed to it, for it was made, practically, without resistance and along a route where no considerable force of the enemy could have been encountered. It was not a venture in the dark with a conclusion to be determined by circumstances; for the authorities at Washington were fully advised of its author's purpose, and Gen. Sherman was assured that he would meet a formidable fleet at Savannah before he undertook it. It was no more nor less than the yielding, by this most typical barbarian conqueror of the Nineteenth century, to the spirit of pillage and excess which distinguished his prototypes in the days of the Goths and Vandals, when the homes and firesides of their enemies were at their mercy. It was a campaign remarkable only for the revival of military methods abandoned since Attila the Hun. It was, nevertheless, as carefully planned as it was ruthlessly executed. It was no sudden impulse which laid the torch to every roof-tree upon the invading army's path. It was no spirit of retaliation for vigorous but ineffective resistance which goaded these conquerors to excess, for out of 62,204 men who began the march but 103 lost their lives before they reached Savannah. It was simply the grasping of the amplest opportunity by a man who glories in looting and destruction, and to whom human misery was a subject for jest.

At the outset let us understand that General Sherman, through all that portion of his career which began with the destruction of Atlanta, was acting upon a plan and a theory devised and adopted weeks before; that his own actions and that of his army were in no sense impulsive, but in every way controlled by premeditation, and that our authority for such a conclusion lies in the repeated statements of the General himself.

With the brutal frankness which was one of his characteristics, he wrote on September 4th, 1864, in a letter to General Halleck, which he reproduces in his autobiography: "If the people raise a howl against my barbarity and cruelty, I will answer that war is war and not popularity-seeking." "I knew, of course," he says, "that such a measure would be strongly criticized, but made up my mind to do it with the absolute certainty of its justness, and that time would sanction its wisdom. I knew that the people of the South would read in this measure two important conclusions; one that we were in earnest, and the other that if they were sincere in their common and popular clamor 'to die in the last ditch,' the opportunity would soon come."

The cold-blooded candor of this statement leaves little doubt of the temperature of the well-springs which fed that organ of General Sherman corresponding to the heart of an ordinary man; but if evidence were wanting of his absolute unconcern for the sufferings of others when his own plans might be interfered with to the slightest degree, it might be found in his answer to General Hood's proposition for an exchange of prisoners. "Some of these prisoners," he says, " had already escaped and got in, and had described the pitiable condition of the remainder." He had at that time about two thousand Confederate prisoners available for exchange. " These I offered to exchange for Stoneman, Buell, and such of my own army as would make up the equivalent; but I would not exchange for his prisoners generally, because I knew these would have to be sent to their own regiments away from my army, whereas all we could give him could at once be put to duty in his immediate army." No possible suffering which his unfortunate companions in arms could be forced to bear by reason of the Confederates' lack of supplies with which to feed and clothe them, could induce him to exchange for men who would not strengthen his own immediate army !

Geneseric, the Vandal, is said to have been " cruel to blood thirstiness, cunning, unscrupulous and grasping ; but he possessed great military talents and his manner of life was austere." Let the impartial reader of history say how nearly the barbarian who marched to the sea in the nineteenth century, approached to his prototype of the fifth century. One is not surprised, therefore, to find this man writing to General Hood on September 7th, 1864, that he "deemed it to the interest of the United States that the citizens now residing in Atlanta should remove."

In the midst of a region desolated by war, their

fathers, husbands, brothers, sons, in the army hundreds of miles away, it was "deemed to be in the interest of the United States" that the helpless women and children of Atlanta should be driven from their homes to find such shelter as God gives the ravens and the beasts of the wood. It was a course that wrung from General Hood these forceful words of reply:

"Permit me to say that the unprecedented measure you propose transcends, in studied and ingenious cruelty, all acts ever before brought to my attention in the dark history of war. In the name of God and humanity I protest, believing that you will find you are expelling from their homes and firesides the wives and children of a brave people." To this burning arraignment General Sherman could find no better answer than argument concerning the right of States to secede. But it was followed on September 11th by an appeal from the mayor and councilmen of Atlanta which would have touched a heart of stone. It was humble, it was earnest, it was pitiful. It provoked these words in reply: "I have your letter of the 11th in the nature of a petition to revoke my orders removing all the inhabitants from Atlanta. I have read it carefully, and give full credit to your statements of distress that will be occasioned, and yet shall not revoke my orders, because they were not designed to meet the humanities of the case, but to prepare for the future struggles in which millions of good people outside of Atlanta have an interest."

The same unalterable resolution must have dominated Geneseric, the Vandal, when he prepared for his fourteen days sacking of Rome. The vandal of the fifth century had at least the pretext of reprisal for his actions; the vandal of the nineteenth century could find no better plea for his barbarity than that it might wring the hearts of absent men until they would sacrifice principle and honor for the relief of their loved ones.

President Davis says: "Since Alva's atrocious cruelties to the non-combatant population of the low countries in the sixteenth century, the history of war records no instance of such barbarous cruelty as this order designed to perpetrate. It involved the immediate expulsion from their homes and only means of subsistence of thousands of unoffending women and children, whose husbands and fathers were either in the army, in Northern prisons, or had died in battle."

At the time appointed the women and children were expelled from their houses, and, before they were passed within our lines, complaint was generally made that the Federal officers and men who were sent to guard them had robbed them of the few articles of value they had been permitted to take from their homes. The cowardly dishonesty of the men appointed to carry out this order, was in perfect harmony with the temper and the spirit of the order.

It was on the 12th day of November, 1864, that "The March to the Sea" began. Hood's army had been followed to Tennessee, and Sherman's forces had destroyed the railroad during their return trip to Atlanta. They were now ready to abandon the ruins of the Gate City for fresher and more lucrative fields of havoc. It is fair to General Sherman to say that his

plans and intentions had been fully communicated to
the authorities at Washington, and that they met
with the thorough approbation of General Halleck,
then Chief of Staff.

General Halleck will be remembered as the hero
who won immortal fame before Corinth. With an
immensely superior force he so thoroughly entrencned
himself before that city that he not only held his position during General Beauregard's occupancy of the
town, but retained it for several days after the Confederate evacuation. He retired from active service after
this, his only piece of campaigning, to act in an advisory capacity at Washington, and it was he who
wrote these encouraging words to Sherman at Atlanta :
" The course which you have pursued in removing
rebel families from Atlanta, and in the exchange of
prisoners, is fully approved by the War Department.
. . . . . . Let the disloyal families thus stripped
go to their husbands, fathers, and natural protectors
in the rebel ranks. . . . . . . I would destroy
every mill and factory within reach, which I did not
want for my own use. . . . . . . I have endeavored to impress these views upon our commanders for
the last two years. *You are almost the only one who
has properly applied them.*" These words of encouragement fell upon willing ears. No one knew better
than Sherman how to read the sentiments between
those lines ; he understood the motives which moved
their doughty author as thoroughly as when later
the same hand gathered courage to advise him in
plain unvarnished words to wipe the city of Charleston off the face of the earth, and sow her site with

salt. The valiant Chief of Staff, who urged on campaigns from a point sufficiently to the rear, had found at last a man who would carry ont his instructions, and the war upon women and children was about to begin.

General Halleck was not the sole confidant of General Sherman's plan. Less than a month before the memorable march was undertaken, he telegraphed to General Grant: "I propose that we break up the railroad from Chattanooga forward, and that we strike out for Milledgeville, Millen and Savannah. Until we can repopulate Georgia, it is useless for us to occupy it, but the utter destruction of its roads, houses and people will cripple their military resources. I can make this march, and make Georgia howl !"

Sir Walter Raleigh conceived and attempted to execute the plan of exterminating the Irish race, and colonizing their lands from England. The Sultan of Turkey is about to carry out a similar policy with his Armenians.

The difference between these other exterminators and Sherman, is that they expected to be met at the doors of the homes they intended to destroy by men capable of offering resistance, while the American General knew he would have to do with women and children alone.

He evidently met with some expostulation from General Grant, for he afterwards telegraphed him that he would "infinitely prefer to make a wreck of the road and the country from Chattanooga and Atlanta, including the latter city, send back all wounded and unserviceable men, and with the effective army move through Georgia, smashing things to the sea."

Receiving no answer to this latter dispatch, he did not hesitate to execute the campaign as he had planned it, and in his own language proceeded to "make the interior of Georgia feel the weight of war."

Sherman and his staff rode out of the Gate City at 7 o'clock in the morning of the 16th. "Behind us," he says, "lay Atlanta, smouldering and in ruins, the black smoke rising high in the air and hanging like a pall over the ruined city. Some band, by accident, struck up the anthem of 'John Brown's soul goes marching on'. The men caught up the strain, and never before or since have I heard the chorus of 'Glory, glory, hallelujah!' done with more spirit or in better harmony of time and place." To the credit of the slandered soul of that other marauder, let us say, that John Brown's lawless warfare was upon men alone, and that booty formed no part of his incentive.

Knowing that no effective resistance was to be expected, Sherman so scattered his columns that the sixty-mile "swath" which it was his purpose to devastate, was covered by them with ease. In order that the work might be thoroughly and effectively done, a sufficient number of men were detailed for that branch of military service peculiar to Sherman's army, and known as "bummers."

"These interesting individuals always," says the General, "arose before day and preceded the army on its march." "Although this foraging was attended with great danger and hard work, there seemed to be a charm about it that attracted the soldiers, and it was a privilege to be detailed on such a party." "No doubt," he adds with that same blunt frankness, "many acts of pillage, robbery and violence were committed by these parties of foragers usually called 'bummers'; for I have since heard of jewelry taken from women, and the plunder of articles that never reached the commissary." But these playful fellows, in spite of such indiscretions, were never more to the General than an exhibition of that charming humor invariably apparent in him in the presence of human suffering.

We may gather an idea of them from the following description given by a correspondent of the New York Herald, who accompanied the army: "Any man who has seen the object that the name applies to will acknowledge that it was admirably selected. Fancy a ragged man, bleached by the smoke of many a pine-knot fire, mounted on a scraggy mule without a saddle, with a gun, a knap-sack, a butcher-knife and a plug hat, stealing his way through the pine forests far out in the flanks of a column, keen on the scent of rebels, or bacon, or silver spoons, or coin, or anything valuable, and you have him in your mind. Think how you would admire him if you were a lone woman, with a family of small children, far from help, when he blandly inquired where you kept your valuables! Think how you would smile when he pried open your chests with his bayonet, or knocked to pieces your tables, pianos and chairs, tore your bed clothing into three-inch strips and scattered them about the yard. The 'bummers' say it takes too much time to use keys. Color is no protection from the rough raiders. They go through a negro cabin in search of diamonds and gold watches with just as

much freedom and vivacity as they 'loot' the dwelling of a wealthy planter. They appear to be possessed of a spirit of 'pure cussedness.' One incident, illustrative of many, will suffice. A bummer
stepped into a house and inquired for sorghum. The
lady of the house presented a jug, which he said was
too heavy, so he merely filled his canteen. Then taking a huge wad of tobacco from his mouth he thrust
it into the jug. The lady inquired, in wonder, why
he spoiled that which he did not want. 'Oh, some
feller'll come along and taste that sorghum and think
you've poisoned him, then he'll burn your d——d old
house.' There are hundreds of these mounted men
with the column, and they go everywhere. Some of
them are loaded down with silverware, gold coin, and
other valuables. I hazard nothing in saying three
fifths (in value) of the personal property of the country we have passed through was taken by Sherman's
army."

In an address delivered before the Association of
the Maryland Line, Senator Zeb Vance, of North
Carolina, has laid the vigorous touch of his characteristic English upon the void until it stands out in
barbarous bold relief, so far beyond the pencil of the
present writer that he best serves his readers by
quoting: "With reference to his famous and infamous march, I wish to say that I hope I am too
much of a man to complain of the natural and inevitable hardships, or even cruelties of war; but of
the manner in which this army treated the peaceful
and defenseless inhabitants in the reach of his columns, all civilization should complain.

"There are always stragglers and desperadoes following in the wake of an army, who do some damage to and inflict some outrages upon helpless citizens, in spite of all efforts of commanding officers to restrain and punish ; but when a General organizes a corps of thieves and plunderers as a part of his invading army, and licenses beforehand their outrages, he and all who countenance, aid or abet, invite the execration of mankind. This peculiar arm of military service, it is charged and believed, was instituted by General Sherman in his invasion of the Southern States. Certain it is that the operations of his 'Bummer Corps' were as regular and as unrebuked, if not as much commended for efficiency, as any other division of his army, and their, atrocities are often justified or excused, on the ground that 'such is war.'

"In his own official report of his operations in Georgia, he says : 'We consumed the corn and fodder in the region of country thirty miles either side of a line from Atlanta to Savannah, also the sweet potatoes, hogs, sheep and poultry, and carried off more than ten thousand horses and mules. I estimate the damage done to Georgia at one-hundred million dollars, at least twenty million of which inured to our benefit, and the remainder was simply waste and destruction !' · · · · The 'remainder' delicately alluded to, that is say damage done the unresisting inhabitants to over and above the seizing of necessary army supplies, consisted in private houses burned, stock shot down and left to rot, bed clothes, money, watches, spoons, plate and ladies' jewelry stolen, etc., etc. A lane of desolation sixty miles wide through the heart of three great states, marked by more burnings and destructions than ever followed in the wake of the widest cyclone that ever laid forest low ! And all done, not to support an invading army, but for ' pure waste and destruction'; to punish the crime of rebellion, not in the persons of those who had brought these about, but of peaceful non-combatants, the tillers of the soil, the women and the children, the aged and feeble, and the poor slaves ! A silver spoon was evidence of disloyalty, a ring on a lady's finger was a sure proof of sympathy with rebellion, whilst a gold watch was *prima facie* evidence of the most damnable guilt on the part of the wearer. These obnoxious earmarks of treason must be seized and confiscated for private use—for ' such is war !' If these failed, and they sometimes did, torture of the inhabitants was freely employed to force disclosure. Sometimes with noble rage at their disappointment, the victims were left dead, as a warning to all others who should dare hide a jewel or a family trinket from the cupidity of a soldier of the Union. No doubt the stern necessity for such things caused great pain to those who inflicted, but the Union must be restored, and how could that be done whilst a felonious gold watch or a treasonable spoon was suffered to remain in the land, giving aid and comfort to rebellion ? For 'such is war.' Are such things war indeed ? Let us see. Eighty-four years before that time, there was a war, in that same country ; it was a rebellion, too, and an English nobleman led the troops of Great Britain through that same region, over much of the same

25

route, in his efforts to subdue that rebellion. The people through whose land he marched were bitterly hostile, they shot his foraging parties, his sentinels and stragglers, they fired upon him from every wood.

"He and his troops had every motive to hate and punish those rebellious and hostile people. It so happens that the original order-book of Lord Cornwallis is in possession of the North Carolina Historical Society. I have seen and read it. Let us make a few extracts and see what he considered war, and what he thought to be the duty of a civilized soldier towards non-combatants and the helpless:

"'CAMP NEAR BEATTY'S FORD,
January 28, 1781.

"'Lord Cornwallis has so often expressed the zeal and good will of the army that he has not the slightest doubt that the officers and soldiers will most cheerfully submit to the ill conveniences that must naturally attend war, so remote from water carriage and the magazines of the army. The supply of rum for a time will be absolutely impossible, and that of meal very uncertain. It is needless to point out to the officers the necessity of preserving the strictest discipline, and of preventing the oppressed people from suffering violence by the hands from whom they are taught to look for protection.'

"Now, General Sherman was fighting, as he said, for the sole purpose of restoring the Union, and for making the people of the rebellious States look to the United States alone for protection; does any act or order of his anywhere indicate a similar desire of protecting the people from suffering at the hands of those whose duty it was to protect them? Again:

"'HEADQUARTERS, LANSLER'S PLANTATION,
February 2, 1781.

"'Lord Cornwallis is highly displeased that several houses have been set on fire to-day during the march—a disgrace to the army—and he will punish with the utmost severity any person or persons who shall be found guilty of committing so disgraceful an outrage. His lordship requests the commanding officers of the corps will endeavor to find the persons who set fire to the houses to-day.'

"Now think of the march of Sherman's army which could be discovered a great way off by the smoke of homesteads by day and the lurid glare of flames by night, from Atlanta to Savannah, from Columbia to Fayetteville, and suppose that such an order as this had been issued by its commanding officers and rigidly executed, would not the mortality have been quite equal to that of a great battle?

"Arriving in Fayetteville on the 10th of January, 1865, he not only burned the arsenal, one of the finest in the United States, which perhaps he might properly have done, but also burned five private dwelling houses near by; he burned the principal printing offices, that of the old 'Fayetteville Observer;' he burned the old Bank of North Carolina, eleven large warehouses, five cotton mills and quite a number of private dwellings in other parts of the town, whilst in the suburbs almost a clean sweep was made; in one locality nine houses were burned. Universally houses

were gutted before they were burned, and after everything portable was secured the furniture was ruthlessly destroyed, pianos on which perhaps rebel tunes
had been played—' Dixie' or 'My Maryland'—disloyal
bureaus, traitorous tables and chairs were cut to pieces
with axes, and frequently, after all this damage, fire
was applied and all consumed. Carriages and vehicles
of all kinds were wantonly destroyed or burned;
instances could be given of old men who had the shoes
taken from their feet, the hats from their heads and
clothes from their persons; and their wives and children subjected to like treatment. In one instance, as
the marauders left they shot down a dozen cattle belonging to an old man, and then left their carcasses
lying in the yard. Think of that, and then remember
the grievance of the Pennsylvania Dutch farmers who
came in all seriousness to complain to General Long-
street in the Gettysburg campaign, of the outrage
which some of his ferocious rebels had committed
upon them *by 'milking their cows.'* On one occasion,
at Fayetteville, four gentlemen were hung up by the
neck until nearly dead to force them to disclose where
their valuables were hidden, and one of them was shot
to death. Again:

" 'HEADQUARTERS DOBBINS HOUSE,

February 17, 1781.

" 'Lord Cornwallis is very sorry to be obliged to call
the attention of the officers of the army to the repeated
orders against plundering, and he assures the officers
that if their duty to their King and country, and their
feelings for humanity are not sufficient to force their

obedience to them, he must, however reluctantly, make use of such powers as the military laws have placed in his hands. . . . . It is expected that Captains will exert themselves to keep good order and to prevent plundering. Any officer *who looks on with indifference and does not do his utmost to prevent shameful marauding, will be considered in a more criminal light than the persons who commit these scandalous crimes*, which must bring disgrace and ruin on his Majesty's service. All foraging parties will give receipts for supplies taken by them.'

"Now, taking it for granted that Lord Cornwallis, a distinguished soldier and a gentleman, is an authority on the rights of war, could there be found any where a more damnatory comment upon the practices of General Sherman and his army? Again:

" 'HEADQUARTERS, FREELANDS,
February 28, 1781.

" 'Memorandum:—A watch found by the regiment of Bose. The owner may have it from the adjutant of the regiment upon proving property.' Another:

" 'SMITH'S PLANTATION, March 1, 1781.

" ' Brigade Orders. A woman having been robbed of a watch, a black silk handkerchief, a gallon of peach brandy and a shirt, and as, by the description, by a soldier of the guards, the camp and every man's kit is to be immediately searched for the same by the officers of the Brigade.'

"Are there any poets in the audience, or other persons in whom the imaginative faculty has been largely cultivated? If so, let me beg him to do me the favor of conceiving, if he can, and make manifest to me, the idea of a notice of a lost watch being given, in general orders, by William Tecumseh Sherman, and the offer to return it on proof of property by the rebel owner! Let him imagine, if he can, the searching of every man's kit in the army for a stolen watch, a shirt, a black silk handkerchief and a gallon of peach brandy! Sherman says 'such is war.' I venture to say that up to the period when that 'great march' taught us the contrary, no humane general or civilized people in Christendom believed *that* '*such was* war.' Has civilization gone backward since Lord Cornwallis' day? Have arson and vulgar theft been ennobled into heroic virtues? If so, when and by whom? Has the art of discovering a poor man's hidden treasure by fraud or torture been elevated into the strategy which wins a campaign? If so, when and by whom?

"No, it will not do to slur over these things by a vague reference to the inevitable cruelties of war. The time is fast coming when the conduct of that campaign will be looked upon in the light of real humanity, and investigated in the real historic spirit which evolves truth; and all the partisan songs which have been sung, or orations which subservient orators have spoken about that great march to the sea; and all the caricatures of Southern leaders which the bitterness of a diseased sectional sentiment has inspired; and all the glamour of a great success, shall not avail to restrain the inexorable, the illuminating pen of history. Truth, like charity, never faileth. Whether there be prophecies, they shall fail, whether there be tongues they shall cease; whether there be knowledge, it shall vanish away ; but when the truth, which is perfect, has come, then that which is in part shall be done away.

"Now let us contrast General Sherman with his greatest foe; likewise the greatest, the most humane general of modern times, and see whether he regarded the pitiless destruction of the substance of women and children and inoffensive inhabitants a legitimate war:

" 'HEADQUARTERS ARMY OF NORTHERN VA.,
June 27, 1863.

" 'General Order No. 73. The commanding general has observed with marked satisfaction the conduct of troops on this march. There have, however, been instances of forgetfulness on the part of some that they have in keeping the yet unsullied reputation of this army, and that the duties exacted of us by civilization and Christianity are not less obligatory in the country of an enemy than in our own. The commanding general considers that no greater disgrace could befall the army and through it our whole people, than the perpetration of barbarous outrages upon the unarmed and defenceless, and the wanton destruction of private property, that have marked the course of the enemy in our country. . . . It will be remembered that we make war only upon armed men.
R. E. LEE, General.'

"The humanity and Christian spirit of this order was such as to challenge the admiration of foreign nations. The 'London Times' commented upon it, and its American correspondent said : 'The greatest surprise has been expressed to me by officers from the Austrian, Prussian and English armies, each of which has representatives here, that volunteer troops, provoked by nearly twenty-seven months of unparalleled ruthlessness and wantonness, of which their country has been the scene, should be under such control, and willing to act in harmony with the long-suffering and forbearance of President Davis and General Lee.'

"To show how this order was executed, the same writer tells a story of how he witnessed with his own eyes General Lee and a surgeon of his command repairing the damage to a farmer's fence. Colonel McClure, of Philadelphia, a Union soldier himself, bears witness to the good conduct of Lee's ragged rebels in that famous campaign. He tells of hundreds of them coming to him and asking for a little bread and coffee, and others who were wet and shivering asking permission to enter a house, in which they saw a bright fire, to warm themselves until their coffee should be ready. Hundreds of similar instances could be given, substantiated by the testimony of men on both sides, to show the splendid humanity of that great invasion. Blessed be the good God, who, if in His wisdom denied us success, yet gave to us and our children the rich inheritance of this great example.

" Major General Halleck, the commander-in-chief, under the President, of the armies of the Union, on the 18th of December, 1864, dispatched as follows to Sherman, then in Savannah : 'Should you capture Charleston, I hope that by some accident the place may be destroyed ; and if a little salt should be sown upon its site it may prevent the growth of future crops of nullification and secession.' On December 27th, 1864, Sherman made the following answer : ' I will bear in mind your hint as to Charleston, and don't think "salt" will be necessary. When I move, the 15th corps will be on the right of the right wing, and their position will bring them naturally into Charleston first, and if you have watched the history of the corps you will have remarked that they generally do their work up pretty well. The truth is, the whole army is burning with insatiable desire to wreak vengeance upon South Carolina. I almost tremble at her fate ; but feel that she deserves all that seems to be in store for her. . . I look upon Columbia as quite as bad as Charleston.' Therefore Columbia was burned to ashes. And though he knew what was in store for South Carolina, so horrible that he even trembled, he took no steps to avert it, for he felt that she deserved it all. Did she, indeed ? What crime had she committed that placed her outside the protection of the law of civilized nations ? What unjust, or barbarous, or brutal conduct had she been guilty of to bring her within the exceptions laid down by the writers on the laws of war as authorizing extraordinary severity of punishment ? They are not even imputed to her. South Carolina's crime, and the crime of all the seceding States, was that of a construction of the constitution of the United States differing from that of General Sherman and the 15th corps—which 'always did up its work pretty well.' Happily the Divine Goodness has made the powers of recuperation superior to those of destruction ; and though their overthrow was so complete that ' salt ' was not needed as the type of utter desolation, Marietta and Atlanta are thriving and prosperous cities."

Governor Vance does not wish to confine himself, in quoting, to Southern testimony. There are plenty of honest and truthful soldiers in the Federal army, who served in its ranks, to tell all we want and more. This is what one of them says, writing to the "Detroit Free Press" of that campaign: "One of the most devilish acts of Sherman's campaign was the destruction of Marietta. The Military Institute and such mills and factories as might be a benefit to Hood could expect the torch, but Sherman was not content with that; the torch was applied to everything, even the shanties occupied by the negroes. No advance warning was given. The first alarm was followed by the crackling of flames. Soldiers rode from house to house, entered without ceremony and kindled fires in garrets and closets, and stood by to see that they were not extinguished." Again he says: "Had one been able to climb to such a height at Atlanta as to enable him to see for forty miles around, the day Sherman marched out, he would have been appalled at the destruction. Hundreds of houses had been burned; every rod of fence destroyed; nearly every fruit tree cut down, and the face of the country so changed that one born in that section could scarcely recognize it. The vindictiveness of war would have trampled the very earth out of sight, had such a thing been possible."

One cold and drizzly night in the midst of this marching General Sherman found shelter and warmth beneath the roof of a comfortable plantation home.

" In looking around the room," he says, " I saw a small box, like a candle box, marked ' Howell Cobb,' and, on inquiring of a negro, found we were at the plantation of General Howell Cobb, of Georgia, one of the leading rebels of the South, then a General in the Southern army, and who had been Secretary of the Treasury in Mr. Buchanan's time. Of course we confiscated his property, and found it rich in corn, beans, peanuts, and sorghum molasses. Extensive fields were all around the house. I sent word back to General Davis to explain whose plantation it was, and to instruct him to spare nothing. That night huge bonfires consumed the fence-rails, kept our soldiers warm, and the teamsters and men, as well as slaves, carried off an immense quantity of corn and provisions of all sorts."

Do the records of civilized warfare furnish a parallel to this petty and mercenary wreaking of spite upon the helpless home of a gallant foeman ?

The General furnished us with proof of how worthy of their selection his staff-officers proved during that memorable raid. While camped that night on Cobb's plantation, Lieutenant Snelling, who was a Georgian commanding his escort, received permission to visit his uncle, who lived some six miles away.

"The next morning," says the General, "he described to me his visit. The uncle was not cordial by any means to find his nephew in the ranks of the host that was desolating the land, and Snelling came back, having exchanged his tired horse for a fresher one out of his uncle's stables, explaining that surely some of the 'bummers' would have got the horse had he not."

It was the eternal fitness of things that the staff-officers of this prince of free-booters should be renegades capable of stealing from their nearest kin.

The unfailing jocosity of this merry marauder breaks out in his recital of a negro's account of the destruction of Sandersville : "First, there came along some cavalrymen, and they burned the depot; then came along some infantrymen, and they tore up the track and burned it, and, just before they left, they sot fire to the well !" The well, he explains, was a boxed affair into which some of the debris was piled, and the customary torch was applied, making the negro's statement literally true. This was one of the incidents to leaving the pretty town of Sandersville a smoking mass of ruins.

But why enumerate further details of an unresisted movement which cost Sherman one hundred and three lives, and the State of Georgia one hundred million dollars, twenty millions of which he frankly states he carried off, and eighty millions of which he destroyed ? It began in shame at Atlanta—it passed with a gathering burden of infamy to Savannah. Starvation, terror, outrage hung upon its flanks and rear. Its days were darkened by the smoking incense from unparalleled sacrifices upon the altar of wantonness; its nights were lurid with flames licking the last poor shelter from above the heads of subjugated wives and children.

Its history is the strongest human argument for an orthodox hell.

TESTIMONIALS.

STATE OF GEORGIA,
EXECUTIVE OFFICE,
ATLANTA, September 1st, 1894.

"Life in Dixie During the War," by Miss Mary A. H. Gay, presents a striking picture of home life among our people during that dark period of our history.

While such presentation is hardly looked for in more elaborate history of those times, Miss Gay's conception was a wise one, and the record she has given will preserve a most desirable part of the history of our section.

Her book deserves to be widely circulated.

W. J. NORTHEN,
Governor.

"LIFE IN DIXIE DURING THE WAR."

This handsome volume from the pen of Miss Mary A. H. Gay, whose many acts of self-denial entitle her to the name of philanthropist, will meet with a hearty welcome from her wide circle of friends. But a casual glance at the volume leads us to conclude that outside of this circle, even with the reader who will look into it as a key to the history of the "times that tried men's souls," it will be a book of more than passing

interest. The author writes with the feelings of a
partisan, but time has mellowed her recollections of
these stormy times, and even the reader whose sympa-
thies were with the other side will agree with Joel
Chandler Harris in his introduction to the book. In
its mechanical get-up, the book is a gem.—*Atlanta
Constitution*, December 18, 1892.

"LIFE IN DIXIE."

Miss Mary A. H. Gay has published a volume
entitled "Life in Dixie During the War," which
should be in every Southern home. It is one of the
truest pictures of the life of our people during the war
that has yet been drawn. In fact, it could not be
better, for it shows things just as they were. The
struggles and sufferings of the Southern people during
that awful period exhibited a heroism that has seldom
been matched in the world's history. Miss Gay was
among them. She looked on their trials with sympathetic eyes and suffered with them. Fortunately she
is gifted with the power of describing what she saw,
and her book will be a classic of war literature. Its
every page is interesting. The story of Dixie during
the war reads like romance to the generation that has
arisen since, but it should have for generations an
interest as deep as that with which it is read by those
who lived and acted amid the scenes it records. It
shows how grand was the courage and virtue, how
sublime the faith and endurance of the men and
women of the South throughout that terrible ordeal.
It is a book that will live, and one that will give to

the world a true representation of the conduct of a noble people in affliction. Miss Gay has made numerous contributions to our literature which mark her as a woman of rare capacity and exquisite feelings, but she has done no work that is worthier of gratitude and praise than that embodied in "Life in Dixie."— *The Atlanta Journal*, January 17, 1893.

"LIFE IN DIXIE."

Miss Mary Gay's recent book, "Life in Dixie During the War," is rapidly winning favor with the public. Some of our most distinguished writers speak of it in very high terms as a notable contribution to our history. The Rev. Dr. J. William Jones says of it :

" 'Life in Dixie During the War' is a charming story of home-life during those dark days when our noble women displayed a patient endurance, and active zeal, a self-denying work in the hospitals, a genuine patriotism, a true heroism which equalled the record of their fathers, husbands, sons and brothers in the army.

"But Decatur, near Atlanta, was the scene of stirring events during Sherman's campaign against the doomed city, and Miss Gay's facile pen vividly portrays historic events of deepest interest.

"Visits from the soldier boy to the old home, letters from the camp, visits to the camps and hospitals, the smoke and changing scenes of battle in the enemy's lines, refugeeing, and many other events of those stirring days, are told with the vividness of an eye-witness and the pen of an accomplished writer.

"It is, in a word, a vivid and true picture of ' Life in Dixie During the War,' and should find a place not only in our Southern homes, but in the homes of all who desire to see a true account of the life of our noble women during those trying days.

"REV. JOHN WILLIAM JONES.' "
The Constitution, May 2nd, 1893.

The "Confederate Love Song," by Miss Mary A. H. Gay, of Decatur, was written during the late war. It is a charming bit of verse, and forms one of a galaxy of beautiful songs from the same true pen.   In 1880, Miss Gay published a volume of verses which received the unusual compliment of public demand for no less than eleven editions.   The author's life is one of the most beautiful; it is, therefore, quite natural that her poetry should partake of the simple truth and sincerity of that life, consecrated as it is, and ever has been, to the noblest work.—*Atlanta Constitution.*

Miss Gay's Book, "Life in Dixie During the War." —Editor "*Sunny South:*" Permit me to say a few words through the columns of your widely read and popular paper about Miss Mary A. H. Gay's " Life in Dixie During the War," the second and enlarged edition of which book has just been issued from the press.

The fact that a second and enlarged edition has been called for is proof that the merits of this genuine Southern story has been appreciated by our people. Not only has the author in her book perpetuated

interesting and historically valuable material of merely
local character, but, to the careful reader, she also
presents matter that goes to the deep moral, social
and political roots of the cause of the people of the
South, that grew and flowered into the crimson rose
of war, which the South plucked and wore upon her
heart during four of the most tragic yet glorious
years recorded in history.

But the chief charms of the book are its simple,
earnest, homely style, its depth of womanly and loyal
feeling, and the glimpses we get of the homes and
hearts of our people during these years of patient suffering and "crucifixion of the soul;" and along with
the passion and the pain, we are presented with
pictures of our people's frequently laughable "makeshifts" to supply many of the common necessaries of
life and household appliances of which the stress and
savage devastation deprived nearly every Southern
family. Above all we are impressed by the more
than Spartan heroism, the tender love, the unwavering
loyalty, the devoted, self-sacrificing spirit of our noble
Southern womanhood, of which this book speaks so
eloquently in its *naive* simplicity, and of which traits
of character, the modest author herself is a living and
universally beloved example.

The book deserves a place in the hearts and homes
of our people. Surely the patriotic motives that
inspired its author to write it is the only passport it
needs to public favor and patronage.

CHARLES W. HUBNER,
"*Sunny South*," Atlanta, Ga., November 3, 1894.

26

A WAR STORY.

Even in these piping times of peace (peace as far as our own borders are concerned, at any rate)—there is a relish in a war story. And when the scene is laid right here in Georgia, in Decatur, in Atlanta; when familiar names come up in the course of the narrative, and familiar events are pictured by an honest eye-witness; when all through the little volume you feel the truthfulness of the writer, and know that the incidents she narrates happened just so; when, too, you see the writer herself—see her to be an old lady now, who really was a heroine in her young days; and then read the simple, personal narrative—now stirring, as the battle-guns sound—now touching, as some dear one falls; with all this combination of interest, a war story claims and holds the attention.

Such is the little book, called "Life in Dixie," written by Miss Mary Gay, and telling of those stirring times in and about Atlanta, back yonder in the sixties.

There are some vivid pictures in that modest little volume, as well as some interesting facts. Miss Gay was in the thick of the strife, and tells what she saw in those dark days.

Among the well-known characters, associated with the recorded events, we find Mrs. L. P. Grant, Mr. and Mrs. Posey Maddox, Dr. J. P. Logan and many others.

A most interesting fact disclosed in those pages is the surprising one that two sisters of Mrs. Abraham Lincoln married Alabama officers in the Confederate army; there is recorded the public presentation, by those two ladies, of an elegant silk banner made for a gallant young company in Georgia's daughter-State. Thus conspicuous were those women in the Southern Confederacy, while their sister and her dearest interests lay on the other side.

Another matter of history which will be interesting to the present generation of readers, however much we may have read of the mammoth prices for the necessaries of life in those hard days, is the following list of articles, with the cost thereof in Confederate money, bought by Miss Gay, after a ride of forty miles to obtain them:

One bushel of meal, $10.00; four bushels of corn, $40.00; fifteen pounds of flour, $7.50; four pounds of dried apples, $5.00; one and a half pounds of butter, $6.00; a bushel of sweet potatoes, $6.00; three gallons of syrup, $15.00; for shoeing the horse, $25.00; for a night's lodging for self and horse, at Mrs. Born's, $10.00.

Then, the vehicle in which the trip for these supplies was made!

It was contrived by "Uncle Mack," a dusky hero of those times. "It was a something he had improvised which baffled description," writes Miss Gay, "and which, for the sake of the faithful service I obtained from it, I will not attempt to describe. Suffice it to say that it carried living freight over many a bridge; and in honor of this, I will call it a wagon."

The horse, which the author herself captured to draw this remarkable vehicle, was equally remarkable, and his subsequent history is one of the most interesting bits of narrative in the book. I wish I could give it all in Miss Gay's own words, but my space does not admit of that.

But there is not a child in your household who would not be interested in the account of how the poor starved horse was lassoed and secured—how he was fed and strengthened, and cared for, and finally harnessed up with ropes and pieces of crocus sacks ; how the letters, "U. S." were found branded on each of his sides, causing his mistress to name him "Yankee"; how she grew to love him so that she deemed that name ill-fitting, and decided to re-christen him "Johnnie Reb.," which she did one day with effective ceremonial by a brook-side; how he rendered invaluable service to his mistress many and many a time, and was a treasured member of the little family that passed such stormy times in the war-stricken village of Decatur; all this is worth reading, told, as it is, with a gentle humor, and a strict truthfulness which is the chief charm of that historic picture. For it is historic. And it were well for the rising generation to read its vivid portrayals of that period.

And though Miss Gay was evidently an ardent secessionist, and is now, I fancy, one of the altogether unreconstructed few, her book contains records of more than one kindness received at the hands of officers of the United States army—kindness proffered, too, in the face of her fearless avowal of opinion.

Some parts of the book (I will add, if the gentle author will allow me) seem somewhat too bitter towards our brethren of the North. But this criticism is from the standpoint of one who knew not the horrors of that dreadful war. If I had seen the desolation and destruction which followed it in the wake of Sherman's army, as Miss Gay saw it and suffered by it (through mother and brother and friends, as well as through personal privation),—if I had thus suffered, doubtless I, too, would be unable to look impartially upon these Federal leaders and their actuating motives—unable to see that, though Sherman was a most unmerciful conqueror, he was not altogether a fiend.

But there is only a touch of this severe judgment in Miss Gay's little book. The greater portion of it is simply historic—a faithful chronicling of events experienced by the writer herself, who was a veritable heroine in those days of horrors.

Miss Gay is to be congratulated upon the fact that "Life in Dixie" is entering upon its second edition. Let me suggest that you get it for your children, you parents. The rising generation should learn of the stirring events which happened right here in Atlanta thirty years ago.

The story will hold their attention and interest throughout—the soldier-brother who fell in the strife, the faithful black Toby sketched so tenderly, the perilous trip of Miss Gay herself, as she carried the blankets and overcoats through the enemy's ranks to the boys in gray—all this will vastly entertain those young folks, at the same time it teaches them of the Battle of Atlanta, and the concurrent events.—EMEL JAY, in *The Atlanta Journal,* November 24th, 1894.

"Emel Jay" is Miss Mary L. Jackson, daughter of the late Hon. James Jackson, Chief Justice of the Supreme Court of Georgia.

"Life in Dixie During the War" is the title of a volume just perused which transcends in interest, truth and beauty all the historical tomes and garlanded fiction to which that epoch has given birth. It embraces the personal experiences and observations of a woman, gifted far beyond the ordinary, who came in contact with the sadness, the bloodshed and the misery of the unhappy struggle. A loved brother laid down his life on the bloodiest battle-field, friends parted and vanished from her, and wealth was swallowed in the maw of destruction.

She tells her story—for story it is—with an exquisite grace, and with a woman's tenderness and sympathy for the people she loved and the cause she adored. Her language is lofty upon occasion, her memories perhaps too keen, her gentleness possibly too exclusive to her own, but her work is done with a fidelity and consistency beyond comparison. The scene is Decatur, Ga., but threads, visible or invisible, reach to every hamlet and entwine every heart in the evanished Confederacy. The heroism of men, the daring of boys, the endurance of women, alike are painted with a skill that requires no color.

Those who wish to embalm their recollections of home-life during the war, and those who desire to know what it was, should read this book. It is one of the records of the past that should be in every library. It is beautifully printed, neatly cloth-bound, and contains 300 pages.—*The Tampa Daily Times*, January 17, 1895.

FROM THE OTHER SIDE.

EVANSTON, ILL., December 30th, 1895.
Mary A. H. Gay:

DEAR MADAM: Allow me to thank you for giving
to the world inside home life in the South during the
war. All histories of the war that have been written
have been confined to battles and movements of
armies, which are so likened to the histories of other
wars that when you have read one you may say that
you have read them all. But yours gives a local and
romantic description of real life, and I feel like con-
gratulating you and calling the scenes in which you
played so important a part the heyday of your existence. I take it you were the daughter, pampered and
cuddled child, of rich and influential people, and had it
not been for the war you would have been raised with
much pomp, arrogance and importance of family,
which, in the very nature of your surroundings, would
have destroyed all the finer and nobler traits which
want and misery have developed into a grand, noble,
self-sacrificing and heroic woman. And although you
portray the scenes freighted with misery, want and
desolation, yet they were halcyon days to one like you,
romantic, energetic, patriotic and self-sacrificing, and
now, as you are passing down the shady lane of life,
you live in the memories of the past, the part you
played in the heroic struggle, and the noble womanhood developed ; and the assurance that you did well

your part in the great tragedy strews roses and garlands along the path of your declining years.

"I follow you through all these stirring scenes ; I sit beside you in your hours of gloom and blighted hopes ; I follow you beside the ox-cart that drew its freight of human misery ; I walk with you into the woody retreats and sit beside you upon the banks of the limpid stream and mix my tears with yours ; I tramp with you over the scenes of desolation ; I sorrow with you over the death of Toby ; I mourn with you over the sudden death of noble Thomie ; I sit beside the death-bed of your sainted mother and mingle my tears with yours ; I gladly accompany you on your weary tramp with your much-loved 'Yankee' or Johnnie Reb ; I gather with you the leaden missiles of death to buy food for starving friends and fellow-sufferers ; I pass with you through all the scenes that are freighted with hope, love, despair and expectation ; I am your friend and sympathizer in all your misfortunes, and yet I am one of those ' accursed' Yankee soldiers who have been the bane of your life.

"The strange blending of pathos and diplomacy on pages 91 and 92 may be said to be amusingly expressive. Chapter 13 is intensely interesting, dramatic and romantic ; still I see no reason that I should speak of these isolated passages, for the whole book is equally interesting, and would foreshadow for it a large sale in the North if properly handled. As to the mechanical construction of the book, I am much pleased with your language, as it is free from Carlylism and ostentatious English, which mars so much of the writings of many of our modern authors. I hold that when a book is overloaded with this disgusting use of the dictionary it is what Goldsmith terms 'display of book learned skill.'

The book was kindly sent me by a lady friend in Atlanta, Mrs. Delbridge, and I hope when I visit Atlanta again I may have the pleasure of meeting the authoress that nature has endowed with such wonderful power of description."

Most respectfully,

CHARLES AIKIN.

Published in *The Atlanta Constitution* January 5th, 1896.

"LIFE IN DIXIE DURING THE WAR,

is the title of one of the best series of sketches that has been written about the 'late unpleasantness.' It contains the record of one woman's experience during the five years of warfare between the North and the South. The author, Miss Mary A. H. Gay, of Decatur, Georgia, one of the most graceful writers in the South, has handled the subject in a masterful manner. 'Truth is stranger than fiction,' and the work abounds in truth. The volume ought to be on sale at every news-stand in the South. The book has been described as containing 'a living picture of those trying times—not to stir up bitter feelings and hatred, but a history, and such history as cannot be obtained in any other form.' Miss Gay was in the thick of the strife, ' and in a modest way shows herself a heroine worthy of any romance.' Her pen describes scenes that bring tears for the pain and suffering, and laughter at the 'makeshifts resorted to by those noble people in the hour of actual need. 'Some parts of the narrative may be judged as rather bitter towards the enemy by those who know not the horrors of that war. But let such critics put themselves in the wake of Sherman's army and suffer as the writer, and they will feel more charitable towards her who, in recalling those experiences, finds it hard to love all her enemies. There is only a touch of this old-time bitterness, however ; most of the book is simply historic, and Miss Gay does not hesitate to record many kindnesses received at the hands of Federal officers.' Such a valuable contribution to the history of the war should be prized. It is a vivid chronicle, and the rising generation should learn of those stirring events. They will read with unflagging interest to the end of the narrative. We wish for it a wide circulation."—*The Arkansas Gazette*, March 10th, 1896.

LIFE IN DIXIE DURING THE WAR.

BY MARY A. H. GAY, DECATUR, GA.

We endorse most heartily the praise bestowed on this modest volume by the general press. Within the same scope we do not believe a truer or more sympathetic picture of the ghastly war time has ever been written. It is not fiction, but a faithful presentation of one woman's experience during the five years that bounded the war between the States.

The writer was in the very thick of the strife, and while with admirable modesty she has endeavored to keep herself out of her book, it is clear that she was one of the heroic and indefatigable women who brought into scenes of suffering the ministry of tenderness. The recital of events as they were, brings humor into the book, whose tenor in the main, however, is necessarily sad.

By those to whom the war is simply a tale that is told, there are parts of the book in which the writer will be accused of undue bitterness. However, no such critics, we think, will be found among the people to whom the war was a reality. Miss Gay records, without hesitation, many kindnesses received at the hands of the Federal officers.

Texas soldiers of Granbury's brigade, Cleburne's division, and Hood's corps, figure conspicuously and by name in the book. Miss Gay visited Hood's headquarters twice while the brigade was encamped in Georgia, the last time just before they left Georgia for the fatal march into Tennessee. The night-scene she describes near Jonesboro, where they were encamped, is most graphic and pathetic. Miss Gay is the woman who collected the money to have the soldiers who fell at Franklin, Tennessee, reburied, when she heard that the owners of the battlefield said their graves should be ploughed over. She collected $7,000, and her name is engraved on the silver plate on the entrance gate at the McGavock cemetery, which she so largely helped to build. — *The Richmond Times*, Feb. 16, 1896.

LIFE' IN DIXIE DURING THE WAR.

The following deserved complimentary notice of the book, "Life in Dixie During the War," written by Miss Mary A. H. Gay, of Georgia, we clip from the New York Times : "Joel Chandler Harris' brief introduction to Miss Gay's reminiscences of the civil war tells of the authenticity of this simple story, and how a book of this character is of that kind from whence 'history will get its supplies.' The dark days are described with absolute fidelity, and this is a quality we may look for in vain 'in more elaborate and ambitious publications.' Think of the strangeness of things, the breaks in families, when the author tells how, at the presentation of a flag, the banner was made for a company of Confederate soldiers by Miss Ella Todd and Mrs. White, of Lexington, Kentucky, the sisters of Mrs. Abraham Lincoln, the wife of the great President.

It was in and around Decatur, Georgia, where the author now lives, that, in the storm and heat of the war, heroically and unflinchingly the women of the South did their duty in helping those in the field. You will find no incidents of the war which do not show the colored man in the South at his best. Miss Gay describes their devotion and what true friends they were. The author tells how more than once she was near starvation. It happened that the house in which she lived became the headquarters of a troop of United States Cavalry. Very possibly bureau drawers became convenient feed troughs for horses. After the cavalry had left there was not a morsel to eat. The famished children, white and black, were crying for food. The day was spent by the women picking up grains of corn from the cracks and crevices in bureau drawers, and other improvised troughs for Federal horses. In this way, by diligent and persevering work, about a half bushel of corn was obtained. The corn, having been thoroughly washed and dried, was taken to a small mill and coarsely ground, and served to give the hungry ones their bread. The utter destitution of the people after the fall of Atlanta is shown in this way: Lead was in demand, and on the battlefields around Atlanta it could be picked up, pellet by pellet. Delicately nurtured women dug up the spent minie balls from the frozen clods and exchanged them for bread.—The Mechanicsburg, Pa., *Free Press*, February, 20, 1896.

LIFE IN DIXIE DURING THE WAR.

BY MARY A. H. GAY, DECATUR, GA.

Of the numerous stories which have had as their basis the war between the States, there are few truer pictures, in our opinion, than that presented by a Southern woman in this volume, with a telling preface by Joel Chandler Harris. The writer's home was in Decatur, but the stories include the history of the entire section, and give much very interesting information relative to life in Atlanta, particularly during the war era. Miss Gay was in the very heart of the strife, and she describes with the vigorous pen of one to whom the matter is a vital reality.—*The Southern Churchman*, Richmond, Va., March 12, 1896.

LIFE IN DIXIE DURING THE WAR.

The volume written and published by Miss Mary A. H. Gay, of Georgia, entittled "Life in Dixie Dur-the War," is one of the few books in the flood tide of literature on the great civil conflict that many will read with interest, because it is a woman's story of actual life in Dixie from the beginning to the close of the great conflict. We have volumes in abundance which tell of the great battles of the war, of the achievement of heroes and the sacrifices which attended the victories, but the story of the home life of Southern people during the war must ever be of absorbing interest to every American. They are our people, our countrymen, sharing the common inheritance of heroism in all the conflicts of the Republic, and that part of the history of the war of the rebellion that is least understood is the extraordinary sufferings and sacrifices of the Southern women, who heroically aided their fathers, husbands, sons and brothers in the unequal contest. Miss Gay gives a plain unvarnished story of life in Georgia during the war, and of the many sad sacrifices to which the families of Southern people were subjected. One of the noticeable features of this story, commencing with the expression of confident hope for the success of the Confederacy and ending in the starless midnight of gloom that attended the surrender of Lee and his legions, is given in the description of a presentation of a silken banner to the Magnolia Cadets when the war began. The banner was prepared and finished by Mrs. Dr. White, of Lexington, Kentucky, and her sister Miss Todd, sisters of Mrs. President Lincoln, and they were presented to the enthusiastic audience by Captain Dawson, who subsequently married Miss Todd.

Miss Gay's volume is full of interesting incidents, showing the heroism and sublime faith and endurance of the women of the South during the terrible ordeal. Like all Southern women, she was intensely devoted to the Southern Cause, and often exposed herself to great peril to serve the Confederacy. More than once she took her life into her hand to aid the hopeless cause in which the Southern armies had engaged. It was principally by her efforts that money was raised to entomb the Confederates that fell at the bloody battle of Franklin, Tennessee. Her name is engraved on a silver plate that is mounted on the entrance gate of the cemetery, and there are few who will not become readers of her book. It is in every way interesting to people both North and South, and should have a very wide circulation.—From *The Times*, Philadelphia, Pa., May 27, 1896.

LIFE IN DIXIE DURING THE WAR.

Many stories of the late war have been written, some from the stand point of the "Blue," and some from the "Grey," but we doubt whether a truer picture of real war times in the South has ever been depicted than the one found in this modest little volume. There is no fiction in it, but it is the record of one woman's experiences during the war.

Her home was in Decatur, Georgia, but her narrative includes the history of all that portion of

country.   Very few persons who did not live in that
section know or remember to what extent those people
suffered.   And we would commend them to this book
—a living picture of those trying times—not to stir up
bitter feelings and hatred, but because it is history,
and such history as cannot be obtained in any other
form.

Miss Gay was in the thick of the strife, and in a
modest way she shows herself a heroine worthy of any
romance.   Her pen describes scenes that bring tears
for the pain and suffering, and laughter at the "makeshifts " resorted to by these noble people in the hour
of actual needs.   Some parts of the narrative may be
regarded as rather bitter towards the enemy by those
who know not the horrors of that war.   But let such
critics put themselves in the wake of Sherman's army,
and suffer as the writer did, and we think they will
feel more charitably towards her, who, in recalling
those experiences, find it hard to love all her enemies.
There is only a touch of this old time bitterness, however ; most of the book is simply historic, and Miss
Gay does not hesitate to record many kindnesses
received at the hands of the Federal officers.   Such a
valuable contribution to the history of the war should
be prized.   It is a vivid chronicle and the rising
generation should learn of those stirring events.
They will read with unflagging interest to the end of
the narrative.   We wish for it a wide circulation.—
" *The Christian Observer*," Louisville, Kentucky, May
8th, 1896.

Commendatory notices have also appeared in "The

Hampton (Florida) *Advocate*," "The Decatur
Record," "The DeKalb County *New Era*," " The Wes-
leyan *Christian Advocate*," *etc.*

The following letter was written to Mr. C. D.
Mitchell, Secretary and Treasurer of Chattanooga
Plow Company, Chattanooga, Tennessee:

CINCINNATI, OHIO, November 30, 1896.
MY DEAR MITCHELL—I have read Miss Gay's book
on "Life in Dixie During the War," and thank you
very much for giving me the opportunity to read it.
I fancy you will think I am a good deal of a "calf,"
but I couldn't help choking up a good many times as
I read of the terrible experience of the poor women
and children and helpless aged people when misfor-
tune placed them in the path of the armies during
that bloody period, and we who were at the front
knew but little of the misery in the wake of the armies.

I was glad to see that Miss Gay speaks kindly of
our command, and that we afforded protection to her
family without leaving any harm to them in any way.

To-day is the anniversary of the death of her
brother, killed in front of our works at Franklin.
When I read of his death the whole bloody scene was
revived, and how useless and fool-hardy that charge
of Cleburne's over the open cotton fields at Franklin
upon our works. The dead were almost countless,
and one long grave was dug for all. I well remember
this immense trench where the Confederates were laid
side by side. I commanded the 1st Batallion that day
at the battle of Franklin, and we had a very warm
time of it. We retreated on Nashville the following

27

day, and I was cut off from the Regiment for a while, but we finally made a big detour and regained our lines. After the battle of Nashville we occupied the Franklin battlefield, and I went carefully over the whole field. Hood's charge upon our Franklin works, if successful, would have been a moderate victory only, but unsuccessful, it was a most terrible loss to him.

At 57 you and I look at things rather different than we did in our youth of 22, and while scars of war may be healed, they are nevertheless not forgotten. With kind regards. Yours very truly,

T. F. ALLEN.

I think General Garrard would like to read this book, if he has not already done so, and if you approve I will send it up to him and return it to you later. At this season of the year he has time to read.

T. F. A.

A Brief Sketch of the Life and Literary Career of Mary Gay

Mary Ann Harris Gay was born in March, 1829, in Jones County, Georgia. Her father was William Gay and her mother the former Mary Stevens, daughter of Thomas Stevens. William Gay was descended from Virginians who migrated through the Carolinas to Georgia. He died within a year or so of his daughter's birth.[1]

In 1833, Mrs. William Gay married Decatur lawyer Joseph Stokes.[2] Following the marriage, the family moved to Cassville on the northwestern frontier of Georgia, where two children were born–Thomas, in 1837, and a daughter, Missouri Horton, in 1838.[3]

In April of 1840, Mary Gay's grandfather Thomas Stevens died leaving part of his estate to Mary Gay's mother with the stipulation that money be held in trust from the sale of certain Twiggs County land for the education of his grandchild Mary Gay.[4]

According to the biographical sketch of Missouri Stokes in Mrs. J. J. Ansley's *History of the Georgia Christian Temperance Union*, the family moved to Marietta in 1845. Mary's first poem "My Valley Home" was published there anonymously the next year.[5]

Following the death of her stepfather, Mary and her family moved to Decatur in 1851. The move to Decatur was probably determined by her deceased grandfather's family and connections in DeKalb County. Thomas Stevens, as a pioneer in the county, purchased lands along the Chattahoochee River and between the forks of Nancy and Peachtree creeks in 1825.[6] In 1831, he bought land lot 143 in Decatur for $400.00.[7] He was also named a trustee of the newly incorporated Decatur Cemetery.[8]

It is not known whether the property to which Mary and her family came was the property purchased by her grandfather in 1831, as the early maps of the city have been destroyed. Also unknown is whether Mary Gay was ever formally educated in accordance with the terms of her grandfather's will.

We do know that she continued to publish poetry, and that her first book appeared anonymously under the title *Prose and Poetry* in 1858,[9] with the second edition the following year in which she was identified as the author.[10] Several of her early poems were republished in this first book, and an idea of Mary Gay's early travels can be gleaned from the date and place name notations with the poems. A poem entitled "Tallassee Falls" carried the notation Montgomery, Alabama, 1850, and "My Childhood Home" Decatur, 1856. "To My Love" was written at Oak Grove, Gordon County, and "The Busy Body" at Adairsville. Her essay "A Vision" published in the 1859 edition of the book, describes the possibility of war between the North and the South. She writes: "...that whether right or wrong our country's privilege shall be defended, and that he who conquers shall find a stubborn foe."

Most of Mary Gay's prose in the 1859 edition of *Prose and Poetry* was written in Decatur. This book went through eleven editions. In the last edition published in 1881, the preface states that these works "...constitute only a very small portion of her writings...." In the eleventh edition of this first book,[11] we also find a letter from William McAdoo, who was to become a cabinet member in the administration of Woodrow Wilson.

McAdoo's reason for writing, in addition to compli-
menting Mary Gay on her most recent publication, was to
request a biographical sketch to be included in a friend's
dictionary of Southern authors.

Following the Civil War, Mary Gay, relying on her
fallen brother's letters, her sister's wartime journal, and her
own memory of the war, began work on the book for
which she would be most remembered, *Life in Dixie
During the War.*[12] In 1892, the book was published with
an introduction by Joel Chandler Harris, and followed by
editions in 1894, 1897, and 1901. These later editions are
longer than the first due to additions to the text itself and
insertion of an appendix of testimonials at the end.

The 1894 edition contains an account of Andrews Raid
as told Mary Gay by Anthony Murphy who was a member
of the Confederate pursuing party that captured the
locomotive *General.* The edition of 1897 included the
initial account plus a second retelling of the event by
William A. Fuller, the conductor of the train pulled by the
General. Fuller was dissatisfied with the account in the
1894 edition.[13]

The first testimonial was printed in the 1894 edition
and was a letter of support and commendation by W.J.
Northen, Governor of Georgia. It had been through his
leadership that Georgia's local option bill had passed in
1886. Mary Gay's sister Missouri, as corresponding
secretary of the Georgia W.C.T.U., acted as one of the
primary leaders in the struggle for local option. Thousands
of names were secured for these petitions through the
activity of the sisters in their little cottage on Marshall
Street in Decatur.[14]

In 1907, Mary Gay published her last book *The Transplanted*, a novel about the antebellum period set in the Mississippi lowlands.[15]

In addition to her writing activities, Mary Gay raised funds for numerous causes, the most notable being for the Confederate Cemetery at Franklin, Tennessee, where her beloved brother Thomie fell in battle. A recent biography of General Pat Cleburne, who was Thomas Stokes' commanding officer and who also lost his life at Franklin, makes use of the letters which his sisters so carefully preserved.[16]

Mary Gay was also largely responsible for raising money for the Alexander H. Stephens Memorial and Library at Crawfordsville.[17] She also solicited funds to construct the little red brick Baptist Church building that stood for many years at the corner of Church and Trinity Streets in Decatur.[18]

On November 6, 1918, shortly before her ninetieth birthday, Mary Gay died and was laid to rest in the old section of the Decatur Cemetery next to her mother and her sister Missouri who had died in the fall of 1910.

A newspaper article in the *DeKalb New Era*, December 5, 1918, written in tribute to Mary Gay and recalling facets of her life and that of her sister Missouri Stokes, closes with the sentence: "A suitable epitaph for each would be, 'She hath done what she could.'"[19]

Gordon Midgette
Executive Director

Carole Stevens
Research Assistant

Notes

[1]Family papers of Annis Gay Mann Richardson of Blakely, Georgia. Photocopy on file Georgia State Department of Archives, Atlanta, Georgia.

[2]Levi Willard, "Early History of Decatur" *DeKalb New Era,* 1920-21. On file DeKalb Historical Society, Old Courthouse, Decatur, Georgia.

[3]Mrs. J. J. Ansley, *History of the Georgia Women's Christian Temperance Union, From Its Organization 1883 to 1907,* pp. 256-258.

[4]Thomas J. Stevens' will, filed July 1837, Bartow County Willis. On file Georgia State Archives.

[5]Ansley, pp. 256-258.

[6]DeKalb County Land Records, Deed Book H, p. 368. On file DeKalb County Courthouse, Decatur, Georgia.

[7]*Ibid,* Deed Book H.

[8]C. M. Candler, "1912 Homecoming Address," *DeKalb New Era Illustrated Trade Edition,* November 14, 1912. P. 46.

[9]Anonymous, *Prose and Poetry* (Nashville, 1858).

[10]Mary A. H. Gay, *Prose and Poetry,* 2nd ed. (Nashville, 1859).

[11]Mary A. H. Gay, *The Pastor's Story, and Other Pieces, or Prose and Poetry,* 11th ed. (1881).

[12]Mary A. H. Gay, *Life in Dixie During the War* (1892).

[13]James G. Bogle, Notes concerning the Great Locomotive Chase were generously supplied to the author by Colonel Bogle, a member of the Civil War Round Table, Atlanta, Georgia.

[14]Ansley, pp. 256-258.

[15]Mary A. H. Gay, *The Transplanted, A Story of Dixie Before the War* (New York and Washington, 1907).

[16]Howell and Elizabeth Purdue, *Pat Cleburne Confederate General, A Definitive Biography* (Hillsboro, Texas, 1973).

[17]W. C. T. U. tribute, *DeKalb New Era*, December 5, 1918.

[18]Adiel J. Moncrief, *Historical Sketch of the First Baptist Church of Decatur, Georgia,* p. 13, On file DeKalb Historical Society.

[19]W. C. T. U. tribute, 1918.

A Eulogy for Mary Gay

(Agnes Lee Chapter U. D. C., *The DeKalb New Era,*
  December 19, 1918)

The following resolutions were unanimously adopted in
regard to the death of Miss Mary A. H. Gay:

WHEREAS, Agnes Lee Chapter learns with sadness of
the death of a charter member, Miss Mary A. H. Gay,
November 8, 1918, and,

WHEREAS, It has pleased our Heavenly Father to
release from earthly infirmity, as the last leaf upon the tree,
this loyal Confederate woman after she had her years—
fourscore and ten—with great and lasting works, and,

WHEREAS, Lovers of Southern History have honored
and appreciated her accomplishments, therefore, be it

RESOLVED, That we acknowledge our debt of
gratitude for her painstaking labor in accumulating and
preserving the Confederate records of DeKalb County and
for her facile pen consecrated to the interest and memory
of the Old South,

RESOLVED FURTHER, That we record our pride in
her literary achievement, and remembering her sacrifices
for the Southern Cause, deem ourselves almost unworthy
of the title – "Daughters of the Confederacy."

Mrs. V. A. S. Moore
Mrs. A. L. Brooks

INDEX